THE FINAL RESOLUTION

THE FINAL RESOLUTION

Combating Anti-Jewish Hostility

Dr. Benzion Allswang

FELDHEIM PUBLISHERS *Jerusalem/New York*

First published 1989 • ISBN 0-87306-455-0

Philipp Feldheim Inc.
200 Airport Executive Park
Spring Valley, NY 10977

Feldheim Publishers Ltd.
POB 6525
Jerusalem, Israel

Printed in Israel

This book is dedicated to my parents
Harry and Betty Allswang
who painstakingly provided their loving support
throughout the years.

Acknowledgments

Special thanks go to Rabbi Harold Shusterman of Congregation Bnei Reuven and Rabbi Baruch Horwitz, Rabbi Zalman Plitnick (of blessed memory), Rabbi Eli Munk (of blessed memory), Rabbi Benzion Lopian, and the entire staff at Yeshivat D'var Yerushalyim in Jerusalem for their concern, character, and wisdom in instructing myriads of young men and women like myself, over the last twenty years, in our invaluable Torah heritage. If not for the aforementioned, this book would not have been written.

I also want to express my appreciation to Rabbi Yehoshua H. Eichenstein, Rabbi Shlomo Rapoport, Rabbi Chaim Tzvi Hollander, Rabbi Yitzhok Wolf, and Avi Meyers for giving of their time to read and critique the manuscript, which added considerably to later drafts.

I am deeply indebted to Dr. John Edwards, Dr. Fred Bryant, Dr. Linda Heath, and Dr. Emil Pasovac of Loyola University of Chicago for their professional contributions to all phases of the studies discussed in the book. Through the continuous objectivity and discipline imposed throughout by Dr. Edwards, the studies attained a level of methodological rigor and integrity that would have been impossible to achieve without him.

In addition, I want to thank the many young men and women who so conscientiously collected data through the intensive months of interviewing, and the Jewish Federation of Chicago, who donated the telephones and space for conducting the surveys.

For precise and dedicated typing services, my warmest thanks go to Sheldon and Joan Allman, who, with remarkable forbearance, put up with my constant corrections and revisions that, of course, needed to be finished by the morrow.

I also want to express my gratitude to Feldheim Publishers for their role in reviewing and critiquing the manuscript, and for their patience and integrity in putting up with my constant revisions.

Special gratitude goes to my immediate and extended family for their extraordinary moral and financial support throughout this several-year endeavor.

Finally, I want to thank my compassionate, patient, and understanding wife Rachel, who unselfishly left her beloved Jerusalem to weather years of fanciful dreams while raising four children in Chicago. Without her, her inspiration, noble character, and gentle personality this work could never have been composed. Just as Rabbi Akiva said of his wife Rachel, so may I say of mine, "Mine and yours are from her."

Contents

I / On Truth

Truth: The state or character
of being true in relation to being.
(Britanica World Language Dictionary)

Truth is posited as most precious, for without truth, life is meaningless and wasteful — where all noble efforts are, in kind, inseparable from self-indulgent ones, and would likewise fade into oblivion. Individual truths and collective truths are inseparable, and for an ideology to qualify as truth, then what is good for the individual must be good for society at large, and what is good for society must be good for the individual. In other words, "truths" which strengthen individual or particular group entities to the exclusion of others are, at best, misleading.

It could be asked why is the issue of truth so important? Should we not worry more about feeding the hungry, clothing the naked, and spreading peace and fellowship to all mankind? In response, if truth was, indeed, an abstract philosophical concept removed from the daily activities of individuals and societies, the answer would be yes. However, if feeding and clothing mankind are dependent on truth (with its corollary in justice), and if peace and love are likewise inextricably connected to truth, then it becomes necessary to push and persevere in one's search for authenticity (in a word, truth).

From a Jewish perspective this quest is paramount. According to traditional Judaism, the foundation of man's relationship to his fellow man and to society at large is based on truth. This tradition should not be taken lightly, for it is the tradition of Abraham, Moses, Joshua, King David, the prophet Isaiah, and multitudes of other Jewish prophets and sages on which Christianity, Islam, and to a great extent all of Western Civilization is based. It is the indigenous tradition of the great thinkers who have literally shaped Western and Eastern thought as we know it today, such as Karl Marx, Sigmund Freud, Albert Einstein, and hundreds of others. It is the tradition which gave to humanity the Ten Commandments, the concept of altruistic love, and justice tempered with compassion, on which the loftiest ideals of mankind are founded. Therefore, in light of its decisively good track record, its commentary on truth (and inversely on non-truth) bears serious attention.

For example, in the book of Exodus it states: "Keep far away from anything false."[1] Likewise, in the book of Psalms it reads: "I hate every false way"[2] and "I hate and abhor falsehood."[3]

The Talmud (that is, the Oral Law tradition, which is complementary to and no less important than the Bible in traditional Judaism) asserts that the world is established on three concepts, "on Judgment, *on Truth*, and on Peace."[4] In other Talmudic literature, the seal of God Himself is said to be truth.[5]

Accordingly, the ancient historian Josephus relates the following story of the Jewish leader and sage Zerubbabel who, in his youth, was a bodyguard of the Babylonian-Median King Darius (some 2,400 years ago). According to Josephus:

> Once when the king (Darius) lay wrapped in deep slumber his guards resolved to write down what each of them consi-

dered the mightiest thing in the world, and he who wrote the wisest saying should be given a reward by the king. What they wrote they laid under the pillow of the king, that he might not delay to make a decision after he awoke. The first guard wrote: "Wine is the mightiest thing there is"; the second wrote: "The king is the mightiest on earth"; and the third, Zerubbabel the Jew wrote: "Women are the mightiest in the world, but *truth* prevails over all." When the king awoke, and perused the documents, he summoned the nobility of his realm, and the three guards as well. Each of the three was called upon to justify his saying. In eloquent terms the first described the potency of wine, when it takes possession of the senses of a man, he forgets grief and sorrow. Still more beautiful and convincing were the words of the second speaker... Finally Zerubbabel depicted the power of women, who rule even over kings. "But," he continued, "Truth is supreme over all; the whole earth asks for truth, the heavens sing the praise of truth, all creation quakes and trembles before truth. Unto truth is the might, the power, and the glory of all times." When Zerubbabel ceased from speaking, the assembly broke out and exclaimed: "Great is truth, it is mightier than all else."[6]

Similarly, a more contemporary leading Jewish thinker of the nineteenth century, Rabbi Samson Raphael Hirsch, wrote in his "How Does Our Time Relate to Truth and Peace?":

Shall we still weep and fast? Has the Exile ended? Has salvation arrived? Is there to be no more Exile? Will the Gentiles' goodwill last?...

To be sure, the time will come at last when the Daughters of Zion will put away their garments of mourning; when the House of Judah will see its days of fasting and grieving transformed forever into days of joy and festivity:...

Is there reason to believe that such a time has come, or that it is even near? You can determine this by assessing whether and in what manner you love truth and peace!

Truth and peace — first truth and then peace; but if truth, then peace as well....

Once the commitment to truth has been made, the attainment of peace is the next task. When peace does not carry with it the denial of truth, when peace does not endanger truth, when peace with other nations is not gained at the expense of truth, then such peace is an exalted possession....

No strife or struggle is unwarranted in defense of truth, even if an entire world were the opponent. In this struggle one must not fear the opposition of the entire world....

A bright future will victoriously arise for us out of the double grave of our past once we love truth together with peace, but never to abandon truth in order to gain peace....

How does our time relate to truth? Is truth most precious to you? *Is truth so important to you, that you desire only that peace which is not built upon the demise of truth?* Or is peace so important to you, that you desire only that truth which is compatible with everything else in your life? *Would you bow only before that truth which has first bowed before you?*

Has not "accommodation" become the great watchword of science and of life, and has not *juste milieu* become the formula for the deception of the generation? Has not shrewdness become the wisdom which communities require from their teachers, and has not silence become the price for which the diploma of shrewdness is earned?

And what about family life, marriage, education, the home, the school — these institutions which determine our present and future well-being? *Is it truth, or is it peace construed as social agreeableness, which governs these institutions and dictates and decides everything for us?*[7]

The Elusive Truth

Is it possible to sort out authentic truth from non-truths so pervasive in an open society like ours? Are we capable of straining out truth from the vast ocean of non-truths currently in vogue? Is this not the tragedy of society itself, in which group entities, throughout history, believed themselves possessors of the truth and massacred savagely to prove their very point?! Would it not be more sensible to accept all versions of truth?

Though ideologically lofty, peaceful co-existence among different frameworks of exclusive truth (for any extended period of time) is historically unfounded. Though a utopian-like tolerance appears optimal, it is psychologically and socially unrealistic. Contrary to Marxian ideology, people require underlying significance to their lives, and are not eternally pacified by the grandeur of ephemeral materialism. They will seek out a deeper and more transcendent meaning to their mundane existence, and without honest direction they will fall prey to the seasoned demagogues, the hate-mongers, the styled psychopaths, who are only too prepared to lead them to the "promised land." Without a sincere and intellectually honest quest for truth we are enervating the masses and creating an emotional vacuum, where the pathologically driven, totalitarian-type individuals or political entities will succeed in all their depravity.

Truth is elusive, and our biases may detach us from our goal. If we become too immersed in our own partialities, we may unwittingly precipitate the very catastrophes we so earnestly try to prevent. To *directly* seek out truth can inadvertently lead to failure, but to *back in* by eliminating non-truths is a viable alternative, and, in a manner of speaking, good science (like the scientist whose primary objective should be the elimination of alternative hypotheses, which enables this scientist to indirectly come closer to the universal laws he/she desires to discover). By eliminating non-truths we come that much closer to truth itself, which provides the impetus and motivation for further effort.

Accordingly, in the Biblical books of Exodus and Psalms mentioned above, the pursuance of truth is transcribed in the negative (that is, the obligatory disassociation from non-truths), for the acquisition of truth is difficult, fraught with obstacles and deception. However, the elimination of non-truths is possible, and can be achieved through dedication and diligence. By eliminating falsehoods (via the evidence) we, perforce, learn to distinguish between non-truths and *possible truths*, and come that much closer to truth itself.

There are many today who purport to have the Truth. They have developed convincing arguments, to which the casual observer is susceptible. To weed out truths from non-truths on the basis of their monolithic arguments is impossible, but to examine their claims or doctrines on the basis of detached skepticism and history is surprisingly effective.

In light of the fact that the Jews have survived as a distinct people for over 3,000 years, and have played an integral role in most major cultures and societies, they become the perfect paradigm from which to understand various "truths." By understanding the Jewish nation (people) historically, we attain an understanding of their historical host societies as well.

In short, the protracted contact between the Jewish culture and others has usually taken the form of discrimination, persecution and, at times, wholesale slaughter. However, the oppression of Jews is different than the oppression of other minority groups (as discussed in chapters II and III), and the delineation of its character takes the individual beyond the limited perception of anti-Semitism into the realm of the broader, more universally significant domain of (what is termed in the present book) the *Anti-Jewish Phenomenon*. By understanding this phenomenon, the individual will learn to be more discerning in his or her quest for truth, and a path can be cleared to make certain truths accessible.

Prior Qualifications

In this book the term "anti-Jewish hostility" is used in lieu of the more commonly applied "anti-Semitism" to denote antipathy towards Jews. This is because the latter is a misnomer. The word Semitism comes from the name Shem, who was Biblically one of Noah's three sons. Therefore, according to the Bible (and assuming all sons were equally prolific), approximately one-third of the world's population today should be inhabited by Shemites (or Semites). *In practice*, anti-Semitism has been used exclusively to denote anti-Jewish prejudice and hostility, and directed against a people who account for considerably less than 1 percent of the world's population. The term anti-Semitism was coined in Germany in the 1870s to denote a "racial" enmity towards Jews, in place of the "dated" religious prejudice engendered in the past. Therefore, if the word anti-Semitism was to be used, this author would be furthering another non-truth rooted in animosity towards both Jews and Judaism.

In addition, this book, *in part*, is adapted from the author's 1985 doctoral dissertation from Loyola University of Chicago entitled: *Anti-Judaism, Anti-Semitism, Anti-Zionism: A Theoretical and Empirical Analysis of the Anti-Jewish Phenomenon Throughout Its History to the Present.* However, to make the book accessible to the non-professional, technical terminology and statistical analyses, presented in the dissertation, were deleted. Nevertheless, any individual or group interested in a more detailed presentation of the *methodology* and *statistical analyses* presented in Chapters VIII, IX, and XI is urged to acquire a copy of the dissertation via University Microfilm International, Ann Arbor, Michigan.

A further qualification, before entering a world of evidence, most probably never experienced by the reader, is *not to skip* chapters. The book was compiled to flow as a complete unit from beginning to end, and because of its radical nature, any skipping or jumping may unjustifiably arouse suspicion, without the required understanding.

The reader is urged to think seriously about the following societal life and death issues. The purpose in writing the book was not to brainwash or propagandize, but to present an analysis of crucial issues based on years of serious research. In conclusion, this book may not have been taken seriously in the past in light of its iconoclastic nature. However, in light of modern man's precarious situation, and because there appears to be, realistically speaking, little "light at the end of the tunnel," the book was now undertaken. Having said all that, I wish the reader an interesting and worthwhile experience and hope to receive stimulating feedback with its completion.

II / Is the Bible Objectively Valid?

We believe what we
want to believe.
(Demosthenes, 348 B.C.E.)

Max Planck, recipient of the Nobel Prize in Physics and past professor at the University of Berlin, declared:

> There can never be any real opposition between religion and science; for the one is the complement of the other. Every serious and reflective person realizes...that the religious element in his nature must be recognized and cultivated if all the powers of the human soul are to act together in perfect balance and harmony. And indeed it was not by accident that the greatest thinkers of all ages were deeply religious souls....Science enhances the moral values of life...because every advance in knowledge brings us face to face with the mystery of our own being.[1]

Professor A. Charniovsky, in *Between Science and Religion,* reflected likewise:

> The astonishing progress in the natural sciences and their applications in the last hundred years has brought many

8

Is the Bible Objectively Valid?

broad sectors of scholars to the opinion that religion and science not only have no common ground, but by their very natures contradict and are inimical to one another... An extreme expression of this philosophical position is the absolute rejection of religion as expendable, even dangerous; religion is deemed a remnant of the distant past, suitable only to a lower level of human culture!...

However, upon deeper examination it becomes clear that the negation of religion has not been founded upon scientific data, but rather on conclusions whose character goes beyond the limits of the scientific method itself.

These conclusions are not proven or logically well founded and very often are rash generalizations at best.

Accordingly, the negation of religion is not, as is generally thought, the result of scientific investigation... Metaphysical speculations are presented as conclusive scientific evidence, with the premeditated intention of opposing and effectively vanquishing any claims of religion.[2]

Before discussing the antecedents, causes and consequences of anti-Jewish hostility, the validity of Old Testament sources, liberally cited throughout this book, requires corroboration. This is because most scholars, in the physical and social sciences alike, tend to ignore religious sources, as if science and religion (in any form) were mutually exclusive. This rule (more appropriately termed the dogma of *Scientism*, not to be confused with the scientific method) is usually accepted as gospel in academia, and precludes any viable integration of the two.

The Jewish sojourn in Egypt, as Biblically recorded, is a case in point of how this perspective of "Scientism" can create an impasse in understanding the "world's greatest hatred." For instance, according to the upcoming analysis in chapter V, to omit the episode in Egypt (and Mesopotamia) only because they are based on Biblical and Oral Law sources, would be to omit the prototype for all subsequent anti-Jewish epochs. This perspective is so pervasive, that despite the fact that the historicity of Egyptian persecution has never been disproven, this author was unable to find one secular source (on anti-Jewish

9

hostility) which gives more than a paragraph (in passing) to the happenings in Egypt.

This lack of perspective when dealing with anti-Jewish phenomena becomes all the more salient when one remembers that both traditional Christianity and Islam have never contested the events in Egypt (with its subsequent culmination at the mountain of Sinai). On the contrary, both Christianity and Islam are dependent on the Egyptian phenomenon, and invoke it as one of the most convincing proofs of God's existence and His relationship to the social world of man. Without this historical foundation, all three religions turn into human fabrications, or as Karl Marx, the "great emancipator," put it, "the opiate of the masses."

In essence, the episode in Egypt, when viewed objectively, satisfies most criteria needed to validate an authentic historical event. An event claimed to have been attested to by some six hundred thousand adult men,[3] in addition to women and children, which changed the way of life of a nation, and eventually the world, could not have been smuggled into the annals of history for all time. Similarly, we accept as fact that there was a Roman emperor called Julius Caesar and a founder of Islam named Muhammed, because it is nearly impossible to introduce fictitious events, witnessed by the masses, into recorded history. This is further corroborated by the fact that, in the case of Egypt, the people who witnessed these events were not members of a primitive servile tribe, but rather a stiff-necked, independently-spirited people. In fact, the Bible itself, in several places, describes the Hebrews' contentious and skeptical nature.[4] However, the events in Egypt are never questioned, though they are referred to repeatedly.[5]

Further support for the events in Egypt concerns the Bible's unflattering description of how the Jewish nation developed. A national history claiming to have evolved via slavery is not to be lightly dismissed. Based on the psychology of political entities, which tend to exaggerate their past in the opposite positive direction, the Jewish people's publicizing of their unattractive origins, based on their own national history book, is not easily discredited. Moreover, after the recorded Exodus from Egypt, Egyptian culture and society came to an abrupt halt, and was not heard from again until hundreds of years later.[6]

That historians and social scientists are reluctant to deal with Biblical history, in any depth, is a consequence of the pseudo-science known as Biblical Criticism, which was popularized in Germany in the nineteenth century. In brief, Biblical Criticism denied the historical accuracy of the Bible and claimed multiple authorship at various stages in history. Its critique, based on Hegelian philosophy, viewed civilization as advancing from the primitive stage and progessively moving westward, until it reached its apex in Hegel's *Germanic culture*. Accordingly, Israel's Bible and its history were reconstructed to fit this chauvinistic mold. Everything was neatly arranged in logical progression, and Israel's religion was depicted as having developed gradually from primitive idolatry to the advanced monotheism of the Prophets.[7] Theories of Biblical Criticism were expanded and refined by various scholars throughout the nineteenth century, and reached their classical formulation in the works of Julian Wellhausen (1844-1918).

What was believed then in the nineteenth century, when there were but few examples of ancient writings, was that phonetic script dated back only to the year 1000 B.C.E. Accordingly, Biblical narratives such as the Jewish exodus from Egypt, the wars of Joshua, and various other Biblical happenings were considered mythologies, written at a later date than traditionally claimed. The common custom, in other cultures, of recording retroactively one's oral traditions provided the basis for this assumption.

In the course of time, however, ancient manuscripts were discovered which set the inception of script back to 1500 B.C.E. In other words, Biblical Criticism is today unable to deny that during the period of the Exodus and of Joshua written records did, in fact, exist. However, this change in fact was not paralleled by a change (or even modification) in perspective.[8]

Wellhausen's theory tried to explain, in natural-rational terms, the formation of the Jewish Bible and the development of Judaism itself. His arguments created a base on which to erect his intellectual edifice. Over the last century, however, his foundations have been completely undermined, and have collapsed one after the other. Proponents of Biblical Criticism today are forced to admit that their "proofs" cannot stand.[9]

In essence, the elaborate edifice of Biblical Criticism was crumbling as quickly as it was being built. One of the first signs came in 1887 when the Tel El Amarna letters were discovered. The letters revealed a well-developed culture in the ancient Middle East as early as the fourteenth century B.C.E. It portrayed a world advanced in intellect, commerce, trade, and diplomacy, and demonstrated that Israel's history began long before the advent of Moses (as Biblically recorded). Since then, the maturing science of archaeology has made hundreds of discoveries, which corroborate the times and happenings cited in the Bible.[10]

One of the foremost authorities on the archaeology of Israel and the Middle East, Professor W. F. Albright of John Hopkins University, declared:

> According to our present knowledge of topography of the eastern delta, the account of the start of the Exodus, which is given in Exodus 12:37 and Exodus 13:20, is topographically absolutely correct. Further proofs of the essentially historical nature of the Exodus-story and the journey in the area of Sinai, Midian, and Kadesh can be supplied without great difficulty, thanks to our growing knowledge of topography and archaeology.
>
> We must content ourselves here with the assurance that the hypercritical attitude, which previously obtained in respect to the historical traditions of Israel has no longer any justification. Even the long disputed date of the Exodus can now be fixed within reasonable limits.... If we put it at about 1290 B.C. [the approximate time period posited by Judaism] we cannot go far wrong.[11]

Is the Bible Objectively Valid?

In his book *Archaeology and the Religion of Israel*, Professor Albright stated similarly:

> The Mosaic tradition is so consistent, so well attested by different pentateuchal documents, and so congruent with our independent knowledge of the religious development of the Near East in the late second millennium B.C., that only hypercritical pseudo-rationalism can reject its essential historicity.[12]

Concerning the seeming difficulties raised by Biblical Criticism, he wrote:

> Hebrew national tradition excels all others in its clear picture of tribal and family origins. In Egypt and Babylonia, in Assyria and Phoenicia, in Greece and Rome, we look in vain for anything comparable. There is nothing like it in the tradition of the Germanic peoples. Neither India nor China can produce anything similar.
>
> In contrast to other peoples, the Israelites preserved an unusually clear picture of simple beginnings, of complex migrations, and of extreme vicissitudes, which plunged them from their favored status under Joseph to bitter oppression after his death. Until recently it was the fashion among Biblical historians to treat the patriarchal sagas of Genesis as though they were artificial creations of Israelite scribes of the Divided Monarchy, or tales told by imaginative rhapsodists around Israelite campfires during the centuries following their occupation. Eminent names among scholars can be cited regarding every item of Genesis (chapters XI-L) as reflecting a later invention, about which nothing was thought to have been known. Archaeological discoveries since 1925 have changed all this. Aside from a few die-hards among older scholars, there is scarcely a single Biblical historian who has not been impressed by the rapid accumulation of data supporting the historicity of the patriarchal tradition....
>
> Numerous recent excavations in sites of this period in Palestine, supplemented by finds made in Egypt and Syria,

give us a remarkably precise idea of patriarchal Palestine, fitting well into the picture handed down in Genesis.[13]

Correspondingly, in his work *Canaanite Israel During the Period of Israeli Occupation*, Dr. Yohanan Aharoni writes:

> Recent archaeological discoveries have decisively changed the entire approach of bible critics. They now appreciate the Torah [Bible] as a historical document of the highest calibre. The approach of bible critics has...been drastically altered because parallel documents have been found which describe the same events, told in biblical narratives, from the perspective of the Egyptians, the Assyrians, or ancient Canaanites. Their fundamental approach (theory) has undergone further alteration because the events described in biblical narratives no longer exist in a historical vacuum. Today we are very familiar with populations and the political picture of the ancient world, and the geographical locations that staged the events of history. We are familiar with the customs and the laws that are described in biblical narratives, as well as the names of the people and places which are mentioned. All of these are compatible with biblical history. No author or "editor(s)" could have put together or invented these stories hundreds of years after they happened. No serious bible scholar remains, who can argue with the fact that these historical events were transmitted with incredible historical accuracy from generation to generation, until our time.[14]

The Ipuwer Papyrus

This author will not burden the reader with the multitude of archaeological finds, made over the last century, which substantively support Biblical history, and conversely, do serious harm to the historical "conclusions" of Biblical Criticism. However, in light of the anti-Jewish hostility below, which depicts the Jews' sojourn in Egypt as the archetype for subsequent anti-Jewish epochs, the following evidence does bear mention.

A papyrus consisting of the words of an ancient Egyptian

named Ipuwer was acquired in 1828 by the Leiden Museum of the Netherlands. According to its first possessor (Anastasi), it was discovered in Memphis, Egypt. The papyrus is presently listed in the museum's catalogue as *Leiden 344*. The papyrus has writing on both sides, with Ipuwer's story on the face and a hymn to some deity on the back. The text of Ipuwer was folded into a book of seventeen pages. Of the first page only a third is preserved, pages 9 to 16 are in bad condition, and only part of the first two lines of the last page remains.[15]

Since its discovery many attempts have been made to translate the text. In 1909 the papyrus, newly translated, was published by Alan H. Gardiner entitled: *The Admonitions of an Egyptian Sage from a Hieratic Papyrus in Leiden.* The papyrus was considered then to have been written around 1500 B.C.E., during the Egyptian "Middle Kingdom," over 200 years before the Hebrew exodus. This date fell nicely into the larger context of the then accepted history of ancient Egypt. In light of the alleged time divergence between the papyrus and Biblical narratives, little attention was paid to the text. In addition, because the Bible was then not accepted as a valid historical document, and because its dating system was seemingly so divergent from all accepted "scientific" theories, the relationship between the Ipuwer text and the "legendary" Hebrew exodus received little attention. However, Professor Immanuel Velikovsky did discern the relationship between the contents of the papyrus and Biblical narratives. He analyzed the papyrus and compared the list of catastrophes and lamentations described by the Egyptian Ipuwer with the Egyptian plagues recorded in the Bible.[16]

The Ipuwer papyrus is a text of lamentations, a listing of fear and destruction. For example:

Papyrus 2:8; Forsooth, the land turns around as does a potter's wheel.
2:11; The towns are destroyed. Upper Egypt has become dry (wastes?).
3:13; All is ruin!

A page from the papyrus Ipuwer[17]

In the words of Professor Velikovsky:

The Leiden Papyrus Ipuwer is a record of some catastrophe followed by a social upheaval; in the description of the catastrophe we recognized many details of the disturbances that accompanied the Exodus as narrated in Scripture. [In addition], the inscription on the shrine from el-Arish contains another version of the cataclysm, accompanied by a hurricane and nine days' darkness; and there we found also a description of the march of the Pharaoh and his army toward the eastern frontier of his kingdom, where he was engulfed in a whirlpool. The name of the Pharaoh is given in a royal cartouche which proves that the text was not regarded by its writer as mythical.[18]

From the style of the papyrus it is clear that Ipuwer is not writing a song of prophecy concerning future events. It is a picture of events he had witnessed. Correspondingly, in accordance with Professor Velikovsky's dating approach (of Egyptian dynasties), the papyrus is associated in time with the traditional Jewish date of approximately 1250 B.C.E. In short, the Ipuwer Papyrus is an Egyptian eyewitness account of events which correspond closely to those recorded in the book of Exodus.[19] The following are samples from the papyrus with corresponding Biblical narratives:

The Ipuwer Papyrus	The Book of Exodus

The Plague of Blood

Papyrus 2:5-6 Plague is throughout the land. Blood is everywhere.	Exodus 7:21...there was blood throughout all the land of Egypt.
Papyrus 2:10 The river is blood.	Exodus 7:20... all the water that was in the river was turned to blood.
Papyrus 2:10 Men shrink from tasting — human beings, and thirst after water.	Exodus 7:21... and the river stank, and Egypt could not drink of the water of the river.
Papyrus 3:10-13 That is our water! That is our happiness! What shall we do in respect thereof? All is ruin!	Exodus 7:24 And all the Egyptians dug round about the river for water to drink, but they could not drink of the water of the river.

The Plague of Hail and Fire

Papyrus 2:10 Forsooth, gates, columns and walls are consumed by fire.	Exodus 9:23-24...The fire ran upon the ground...there was hail and fire mingled within the hail, very grievous.
Papyrus 9:2-3 Behold, cattle are left to stray, and there is none to gather them together. Each man fetches for himself those that are branded with his name.	Exodus 9:19-20... gather thy cattle, and all that thou hast in the field.... He that feared the word of God among Pharaoh's servants... made his cattle flee into the houses. And he that disregarded God's word left his...cattle in the field.
Papyrus 4:14 Trees are destroyed. 6:1 No fruit nor herbs are found....	Exodus 9:25... and the hail smote every plant in the field and broke every tree of the field.

The Ipuwer Papyrus	The Book of Exodus

The Plague of Locusts

It was after this plague that the fields became utterly barren. Like the Book of Exodus, (9:31-32 and 10:15) the papyrus relates that no duty could be rendered to the crown, and as in Exodus 7:21 ("And the fish that was in the river died") there was no fish for the royal storehouse.

Papyrus 10:3-6 Lower Egypt weeps ....The entire palace is without its revenues. To it belong (by right) wheat and barley, geese and fish.

Papyrus 6:3 Forsooth, grain has perished on every side. 5:12 Forsooth, that has perished which yesterday was seen. The land is left over to its weariness like the cutting of flax.

Exodus 10:15...There remained not any green thing in the trees or in the herbs in the fields throughout all the land of Egypt.

Papyrus 6:1 No fruit nor herbs are found... hunger.

The statement that the crops of the fields were destroyed in a single day ("which yesterday was seen") excludes drought, the usual cause of a bad harvest; seemingly only hail, fire or locusts could have left the fields as though after "the cutting of flax." The plague is described in Psalms 105: 34-35 in these words: "... the locusts came, and caterpillars, and that without number. And did eat up all the herbs in their land, and devoured the fruit of their ground."

18

Is the Bible Objectively Valid?

The Ipuwer Papyrus	The Book of Exodus

The Plague of Pestilence

Papyrus 5:5 All animals, their hearts weep, cattle moan....	Exodus 9:3...the hand of the Lord is upon thy cattle which is in the field, upon the horses, upon the asses, upon the camels, upon the oxen, and upon the sheep.

Death of All First-Born Egyptians

Papyrus 4:3 and 5:16 Forsooth, the children of princes are dashed against the walls. 6:12 Forsooth, the children of princes are cast out in the streets.	Exodus 12:27 [The Angel of the Lord] passed over the houses of the children of Israel in Egypt, when he smote the Egyptians, and delivered our houses.
In the papyrus: The residence is overturned in a minute.	Exodus 12:30 And Pharaoh rose up in the night, he, and his servants, and all the Egyptians; and there was a great cry in Egypt: for there was not a house where there was not one dead.
Papyrus 6:3 The prison is ruined.	Exodus 12:29 And it came to pass, that at midnight the Lord smote all the firstborn in the land of Egypt, from the firstborn of Pharaoh that sat on his throne unto the firstborn of the captive that was in the dungeon.
In the papyrus (2:13) it is written: He who places his brother in the ground is everywhere.	Exodus (12:30):...there was not a house where there was not one dead.
The papyrus (3:14): It is groaning that is throughout the land, mingled with lamentations.	In Exodus (12:30):... there was a great cry in Egypt.

The Final Resolution

The Ipuwer Papyrus	The Book of Exodus

The Exodus

Papyrus 4:2 Forsooth, great and small say: I wish I might die. 5:14 Would that there might be an end of men, no conceptions, no births! Oh, that the earth would cease from noise, and tumult be no more!	Exodus 12:33 And the Egyptians were urgent upon the people, that they might send them out of the land in haste; for they said, We be all dead men.
(The following lines speak of a population escaping a disaster.) "Men flee"....Tents are what they make like the dwellers of the hills" (Papyrus 10:2).	In the Book of Exodus it is said that the Israelites left the country "in haste" (12:33) and "could not tarry" (12:39). A "mixed multitude" of Egyptians joined the Israelite slaves, and with them made haste toward the desert (Exodus 12:38). Their first brief stop was at Succoth (13:20) — which in Hebrew means "huts."
Papyrus 7:1 Behold, the fire has mounted up on high. Its burning goes forth against the enemies of the land.	Exodus 13:21...by day in a pillar of cloud, to lead them the way; and by night in a pillar of fire, to give them light; to go by day and night.[20]

The Bible and the Computer

In addition to the archaeological finds made over the last century, which significantly upset both the historical and philosophical foundations of Biblical Criticism, the literary basis, as well, has recently come under attack. The threat to Biblical Criticism, in regard to its literary interpretations, has come from the paragon of technology itself, *the computer.*

In brief, Biblical critics in the nineteenth century attempted to reconstruct the Bible's literary history to accompany its alleged mythical character. For example, the book of Genesis was interpreted as having at least three authors. Nineteenth-century critics theorized that there once existed a Judahite history, which commenced well before the Hebrew Patriarchs

20

and preserved the tradition of calling God's name YHWH (the *J source*). Later on, they concluded, an Ephraimite historical sequel appeared, which began with the first Jewish Patriarch Abraham, and used a second term denoting God's name, Elohim (the *E source*). They posited a third source (P), which they claimed was of priestly origin, and was added centuries after sources J and E. Each source was said to have its own literary style, and allegedly displayed its own distinctive religious outlook. This general reapportionment of the Book of Genesis is better known as the *Classical Three-Source Hypothesis* of the Graf-Wellhausen School of Biblical Criticism.[21]

However, in one of the major technical universities in the world (*The Technion; The Israel Institute of Technology*), data have recently been presented which critically damage the above perspective.[22] The goal was to create an objective approach from which to evaluate the basic postulates of "Classical Biblical Criticism." The approach became possible with the advent of the computer and the combined expertise of four disciplines (Biblical, Linguistic, Statistical, and Computer Science).

In brief, Biblical portions ascribed by the Graf-Wellhausen school of Biblical Criticism to *source J* (YHWH) and *source E* (Elohim) were extracted and compared with each other. After taking 54 variables into consideration, the computer concluded that the probability of *source J* and *source E* resulting from the same author was *82 percent*. How high this percentage is, is more fully appreciated when compared with the probability that the German philosopher Kant or the German poet Goethe had, in actuality, written their own literary works. The probabilities, according to the computer, that Kant had independently written Kant, or that Goethe had written Goethe were 8 and 22 percent respectively![23]

Correspondingly, Biblical scholar Dr. Moshe Katz and computer expert Dr. Menachem Wiener, also of the Israel Institute of Technology, have in recent years researched the hypothesis that relevant words are concealed in the Hebrew text of the Old Testament (more specifically, the Pentateuch) and may be reproduced by separating out letters at fixed intervals. Using this approach, they found *hundreds* of significant words and concepts revealed throughout the Pentateuch which relate to the text at hand.[24]

Dr. Katz, explaining his findings to journalists, stated that the empirical evidence dispels the belief that the Bible is a collection of various documents composed and edited by different people at different times. "The patterns of letters," he said, "repeated throughout the text, dismiss the theory [i.e. of Biblical Criticism] in light of the fantastic statistical probability of such patterns occurring wholly by chance, at times reaching 1:3 million" (i.e., the probability of one in three million).[25]

In assessing the above findings, the conclusions are: (1) Either the computer is correct and the literary basis of Biblical Criticism, (like its already defunct historical and philosophical foundations) has been struck a fatal blow, or (2) the computer is incorrect, which would imply that our "Critical" methodology is so *unreliable* (after two centuries of refinement!), as to make the "science" of Biblical Criticism functionally useless at best.

In short, the pseudo-science of Biblical Criticism should be a thing of the past. *Philosophically*, Germany was not the apex of civilization. *Historically*, the multitude of archaeological discoveries, over the past century, not only fail to invalidate Biblical happenings but significantly support them. And, from the *literary* perspective, the computer has struck Biblical Criticism a fatal blow. *Ironically, however, Biblical Criticism today is still taught and disseminated in both American and European academia as the "higher" form of Biblical interpretation.*

If the world of Biblical Criticism was not so compelled to espouse its own type of religion, it would quickly discern its irrationality. For example, suppose the evidence was reversed. That is, suppose, hypothetically, that the scientific and historical evidence which refutes classical Biblical Criticism was now used to support it, and further suppose that any salvaged support in behalf of Biblical Criticism was now used to refute it. *Is anyone naïve enough to believe that if the cards, indeed, switched hands, that anyone would deny the theory of Biblical Criticism?*

This irrationality clothed in scholarship is comparable to a story related by Rabbi Adin Steinsaltz, who is head of the Israel Institute for Talmudic Publication and prize-winning essayist on Jewish philosophy. While lecturing at Northwestern University in the spring of 1986, he cited a study done in the United States some fifteen years prior. The study surveyed college instructors throughout the country and among the many questions was: "Do you believe in God and why or why not?" Results showed that the great majority of college instructors in the *Liberal Arts* and *Social Sciences did not* believe in God, "*in light of contemporary science.*" However, a significant majority representing the *Physical Sciences*, ironically, *did* believe in God. *In short, the paradoxical nature of these results reveal a pseudo-scientific mind-set prevalent in today's academia.*

Correspondingly, "distinguished" Biblical critics, over the last century and a half, seem to have been more interested in denying Biblical authenticity than in actually discovering truth. For example, the Biblical "work of genius" by Wellhausen and his followers was much less objective than its proponents like to admit.

How much did Wellhausen's own biased view of the Bible, which in his own words, "robbed Israel of its old natural heathenism, and put in its stead gloom, puritanism and self-righteousness, deadening the conscience and taking the soul out of religion,"[26] affect his allegedly clear and objective analysis of the same? Other names in the field, such as Eichhorn and Gabler, had an obsessive distrust of Jews as eyewitnesses. They believed that Jews, in particular, were unable to relate true facts without mixing them with biased interpretation. Another Biblical scholar and critic, Franz Delitzsch held Jews responsible for Germany's loss in World War I, and cited "proof" that the Jewish religion fostered ritual murder. His initial attitude towards Judaism as "the Great Deception" was shared by Harnack, Kittel, Duhm, and other well-known Biblical critics in nineteenth- and twentieth-century Germany. Accordingly,

German Biblical scholars Gerhard Kittel and Emanuel Hirsch were Hitler's leading theological supporters, and may be deemed the primary source responsible for the German Churches' silence, during the systematic massacre of six million.[27]

Another early name in this branch of scholarship was the nineteenth-century German born rabbi, Abraham Geiger. Geiger is often considered the most important early proponent of Reform Judaism. Geiger denied the Divine origin of the Pentateuch, scoffed at Jewish dietary laws, and called for the abolition of circumcision. In his essay, *The Uselessness and Evil Consequences of Religious Formalism,* he attacked Jewish tradition and maintained that in modern times they undermine deep religious consciousness and moral development. His *hatred* of Jewish tradition reached such heights that he contended that Jews who cling to their traditions are not worthy of civil emancipation! It is little wonder that this "paragon" of Jewish liberalism concluded that Jewish history be broken into four separate epochs, of which the fourth and most advanced was the scholarly Criticism of nineteenth-century Germany.[28]

In conclusion, the view of Werner Keller in his classic *The Bible as History* bears repeating:

> In view of the overwhelming mass of authentic and well-attested evidence now available, as I thought of the skeptical criticism which from the eighteenth century onward would fain have demolished the Bible altogether, there kept hammering in my brain this one sentence: "The Bible is right after all!"[29]

The Academic Bias

Jewish history runs counter to the laws of history. According to the historic law of nations where "might is right," the Hebrew nation's survival is a deviation from the rule. [Christianity and Islam are religious belief systems which have no national origin, and by their own definitions are universal in doctrine and perspective. In addition, their ability to grow (and even to survive) has, most often, depended on their majority status.] Jews not only survived under the most insurmountable odds, but within their hostile and predatory environments they managed to create societies which grew intellectually, spiritually, and when allowed, economically throughout millennia.[30]

Just as the odds against spontaneous formation of a living cell from inanimate matter are astronomically fantastic, so does the continued existence of the Jewish people and the validity of their Bible defy the natural (or consistent) laws of nations. And just as the physical science community religiously accepts this incredible physical theory (and many would argue law) despite much evidence to the contrary,[31] so, too, have social scientists and historians unflinchingly explained the Jewish phenomenon without suggesting the involvement of the super-physical.

Accordingly, secular academia, predicated on the ideals and objectives of the Enlightenment, represented in its original form a severance from the dogma of organized religion. Although a severance was in order, in light of the barbarous activities legitimized in the name of religion (Judaism excluded), an academic community (that bases itself on the scientific method) seeking truth which blatantly avoids the psychological, social, political, and historical ramifications of religious validity is itself dogmatic. Accordingly, contemporary social scientists (following their physical science counterparts' lead) may feel great professional and/or personal pressure to "justify" their non-theological stance in the name of science itself!

Science vs. Religion

Sir Isaac Newton, the celebrated seventeenth-century scientist, proclaimed:

> Whence is it that nature doth nothing in vain, and whence arises all that Order and Beauty which we see in the world? ... whence is it that planets move all one and the same way ... what hinders the fix'd stars from falling upon one

another? How come the bodies of animals to be contrived with so much Art.... Was the eye contrived without skill in opticks and the ear without knowledge of sounds? How do the motions of the body follow from the will, and whence is the instinct in animals?... These things being rightly dispatched, does it not appear from Phenomena that there is a Being incorporeal, living, intelligent, omnipresent, who in infinite space, as it were in his Sensory, sees the things themselves intimately, and thoroughly perceives them, and comprehends them wholly by their immediate presence to himself.[32]

Albert Einstein, some three hundred years later, proclaimed:

The most beautiful experience that we are capable of feeling is that of the mystery of the cosmos. This is the source of true art and science. A human being to whom this experience is foreign, who is incapable of feeling this astonishment and of standing in excitement and awe in the face of ultimate mystery, must be considered dead. His eyes are sealed! It is imperative to know that that which lies beyond our grasp is nevertheless truly real. The mystery of reality is revealed in a supernal wisdom and sublime beauty that shines so exceedingly bright that our impoverished faculties can only comprehend it in the most primitive fashion.[33]

Over the last 150 years other "scientific" theories have been expounded which, like Biblical Criticism, seemingly negate Biblical narratives. The most popularly accepted theory, used consistently to "refute" Biblical doctrines is the theory of evolution. Evolution is presented as *fact* in most elementary, high school, and college textbooks throughout the United States. However, the theory of evolution, like its contemporaries which claim "scientifically" to refute Biblical accuracy (and indirectly the existence of God Himself), is itself based on little more than religious faith.

The famous philosopher of science, Sir Karl Popper of London University, lists seven fundamental requirements for a theory to be considered scientific. Among the list is: *"A theory which is not refutable by any conceivable event is non-scientific.*"[34] And, concerning the theory of evolution, Professor Aaron Katzir writes: "Despite the fact that Darwin's theory of evolution has won wide acceptance, it is nevertheless not experimentally demonstrable, and it is impossible to verify."[35]

According to P. K. Turner, who cites Popper as his source: "Darwinism is not a scientific theory but metaphysical [like religion]... Popper holds that since evolutionary theory cannot make predictions, and cannot therefore be proved false, it is not a scientific theory."[36]

What are the "Proofs" for Evolution?

The "proofs" that proponents of evolution cite are:

PROOF No. 1:   *Fossil beds demonstrate the evolution of one species from another.*[37] Some problems with this "proof" are:

A. In principle, fossils are able to show no more than gradations between species, and gradations between species does not mean that one species evolved from another.[38]

B. Because the principle of gradations is deduced by an arbitrary classification of fossils it is artificial. For example, one can, with equal facility, superimpose on a Neanderthaloid skull the features of a chimpanzee or the lineaments of a philosopher! These restorations of ancient types of man have little, if any, scientific value and can easily mislead the public.[39]

C. When determining age by radioactive carbon 14 (C^{14}) on fossils of cave men, Cro-magnon ape, and Neanderthal man and others, they indicate a relatively young age of several thousand odd years as opposed to the hundreds of thousands of years attributed to them when originally discovered (and which remains the status quo). In addition, carbon, petroleum, and natural gas measurements point to the same.[40]

D. Evolutionists have been unsuccessful in demonstrating a continuity of evolutionary change. Seriously large gaps exist in fossil records. *For example, transitional forms are lacking everywhere.*[41]

E. From a statistical perspective (which is invaluable to the scientific method) the absence of transitional forms (species) is strong enough evidence to suggest that, in actuality, there never were![42]

F. "...According to most paleontologists the principle feature of individual species within the fossil record is *stasis*, not change."[43]

G. Fossils discovered in "wrong" strata of rock. For example, the Seymuria, which is believed to be "the transition" between amphibians and reptiles, has been discovered in Permian formations, whereas the earliest reptiles have been found in the Pennsylvanian formations which, according to geologists, preceded the Permian by some 20 million years![44]

PROOF No. 2: *"Vestigal limbs" are seen as indicating evolution.*[45] This "proof" fails to stand because:

A. Vestigal limbs most always demonstrate degenerate and destructive mutations, as opposed to the evolutionary and constructive mutations they are posited to represent.[46]

B. Because no obvious functions have been found for certain limbs, we are not compelled to conclude that they do, in fact, have no function. For example, at one time the thyroid, the thymus gland, the appendix, and the tonsils, were all considered useless.[47]

PROOF No. 3: *Biochemical similarities are seen as indicating evolution.*[48] This "proof" fails to hold up because:

A. The fact that similarities exist among species does not imply that they were generated one from the other.[49]

B. The chemistry of the body is involved in most sicknesses so that the similarity between illnesses (among men and animals) stands in direct contradiction to the theory of evolution (i.e., where is the evolutionary process?).[50]

C.   Comparisons among cytochrome C sequences do not fit the phylogenetic classification.[51]

**Postulates Upon Which the
Theory of Evolution is Based**

The theory of evolution is based on several assumptions which are interrelated, and with the collapse of one the entire theory falls. It may be likened to a tower of blocks where one block rests on the other. Once one block is removed the entire tower collapses.[52]

POSTULATE No. 1:   *"There was an appropriate substrata to the terrestrial globe, which had a reducing atmosphere."*[53] Some facts which contradict this postulate are:
    A.   Among the gases that escape from beneath the earth's crust, there are oxidizing gases and not only reducing gases.[54]
    B.   Oxygen is continually generated by the effects of primary or secondary cosmic radiations and photolysis via ultraviolet rays that arrive from the sun. More specifically, in the absence of the protective ozone belt around the earth's primitive atmosphere, oxygen would have been generated by intensified photolysis.[56]
    C.   Strata rich in the mineral magnetite (Fe_3O_4), and the mineral hematite (Fe_2O_3) in pre-Cambrian strata are evidence for an ample supply of oxygen, which was needed for their oxidation.[56]

POSTULATE No. 2:   *"There was a spontaneous generation of simple organic elements, amino acids, sugars, purines, and pyrimidines, etc., that merged in the primitive 'broth.'"*[57] This postulate fails to stand for the following reasons:
    A.   "Thermodynamic calculations predict vanishingly small concentrations of even the simplest organic compounds." In addition, the reactions invoked to synthesize com-

pounds of this sort are much more effective in decomposing them.[58]

B.   The physical chemist, guided by the proven principles of chemical thermodynamics and kinetics, is unable to offer any encouragement to the biochemist, who requires literally oceans full of organic compounds to create even lifeless coacervates.[59]

C.   At least five major factors limit the kinds of compounds that could have been produced in the primitive ocean.
1. Limitations on what can be produced by inorganic means.
2. The fact that organic matter degrades spontaneously with time.
3. Substances destroyed by radiation.
4. The removal of compounds via precipitation and absorption.
5. Chemical incompatibilities among constituents of living matter, where some of the components would react to form nonbiologic substances.[60]

D.   The Viking Space Ship, which landed on Mars, did not find a trace of the simplest biochemical matter. This is highly meaningful, for all the basic elements required for life exist on Mars as well.[61]

E.   The tremendous asymmetry which exists between L molecules versus D molecules.[62]

POSTULATE No. 3:   Spontaneous synthesis of proteins and nucleic acids and their collection in the primal "broth."[63] The unscientific features of this postulate are:
A.   The basic substances would react readily with the tens of thousands of chemical compound species which were formed accidentally, and would leave the process.[64]

B.   Low concentrations in the primal "broth" would prevent the process from proceeding.[65]

C.   The acclaimed scientist, Fred Hoyle, calculated the probability of the 2,000 genes known to us as having been generated by chance from the existing chains of nucleotides. He arrived at the impossible probability of $10\text{-}40{,}000$.[66]

POSTULATE No. 4:   *Spontaneous generation of fixed indepen-dent complex biological systems from simple elements of an earlier stage.*[67] This postulate fails to stand because:

    A.   The transition from molecules to a living cell is a "fantastic leap of faith" which finds no comparison in any known process.[68]

    B.   The spontaneous generation of living cells totally contradicts the Second Law of Thermodynamics.[69]

    C.   The celebrated Chemist-Physicist, Ilya Prigogine, recipient of two Nobel Prizes in chemistry claimed: "The statistical probability that organic structures, and the most precisely harmonizied reactions that typify living organisms would be generated by accident is *nil.*"[70]

    D.   George Wald, the Nobel Prize recipient in physiology concluded that: "One has only to contemplate the magnitude of this task to concede that the spontaneous generation of a living organism *is impossible.*"[71]

POSTULATE No. 5:   *Constructive mutation of species via the process of natural selection.*[72] This postulate is unsatisfactory because:

    A.   The process of natural selection appears unable to generate new species. For example, the combined effect of 1,000 mutations on one fruit fly (a scientific impossibility) would leave us with no more than a fruit fly.[73]

    B.   The potential for amplifying or strengthening the characteristics of a species beyond a certain range is limited. For example, in an experiment conducted on 20 generations of fermentation fruit flies, scientists succeeded in magnifying their number of bristles from 36 to 56 but not further. When 56 bristles were reached the flies became unable to reproduce further, and their death rate rose significantly.[74]

C. Each mutation of itself does not appear to have any evolutionary value. Moreover, each respective change may be fatal to the embryo. However, to say that these changes were harmonized from the beginning would attribute to evolution a predesigned objective which is unconditionally rejected by the theory itself.[75]

How, Then, Did the Theory of Evolution Become so "Scientifically" Popular?

It is not surprising that the theory of evolution became so popular among the masses. Whoever is not privy to the above type of information gets the impression that evolution is a true scientific theory, whose postulates are verifiable and proofs incontrovertible. Almost every educational institution from grammar schools to universities, from textbooks to the mass media portray the theory as fact. With the aid of impressive terminology and pictorial charts, it appears unquestionably scientific. Add to this the fact that it is fostered by the champion of our age, the "objective" scientist, it is not surprising that evolution has become basic "knowledge" in all educational settings. Conversely, its hypothetical nature, its inconsistencies, the multitude of unanswered questions it poses, and the vast number of criticisms it evokes are ignored. However, what should be surprising is how scientists themselves support such theories.

An answer to this question comes from scientists themselves. For example, Professor George Wald, a Nobel Prize recipient in physiology, expressed the problem thus:

> The reasonable view was to believe in spontaneous generation; the only alternative, to believe in a single, primary act of supernatural creation. There is no third position. For this reason many scientists a century ago chose to regard the belief in spontaneous generation as a philosophical necessity.[76]

Accordingly, Professor August Weisman, one of the founders of modern genetics, wrote in his book *The Omnipotence of Natural Selection*:

> Though we may never be able to determine the process by which a new species was generated by means of natural selection in the struggle for survival, we are nevertheless obligated to accept the principle of natural selection because it offers the only explanation of a diversified natural living world, without our having to assume that it was created by a force that desired and created it intentionally...."[77]

Sir Julian Huxley, renowned physiologist and evolutionist, asserted: "Darwin's real achievement was to exclude the idea of God as Creator of all life from the realm of rational analysis...."[78] In other words, it was less important, according to Sir Julian, whether Darwin's theory was valid or not; what was important, however, was that people were now able to explain the life-generating process without postulating the existence of God.

Similarly, the famous scientist and philosopher, Aldous Huxley, wrote the following towards the end of his life:

> I had reasons not to want the world to have meaning, and as a result I assumed the world had no meaning, and I was readily able to find satisfactory grounds for this assumption. ....For me, as it undoubtedly was for most of my generation, the philosophy of meaninglessness was an instrument of liberation from a certain moral system. We were opposed to morality because it interfered with our sexual freedom."[79]

In effect, the technological achievements of the nineteenth century created a misplaced faith in the omnipotence and omniscience of science, and everything "non-scientific" was considered, at best, expendable. Scholars who doubted the power of contemporary science were labeled religionists.[80]

Consequently, a supreme value was conferred upon science, and a religiosity developed to promote its theories, without concern for its ever-mounting opposing data. The evidence presented (via archaeological finds, computer analyses, and others) in support of the Bible, or evidence which refuted mainstream "scientific" theory; was then met by heated *emotionalism.*

Professor Charniovsky, in *Between Science and Religion,* spoke of this type of mind-set:

> Faith in the omnipotence of the natural sciences gave rise likewise to the certainty that they were capable of replacing all other achievements of the human spirit, and among them the place of religion. In the place of religious theology, *a theology of natural science was formulated.*[81]

In conclusion, it is interesting to note that it was the ideology of evolution (that depicted man as a zoological specimen) which helped foster the rise and popularity of Nazism.[82] Hitler, in *Mein Kampf,* summarized the relationship as follows:

> In nature there is no pity for the lesser creatures when they are destroyed so that the fittest may survive. Going against nature brings ruin to man.... It is only Jewish impudence to demand that we overcome Nature![83]

Can the Bible (Old Testament) Be Validated?

According to the *Cartesian gage,* in order to discredit evidence, its implausibility must outweigh its plausibility. In other words, it is wrong to discount evidence on the grounds that there exists some other (however implausible) explanation. Rather, the objective researcher must weigh the strengths of arguments against their weaknesses.

In essence, much of what we "know" is not through direct experience, but through the accumulation of evidence, which leads us to conclude that a given phenomenon is indeed real. For example, do people know for a fact that the earth is round? The answer, for most of us, at least, is no. We conclude the earth is round, not by direct experience, but vicariously through multiple pictures, measurements, and scientific laws, etc. From the perspective of a pig-headed skeptic, the pictures we see may be forged, the measurements and laws a hoax, and the scientific community may (collectively) be conspiring to mislead us! Although possible, we reject the skeptic's claim, for we have too much evidence suggesting the contrary.

In like fashion, do we *know* there is a land called Russia? Most Americans were never there to testify to its authenticity. What we see on televison may be a media canard, and people claiming to have visited may have been brainwashed. Who is right? Is there a Russia or not? Again, most of us must rely on the evidence from sources other than our own senses, to conclude that, in all probability, there truly is a land called Russia! We, not unlike objective researchers, weigh the evidence for and against the existence of a Russia, and based on the evidence decide whether Russia does or does not exist.

Does one know through direct experience who one's real mother and father are? Most of us do not, but we rely on the facts that hospitals usually do not make mistakes, that our parents are not lying to us, and that the physical similarities between ourselves and our parents are not accidental. However, most of us will never know for certain whether our present parents are truly ours. However, we conclude they are on the basis of evidence, which supports the claim that one's parents are truly his. We could go on to demonstrate how much, in essence, we really do not know, but only think we know on the basis of solid evidence.

However, despite our seeming expertise at drawing accurate conclusions from the evidence (data), we do, at times, fail at this task. Our failure to draw accurate conclusions from the evidence is particularly blatant in the areas of *science* and *religion*. In these areas our unusually good logic and decision-making processes falter. For instance, how many scientists today accept the theory of evolution despite the paucity of hard data, and despite the vast amount of evidence to the contrary?

It appears that in these types of issues our personal biases cloud our thinking to such an extent that, if the issues were not emotionally charged, our unusually fine decision-making apparatus would lead us to conclude the very opposite. At the conclusion of this chapter, the reader may have enough information and evidence to decide for himself/ herself what is, most probably, valid or invalid. The evidence must be weighed, and less probable hypotheses must give way to more probable ones. Anyone can be the "devil's advocate," but the individual hungry for truth must be an objective judge, weighing critically the pros and cons.

1. Archaeological Finds

As mentioned above, over the last hundred years, literally hundreds of archaeological finds which directly or indirectly corroborate Biblical narratives from the first book of Genesis to the Prophets and Holy Writings have been uncovered. The findings cover a time period from the creation of the world to the beginning of the Second Jewish Commonwealth (in the fifth century B.C.E.). For example, the Bible explains that less complex organisms were created before more complex ones, and that water-based life and earth vegetation preceded the animal kingdom. This description is now supported by modern geologists.

In brief, archaeological discoveries have been made (and are continuously being made) which substantively support the following Biblical narratives:

A. The Flood of Noah
B. Jewish Patriarchal Life
C. Joseph's Prominence in Egypt
D. Hebrew Bondage in Egypt
E. The Period of the Judges
F. The Jewish Monarchy
G. The Jewish Wars, and
H. The First Exile[84]

2. Six Hundred Thousand Male-Adult Witnesses

The revelation at Mount Sinai, as recorded in the Old Testament, came about in a manner *entirely different* from prophetic revelations described by other religions. For example, both Christianity and Islam claim Divine Revelation via one or a handful of individuals. However, at Mount Sinai, the entire Jewish nation was present. It is difficult to believe that an event attested to by an entire nation is fictitious. Moses himself stressed this point: "With us [i.e., the Revelation was with all of us], us, who are all of us here alive this day."[85]

It is illogical to suggest that one person (or a group of people) brainwashed an entire nation to believe they had witnessed an event that never occurred — in particular this phenomenon which changed the lifestyle of a nation and eventually the world. And by the laws of logic, that which is perceived and attested to by the greatest number of people has the greater historical validity. The Bible itself states:

> For ask now of the days past, which were before you, since the day that God created man upon the earth, and from one end of heaven unto the other, whether there has ever been any great thing as this great thing?... Did ever a people hear the voice of God speaking out of the midst of the fire, as you have heard?... Unto you [the Jewish people] it was shown, that you might know that the Lord, He is God; there is no one else beside Him.[86]

Has, indeed, any nation ever made such a claim?

However, the "argument" is sometimes made that Moses (who had taken them out of bondage) had come to be considered a superman who convinced the people of things that, in actuality, never were. In response, it is highly improbable that a man (even with the stature of Moses) could have contrived phenomena that would be believed by an entire nation. However, this is beside the point, for despite Moses' superior qualities, the Hebrew people never followed him blindly. For example, as soon as the Hebrews encamped by the Red Sea (after their exodus from Egypt) they began speaking against Moses: "Because there were no graves in Egypt, have you taken us away to die in the wilderness?"[87] Later on, it states: "the whole congregation of the Children of Israel murmured against Moses and Aaron in the wilderness,"[88] and the nation's dissatisfaction intensified to such an extent that Moses himself cried to God saying: "They are almost ready to stone me!"[89] Even after the abortive rebellion of Korach and his followers, the Hebrews' independent nature remained remarkably unchanged: "On the morrow all the congregation of the Children of Israel murmured against Moses and Aaron saying, 'You have killed the people of the Lord' [i.e., the rebellious Korach and his followers!]."[90]

From the above and other passages it becomes clear that the Israelites never followed Moses nor any Jewish leader blindly. Jewish leaders throughout history were, in fact, the object of acrimonious criticism. However, despite their independent and rebellious nature, nowhere throughout the Bible did this rebellious and skeptical people ever deny Biblically recorded happenings. On the contrary, Biblical history was often invoked to rebuke and humble the nation collectively.

3. Unflattering Language Suggests Objectivity

In P. Biberfield's work, *Universal Jewish History*, he writes:

> ...it may be said that Biblical sources possess an objectivity and impartiality never matched by human documents. Nowhere on earth do we find the mistakes and blunders of kings so clearly described and condemned as those of the kings of Israel. No other nation has given such unbiased reports of its defects and of the tributes paid to foreign conquerors. The Egyptian historiographers avoided carefully the reports of any humiliating fact. The same was true with the otherwise more reliable Assyrian annals.[91]

As mentioned above, the Hebrew Bible repeatedly talks in highly unflattering terms about the Hebrew (Jewish) people. They are consistently portrayed (*in their own national history book*) as a "stiff-necked", stubborn people who have a penchant for rebelling against authority. Moreover, they have openly admitted that their own national beginnings stemmed from being Egyptian slaves. Has there ever been an official constitution and national history put down in such denigrating terms? All other national histories cover up their blemishes while aggrandizing, romanticizing, and even fabricating their deeds, heroism, and prideful national origins (which were allegedly witnessed by one or a handful of people and/or are rebutted by other contemporaneous historical sources). The fact that Jewish history took the opposite approach in detailing the Jewish people's faults and blunders shrieks of objectivity.

Correspondingly, the Bible openly records the sins of its greatest leader, Moses.[92] Logically, no leader should have had to detail his own sins and inadequacies so conscientiously. Honesty of this sort undermines credibility, and invites disrespect and rebellion — all the more so when it is openly recounted how the leader rebukes, punishes, and criticizes the people (as did Moses). In effect, he would be setting himself up for disqualification on the grounds that he himself is as culpable.

This unwillingness to cover up shortcomings pervades Jewish Biblical history. The *New World Encyclopedia* concludes thus:

> Jewish historiography is unique in its objectivity. It does not deal in flattery or propaganda for the sake of the monarchy. Due to the objectivity of the authors of the Bible [Old Testament], an accurate description of the character of King David has been preserved which relates the very human faults which darken his otherwise extraordinary personality. No other national-historical document faintly compares to the Bible in the honest and uncensored exposé of the sins that stained David's personal life, the rebellions that endangered his monarchy, the isolationist tendencies which continued to exist throughout his reign, and the intrigues that accompanied the coronation of his successor, Solomon. No attempt was made to beautify or hide or obliterate condemning facts, as was common in the courts of all the rulers of the ancient East.[93]

4. The Commandments to Remember

The Jewish nation is repeatedly commanded (in the Bible) to remember events they themselves witnessed. In several places the Bible emphatically commands: *You shall remember!* It is illogical that any nation would bind itself to remember what it allegedly saw and experienced had these events not occurred (especially with regard to the independently spirited Israelites).

Only when it becomes evident that the Bible was not written at a later date or dates, but at the time the events occurred, is it conceivable that the Jewish nation would accept the responsibility to remember.[94] It is absurd to believe that the Hebrews were brainwashed into believing the events, and thereafter were commanded to remember them. For example:

A. *Remembrance of the Exodus:*
    "...in order that you shall remember the day of your leaving the land of Egypt all the days of your life."[95]

B. *Receiving the Torah at Mount Sinai:*
    "Only take utmost care and watch yourselves scrupulously so that you do not forget the things you saw with your own eyes and so that they do not fade from your mind as long as you live. The day you stood before your God at Sinai, when God said to me, 'Gather the people to Me that I may let them hear My words, in order that they may learn to revere Me as long as they live on earth and may so teach their children.' "[96]

C. *Remembrance of the slavery in Egypt:*
    "And you shall remember that you were a slave in Egypt..."[97]

D. *"Remember,* never forget, how you provoked God to anger in the wilderness from the day you left the land of Egypt until you reached this place, you have been rebellious against the Lord."[98]

E. *Remembrance of Amalek:*
   "Remember what Amalek did to you on your journey from Egypt, how he came upon you on the way, struck you in your hind parts, the weak ones following at the rear, and you were tired and exhausted and he was undeterred by the fear of God....Do not forget!"[99]

F. "When, in time to come, your son asks you, 'What do the testimonies and the laws and the legal regulations mean that God has commanded you?,' and you should say to your son, 'We were slaves to Pharaoh in Egypt and God freed us from Egypt with a mighty hand and outstretched arm.'"[100]

G. *Remembrance of the Ten Plagues:*
   "Be not afraid of them [the nations of Canaan]. You have but to bear in mind what God did to Pharaoh and to all Egypt: The wondrous acts that you saw with your own eyes, the signs and the wonders, the mighty hand and the outstretched arm by which God liberated you."[101]

H. *Remembrance of Miriam's leprosy:*
   "Remember what God did to Miriam on the journey after you left Egypt."[102]

I. *Remembrance of the journey in the wilderness:*
   "Remember the entire journey that God has made you travel in the wilderness these past forty years in order to subject you to hardship, to test you and make known what was in your hearts, whether you would keep His commandments or not."[103]

5. The Bible's Anachronistic Nature

A. Malamot, in his *A History of the Jewish People*, writes:

The early history of every nation is shrouded in mystery. Only faint memories of minimal historical value have succeeded in reaching us through the corridors of history. The Nation of Israel is unique among all the nations of the ancient east in its preserving a complex organic transmission, contained in the books of the Pentateuch and Yehoshua [Joshua], concerning its origins and development before it emerged onto the horizon of history as a defined national entity.

The possibility exists that among those nations that settled in close proximity to Israel there were records preserved from the countries of their origins, however, detailed information of origins or uninterrupted historical records of no other nation of the Biblical period has reached us which compares to that of the Biblical account of the patriarchs, the Exodus, or the conquering of the Land.[104]

According to the Jewish philosopher and poet Rabbi Yehuda HaLevi, in his classic work *The Kuzari,* the authenticity of the Old Testament is attested to by its incongruity with the age of its birth, its original and unborrowed nature, and the suddenness with which it came about in an era of violence and superstition.[105]

The Biblical commandments present a gaping departure from the lifestyle and philosophy of the time. For example:

A. To rest on the *Sabbath* day was incongruous with the times.

B. The *rights of slaves,* almost equivalent to that of masters, sharply deviated from the prevailing custom which treated slaves as beasts of burden.

C. The *love for strangers* was indeed strange during that period in history.

D. *Charitable obligations* surpassed social benefits given even today.

E. The seemingly hypersensitive commandment to *protect and provide* special care *for the orphan and widow.*

In short, Biblical laws were totally incompatible with the times: One God with no physical form as opposed to the prevalent idolatries of the time; justice and ethics in place of enslavement and tyrannical oppression, and the *sublimation* of one's instincts in opposition to hedonism.[106]

6. Was Moses an Omniscient Zoologist?

The Bible, without caution, states that there exist four types of animals *in the world* which possess only one of the required two kosher characteristics. In the book of Leviticus it states:

> These are the creatures that you may eat from among all the land animals: any animal that has true hoofs, with clefts through the hoofs, and that chews the cud — such you may eat. The following however, of those that either chew the cud or have true hoofs you shall not eat: the camel — although it chews the cud has no true hoofs: it is unclean for you; the hyrax — although it chews the cud, it has no true hoofs: it is unclean for you; the hare — although it chews the cud, it has no true hoofs: it is unclean for you; and the swine [pig family] — although it has true hoofs, with the hoofs cleft through, it does not chew the cud: it is unclean for you.[107]

The Bible could have listed only the kosher characteristics, and not have endangered its credibility by limiting the kinds of animals who have only one of the two characteristics. The Malbim (Rabbi Meir Leib Weiser), in the nineteenth century, wrote accordingly:

> In the books of Leviticus and Deuteronomy are listed only three mammals that possess the single [kosher] characteristic of chewing their cud...and the only mammal with the single characteristic of split hoofs. In addition, in the book of Deuteronomy a definitive listing of the ten clean animals [i.e., animals with the two kosher characteristics] is given. Naturalists of all eras investigated and examined all manner of animals existing in all locations and climates of the world, but were unable to find one exception to the ten clean animals or the four animals with only one kosher characteristic.[108]

The scientist and world traveler, Kach, concurred. Kach traveled around the world searching for the fifth species. After touring the globe he was unable to discover any exception to the above four. However, the question remains: How did the Bible (3200 years ago) know that only four species would be found possessing one of the two identifiable kosher character-istics?[109] The Talmud itself asks the rhetorical question: "Was Moses a hunter or archer [i.e., someone highly knowledgeable of the animal kingdom]?"[110]

7. Defiance of Human Logic

Several promises are made in the Old Testament which have, according to the laws of nature, *zero probability* of occurring. Moreover, these promises have to do with *this world* and not the next (i.e., after one dies). They are promises whose realization can be observed and refuted (i.e., if they fail to materialize). Their validity and authenticity (or conversely their falsity) may be publicly observed. Other religions make supernatural promises but these promises deal with life after death (Heaven or Hell?), or with future happenings, phenomena impossible to prove or support. In contrast, the Old Testament promises things that could be tested and observed, and thereby refuted. The fact that these out of the ordinary promises were never denied or refuted by the spirited and skeptical Jewish people (throughout hundreds of years of observation) suggests the promises did indeed materialize. Furthermore, it is highly illogical (and veritably imbecilic) for leaders to make unnatural (supernatural) promises which would be observed in the here and now, and which have zero probability of occurring naturally. However, the Bible did make these "ridiculous" types of promises, and to none other than the recalcitrant, independent, and skeptical Hebrew people.

A. In the book of Deuteronomy it states:

Moses then related to them [the Jews] the following com-mandment: "At the end of each seven year period, at a fixed time on the festival of Succoth...when *all* [the people of] Israel come to present themselves before God your Lord in the place He will choose, you must read from this Torah [Bible] before *all* Israel so that they will be able to hear it. *You must gather together the people, the men, women, children and proselytes from your settlements*, and let them hear it. They will thus learn to be in awe of God your Lord, carefully keeping all the words of this Torah."[111]

Correspondingly, in the book of Exodus it states: "Three times each year, *all your males* shall thus present themselves before God the Master, Lord of Israel. [And] when I expel the other nations before you and extend your boundaries, *no one will be envious of your land when you go to be seen in God's presence three times each year.*"[112]

In brief, the above Biblical passages if, indeed, prescribed by mortal man, propose a plan for national suicide! *All males* were commanded to travel to Jerusalem three times yearly. This commandment leaves all borders abandoned (while the women and children stay in constant danger of attack). In effect, they were commanded three times yearly to leave *all* cities and possessions open and accessible to all comers. Why would a mortal lawmaker make an illogical and potentially devastating law which, realistically, portends national suicide? How would this lawmaker be able to keep this grandiose promise throughout history? Has there ever been a similar promise promulgated by other national leaders? And how did this stiff-necked Hebrew people accept and follow this commandment for hundreds of years?

B. In the book of Leviticus it reads:

> The Lord spoke to Moses on Mount Sinai: Speak to the Israelite people and say to them: When you enter the land that I give you, the land shall observe a Sabbath of the Lord. Six years you may sow your field and six years you may prune your vineyard and gather in the yield. But in the seventh year the land shall have a Sabbath of complete rest...you shall not sow your field or prune your vineyard. You shall not reap the aftergrowth of your harvest or gather the grapes of your untrimmed vines; it shall be a year of complete rest for the land.... You shall observe My laws and faithfully keep My rules, that you may live upon the land in security; the land shall yield its fruit and you shall eat your fill, and you shall live upon it in security. And if you should

ask, "What are we to eat in the seventh year, if we may neither sow nor gather in our crops?" *I will ordain My blessing for you in the sixth year, so that it shall yield a crop sufficient for three years.* When you sow in the eighth year, you will still be eating old grain of that crop; you will be eating the old until the ninth year, until its crops come in.[113]

It is difficult to understand the practical reason for this commandment. An entire *agricultural society* is commanded to *totally abandon* its most important (if not only) source of livelihood (with no freezers, food preservatives, or industry to soften the economic and social blow) with a seemingly irresponsible disrespect for the people's future well-being. In short, this commandment, as well, is a plan for national suicide!

What logic could explain a law which submits an entire people to the danger of economic and physical annihilation? What human leader would introduce such laws, least of all to the people of Israel? What ruler could guarantee his subjects' welfare, which only nature could provide? Who would promise a miraculous harvest every sixth year? In effect, the command would delegitimize the entire scheme of Torah observance. If the promise is not reliably kept for one or two seven-year cycles, the peoples' confidence in Torah law would be lost.[114] Moreover, to endanger an entire nation's economy and food supply, in the face of animosity and rivalry among nations, is insane!

C. In the book of Numbers it states:

God spoke to Moses telling him to speak to the Israelites and say to them: [This is the law] if any man's wife is suspected of committing adultery... [this is the case where] the man [had previously] expressed feelings of jealousy against his wife, and she then [may have been] defiled. [However,] he may have expressed such feelings of jealousy against his wife, and she [may not have been] defiled. [The law is] that the man must bring [his wife] to the priest.... In the priest's hand shall be the curse-bearing bitter water. The priest shall administer an oath to the woman, saying to her, "If a man has not lain with you, and you have not committed adultery

so as to be defiled to your husband you shall be unharmed by
this curse-bearing water.... He shall then make the woman
drink the bitter curse-bearing water.... When the woman
drinks the water, if she has been defiled and untrue to her
husband, the curse-bearing water will enter her body to
poison her, causing her belly to blow up and her sexual
organs to rupture.... However, if the woman is pure and has
not been defiled, she will remain unharmed and will subsequently become pregnant [as compensation for being
wrongly accused].[115]

Again, what mortal leader would stake his reputation and
the obedience of his people on supernatural occurrences which
could be openly refuted? And, what type of nation would
blindly accept such "nonsense" when it could be proven otherwise? And yet, one of the most capable leaders in history,
Moses, did present the Jewish people with this seemingly irra-
tional law and promise. Moreover, the proverbial stiff-necked
Hebrews never, over centuries of implementation, questioned
it, its authority, or its validity.

8. The Computer Revolution

Jewish tradition has always claimed that the Bible, as a
God-given instrument, was made to be interpreted on several
levels, from its revealed simple interpretation to its hidden
meaning. According to Nachmanides (the Ramban, 1194-
1270), the *full depth and wisdom* of the Bible "is hidden from the
eyes of all living,"[116] and is "broader than the sea."[117] The same
theme is expressed in the Talmud: "The son of Bog Bog said,
'Turn it [the Bible] over, and [continue to] turn it over, for
everything is in it.'"[118]

Today, some of its hidden esoteric knowledge is becoming
accessible via the computer. The computer was programmed to
scan the entire Bible and mathematically decode passages,
sentences, and words in its original Hebrew form. Its ability to
survey the Bible, in almost any conceivable pattern, was impossible only a generation ago. In Israel, in particular, the investi-

47

gation of Biblical code words is proceeding steadily. Significant code words are being found *everywhere* in the original Hebrew text, according to mathematical procedures.

Furthermore, the same procedures implemented on other books and literary classics *fail* to reveal any consistent intelligible coding, let alone coding which is traditionally and logically connected to the text at hand.[119] Two scientists from Israel's Institute of Technology, Dr. Moshe Katz and Dr. Menachem Wiener, claim that the remarkable aspect of the research is not (necessarily) that words are uncovered by stringing together letters at regular intervals, but that the revealed word, in each instance, bears direct relevance to the text at hand.[120]

These scientists, who use a letter-stripping method, say their evidence "strongly suggests" that the Bible could not have been composed by mortal intelligence. In the words of Dr. Weiner: "Such a phenomenon cannot be explained rationally, so we need a non-rational explanation. And ours is that the Bible was written by God, through the hand of Moses. Clearly, we have not scientifically proved this, but the preponderance of occurrences certainly points to it."[121]

Another institution involved in this type of research is the Meir Institute of Israel. The institute is presently in the process of publishing its computer generated findings which demonstrate the unparalleled depth of Biblical literature.

The following examples represent one type of simple data presently being generated. For this data, the computer was programmed to derive words from Biblical passages, based on equal steps or intervals between letters.

The Holocaust (HaShoah)

Is it possible that the Bible, thousands of years prior, knew of the Nazi Holocaust? In the book of Deuteronomy it reads:

> God said to Moses, "When you go and lie with your ancestors, this nation shall rise up and stray after the alien gods of the land into which they are coming. They will abandon Me and violate the covenant that I have made with them. *I will*

then display anger against them and abandon them. I will hide My face from them and they will be [their enemies'] prey. Beset by many evils and troubles, they will say, "It is because our God is not in our midst that these evils have befallen us." Yet on that day I will keep my countenance hidden, because of all the evil that they have done in turning to alien gods. Therefore write down this poem and teach it to the people of Israel. Make them memorize it, so that this song will be a witness for the Israelites."[122]

Correspondingly, the following is a death-camp description by one World War II survivor:

The Holocaust stands at the center of the events of our generation and in many ways at the center of Jewish history in its entirety. The quintessential element that distinguishes this event was the search for God. Every Jew who remained in the ghettos and the camps remembers the God syndrome that shrouded everything there. From morning till night we cried out for a sign that God was still with us. From the depths of our tragedy, in the face of the piles of dead bodies of our brethren, and the gas chambers, in the face of the most inconceivable wickedness ever perpetrated, we screamed: "Almighty God! Merciful Compassionate God! Where are You?" We sought Him, but we did not find Him. We were always accompanied by the crushing and unsettling feeling that God had disappeared from our midst.[123]

Using the computer, one can see that the aforementioned Biblical passage contains more than it openly reveals. Beginning from the third Hebrew letter *Hay* (ה) in the passage and counting four sets of 50 letters downward, the 50th letter of each set (together with the beginning letter *Hay*) produces the Hebrew letters *Hay, Shin, Vav, Aleph,* and *Hay* (השואה). Its transliteration is *HaShoah* which means in English *The Holocaust*. The *number 50* is also significant (in Jewish tradition) for it represents, among other things, the number of days between the Exodus from Egypt and the giving of the Torah on Mount Sinai.

Correspondingly, the word *Nazi* (In Hebrew, the letters are

Nun, Tzadi, and *Yud* [נצי]) is found in *equal intervals* of *49* letters (7 x 7; seven and multiples of seven are, traditionally, significant) in the Biblical passage dealing with rebuke and punishment for failing to observe the Torah![124]

שמואל יניב, רמז בפרדס ושפות נסתרות בתורה (מכון מאיר: 1984) 201.

Other Examples

The above example describes how the procedure is done. To recapitulate, *real words*, formed by *equal interval spacing between letters* in which the *number* of letter spaces (between the letters forming the word) is, in general, traditionally significant, and where the word formed is a *meaningful part of the Biblical passage at hand* have been decoded in literally *hundreds* of places throughout the *Old Testament. In addition, no other known book, past or present, has similar characteristics.* The following are further examples of *decoded words*, their *context,* and the *number of equal spacing* between letters:

1. *Torah,* equal spacing of 50 letters; in the passage concerning the Creation of the world.[125] (Jewish tradition states that God created the world through the blueprint of Torah.)

2. *God's Name found five times,* in equal spacing of 5, 8, 13, 21, and 34 letters respectively.

$$21 = \begin{array}{c} 5 \\ +8 \\ 13 \\ +21 \\ 34 \end{array} \begin{array}{l} > = 13 \\ \\ > = 34 \end{array}$$

This mathematical configuration is found in the passage concerning sacrificial worship.[126] It could be understood from this passage that the Jewish people are enjoined to sacrifice only and wholly to God Himself.

3. *Torah*, equal spacing of 50 letters; in the passage concerning the boundaries of the new land (i.e., the Land of Israel) the Jews were about to enter.[127] This corresponds to Biblical passages which state that Jewish occupation of and survival in their own land are dependent on Torah observance.[128]

4. *Sabbath, two times*; equal spacing of 50 letters; each concerning Moses's instruction to keep the Sabbath day holy.[129]

5. *Soul*, equal spacing of 39 letters; in the passage concerning the prohibition of doing work and eating on Yom Kippur.[130] According to Talmudic literature, there are 39 major forms of work prohibited on Yom Kippur which if performed intentionally (while being cognizant of the law) will effect an "excision" of the *soul*.

6. *Honor*, equal spacing of 51 letters; in the passage concerning God's furnishing dress for the first man (Adam) and his wife (Eve), and then sending them out to work the land.[131]

7. *Blessing, two times*; equal spacing of 13 and 15 letters; regarding Jacob's final blessing to his son Joseph,[132] who previously (in private) received a double inheritance.

8. *Torah*, equal spacing of 50 letters; in the passage concerning Moses's praise of God, and his concluding instructions to the Israelites.[133]

9. *Leah and Rachel* (Jacob's two wives), equal spacing of 50 letters; concerning Isaac's instructions to his son (Jacob) to take a "wife" from his mother's family.[134]

10. *Moses*, equal spacing of 50 letters; concerning Joseph's last words to his brothers, (that God would eventually redeem the Israelites from Egypt).[135]

9. Old Testament Prophecies

The materialization of Old Testament prophecies, and what they portend for the future is discussed in detail in chapter

X. However, it may be mentioned here that the realization of ancient Jewish prophecy concerning the Jewish people, the Land of Israel, the Torah, and the relationship of the Jewish people to the nations of the world, is without precedent. Similarly, Simcha Meiri, a leading Israeli educator, states thus:

> Try to imagine how amazed we would be if we were to uncover an ancient papyrus thousands of years old which describes events that actually occurred generations later, or even in modern times. It would be that much more astounding if these events were of an extraordinary nature, as were those recorded in Jewish history. But such a manuscript does exist, in fact several do — the book of the Scriptures, which are unquestionably older than the events they describe, and ...these events could not have been anticipated as they run counter to all accepted laws of history.[136]

III / Prerequisites in Understanding

Remember days long gone by.
Ponder the years of each
generation.
(Deuteronomy 32:7)

Father Edward Flannery, in his introduction to *The Anguish of the Jews*, declared:

> Christians, even highly educated ones, are all but totally ignorant of it—except for contemporary developments. They are ignorant of it for the simple reason that anti-Semitism does not appear in their history books. Histories of the Middle Ages — and even of the Crusades — can be found in which the word "Jew" does not appear, and there are Catholic dictionaries and encyclopedias in which the term "anti-Semitism" is not listed.[1]

The present author, some twenty years later, would add that Jews as well (specifically the young adult generation) know little of the sorrow which befell their ancestors throughout recorded history. The Sisyphus-type vicissitudes of the Jewish Patriarchs and Matriarchs are virtually unknown, and the sojourn in Egypt is, in general, misconstrued. Accordingly, the Assyrian slaughter and expulsion, some 2,700 years ago, is

53

unrecognized by even "educated" Jews, and any reference to the great Babylonian and/or Persian exile conjures up images of the "Birth of Civilization" only (as emphasized in general history textbooks). And ancient Greek and Roman savagery remain a possession of the historian. Does anyone know that nineteen hundred years ago the Romans were *crucifying* five-hundred Jews daily? And who is aware that for over one-thousand years Jews, en masse, were pillaged, expelled, and slaughtered in the name of Christianity? How many westerners understand Islam's approach towards Jews and Judaism, an approach which views Jewish subjugation and degradation as "sacred." Who has heard of the Russian folk hero and "freedom fighter" Chmelnitsky who in the seventeenth century fought the Polish (non-Jewish) aristocracy, and in the process wittingly massacred hundreds of thousands of Jewish civilians. And who knows of the Russian pogroms, the Russian revolution, and its ensuing civil war which produced the wholesale slaughter and torture of over half a million Jewish peasants?

Correspondingly, a fixation, common among Jewish people today, is to focus on the Nazi-German holocaust, while bypassing over three millennia of brutal persecution. This obsessive focus is fostered by Jewish organizations of all kinds, and has produced a mind-set incapable of understanding the phenomenon in perspective. Its repetitive nature has repulsed young Jew and Gentile alike, whose perception today of the Jew is that he is more to be envied than pitied. This focus makes it difficult to deal with the problem adequately, and any constructive plan of action following therefrom is doomed. This does not imply that the bestiality of the German people during World War II deserves a respite from condemnation, but that the attempted genocide, carried out by one of the most "civilized" nations in the twentieth century, was little more than the culmination of a millennia old social cancer. *In effect, only historically can anti-Jewish hostility be understood.*

A further problem concerns the type of analyses heretofore presented. Since World War II, there have been several serious English works delineating anti-Jewish hostility with its bloody consequences, but these works do little more than detail its many occurrences.[2] Seemingly, their intent was to prevent future happenings; however, their writings (as conclusive works) are substantively inadequate for the following reasons: (1) anti-Jewish hostility has taken various forms, and has been perpetrated by considerably different ideological entities throughout history, and without a cohesive theory, Jews may be too preoccupied searching out Nazis and criticizing Christianity to deal with the threats facing Jewry today, and (2) criticism and moral exhortations will not change peoples' attitudes and behavior, but may, in fact, produce greater frustration in the potentially hostile population, bringing more suffering in its wake (the "blaming the victim" effect).

Accordingly, the only constructive way to deal with the problem is through logical and concrete action based on *solid theory* and *experience*. Unfortunately, most authors fail on both counts. An exception to the rule is Prager and Telushkin[3] who, unlike others, have developed a theory which is consistent. Nonetheless, their theory is shallow, and their strategies to combat the malady are unrealistic and potentially harmful. In short, their historical-universal reason for Jew-hatred is specifically Jewish (unlike other theorists who posit economic, social, psychological, or political causes, and whose theories may be superimposed on any distinctive ethnic or racial minority). But their exposition is ambiguous and questionable. For example, their claim that anti-Jewish hostility exists, in great part, because Jews have been better educated, less prone to drinking, more charitable with one another, less prone to crime, and have had a more stable family unit than their non-Jewish neighbors is dubious, for it may be argued (however wrongly) that these factors are more a *result* of anti-Jewish hostility than the causes thereof. In addition, *their primary solution* to the problem is that Jews accept the challenge of spreading ethical monotheism (to the world). However, the authors themselves express the irony that it is "the ultimate cause of anti-Semitism which must be fulfilled in order to end anti-Semitism."

Social scientists of different strains have also proposed theories of anti-Jewish hostility, but their theories are ahistorical in nature and cannot deal, on their unilevel of analysis, with *historical* anti-Jewish hostility (that is, their theories are at best dubious when superimposed on various cultures and times). Alternatively (as alluded to above), historical analyses of anti-Jewish hostility are, in general, theoretically amorphous, varying only in their emphasis on detail and era(s) of analysis.

The factual horror stories told by these authors have indeed depicted humanity's lowly state, but have failed miserably in describing the uniqueness of anti-Jewish hostility. *Their topic is Jewish suffering, yet they focus on non-Jewish brutality.* A disinterest in portraying anti-Jewish hatred *per se* is evident, and only their universal message via the Jewish experience, is deemed important. Jews are depicted as qualitatively replaceable by other persecuted and discriminated against groups such as Blacks, women, the American Indian, etc., and only by virtue of the intensity and extensiveness of their suffering do they embody the most complete paradigm from which to portray humanity's sadistic nature. In other words, anti-Jewish hostility, according to these authors, is not different in kind from other forms of group-hostility, and lessons to be learned are not and never intended to be specifically Jewish, but rather universal in scope and application.

It was this a priori intention of admonishing the world (arbitrarily via the Jewish experience) which precluded the analysis of anything distinctively Jewish. In contrast, the present author asserts, at the outset, his disinterest in detailing man's active enmity towards his fellow man (a cursory reading of contemporary newspapers would illustrate the same). By asking the question, "What is fundamentally different about anti-Jewish hostility?" as opposed to the implicit question asked by others, which is; "What has been the general state of prejudice throughout the ages?" the answers, as well, turn out to be different. While other writers present a sad commentary on humanity, in which Jews are little more than arbitrary stimuli on whom frustration and contempt are heaped, the present analysis depicts the anti-Jewish process as qualitatively distinct. Where other writers derive universal lessons from Jewish history (which they hope will benefit other persecuted and discriminated against minority groups), the present author derives Jewish lessons which serve universal ends (that is, for both the oppressed and the oppressors). Following therefrom, it is little wonder why most historians and social scientists fail to discern the following distinctively Jewish anomalies.

Anomaly No. 1

This anomaly is Jewish longevity. Better put, the question is not why Jews have been oppressed throughout millennia (for other groups and nations have suffered at the hands of the more powerful), but rather how they continued to remain a distinct people, under the most unbearable and ironic of circumstances (and most of the time in a foreign land). For example, when Alexander the Great conquered much of the known world, multitudes of ancient cultures were supplanted by the victorious Hellenistic culture. However, this relatively easy process of transplanting Grecian culture throughout the world was ineffective when confronted with Jews and Judaism. The Jews, *in general*, were unwilling to exchange their civil and religious laws, their modes of thinking and acting, and their sacred knowledge for the progressive and sophisticated Hellenistic culture.

When mighty Rome prevailed, all succumbed except for the stubborn Hebrews. (It should be noted that Christianity was originally a Jewish sect, which after estranging itself from its mother nation had no national character or unique lifestyle other than a system of beliefs not too disparate in kind, in the beginning at least, from its mother religion, Judaism.) Over the three-hundred-year period of Roman rule the Jewish people would, once again, learn the cruel lesson of being different. In fact, the Jewish nation was the only nation exiled, en masse, from its homeland (by the Roman legions) with the intent of destroying, once and for all, Jewish nationalism.

During the Dark and Middle Ages, it was the Christian Church which united Europe. Remnants of the Roman Empire, together with groups of invading "barbarians" relinquished their age-old religions in order to embrace this new creed, as embodied in the Jew from the land of Israel, Jesus. All, that is, except for the Jews, who again refused to bow to any bodily form. Their refusal to accept Christianity would, for the following fifteen hundred years, cost them dearly in wealth, security and blood.

Accordingly, from the eighth century onward, the conquering Islamic armies converted whole tribes and nations throughout North Africa, Asia Minor, and the Middle East — all except the Jews (and to a significantly lesser extent Christians) who persistently weathered second class citizenship (with its cruel ramifications) for more than one thousand years thereafter.

Where are the great cultures of the ancient world with their indigenous language, religion and group mores? Where is ancient *Sumeria, Mesopotamia, Egypt, Babylonia, Persia, Greece,* and *Rome*? Where are the mighty powers of the *Hittites*, the *Philistines*, and the *Assyrians*? Where are the ancient nations of the *Phoenecians, Amalekites, Gazathites, Amorites, Gittites, Girgasites, Chaldeans, Canaanites, Midianites, Moabites, Pharzites, Kenites, Jebusites, Zidorians,* and *Sycthians*? And what about the not-so-ancient groups such as the *Mongols, Huns, Goths, Visigoths, Lombards, Celts, Saxons, Berbers, Kazars, Picts, Tartars, Gauls,* and *Vikings* — where are they today? The answer to this question is clear. These nations and literally hundreds of others[4] have been absorbed culturally, religiously, and even ethnically within the flow of history.

All other ancient nations have relinquished their national and/or religious identity (when given the opportunity) to become one with the majority or conquering power. The Jewish people only, amidst untold discrimination and persecution, retained their language, religion, national consciousness, and civil laws for over three thousand years, while oftentimes becoming an integral part of the larger non-Jewish society.

The Jewish people had only to accept the majority culture and/or religion, and seemingly, would have been saved untold accounts of pillage, rape, exile, and slaughter. Why were the Jews different from the other nations and cultures? Were Jewish leaders, throughout history, so uncommonly ingenius and convincing that they succeeded in holding the Jewish nation together for over three thousand years (in highly disparate lands), while the disintegration of other nations was only a matter of military conquest, ideological infiltration, or exile? Were the Jewish people so different in kind, that only they were able to persevere, whereas other nations (under significantly less severe conditions) were, in a matter of time, fully integrated and absorbed?

History pundits, however, are fast to downplay the Jewish longevity phenomenon in light of other ancient peoples currently extant, whose histories (in one form or another) also predate three millennia, such as the Chinese or the Kurds. *Superficially*, their arguments are sound, and in order that one group not deviate from the norm, the issue is usually not scrutinized. However, before comparing the historical continuity of the Jewish nation with others, the following questions should be asked:

QUESTION 1:   *Has this nation had the luxury of living continuously on its indigenous soil throughout millennia?* Both the Chinese and Kurds have always lived in one geographical area. In contrast, the Jewish people since the destruction of the First Temple (some twenty-five hundred years ago), and, more so, after the destruction of the Second Temple (nineteen hundred years ago) have been scattered literally throughout the world.

QUESTION 2:   *Has the continuity of these nations been, in great part, on account of their cultural and physical isolation?* For example, the Chinese had no substantive interaction with Western or Middle Eastern culture up to the nineteenth century. The Kurds, too, had minimal interaction with the West, and to this day are, in general, a pastoral people living in tents. In comparison, the Jews have not only witnessed every Western and Near Eastern physical and cultural revolution over the past three thousand years, but have, more times than not, been an integral feature of non-Jewish society.

QUESTION 3:   *Have the belief systems (that is, the religions) of these ancient nations remained intact?* In a word, "religion" today in China is *Communist controlled*, and the ancient Kurds are today *faithful Muslims*. Judaism, by comparison, is the same basic Judaism with the same Written code (the Bible) and Oral code (the Talmud) throughout millennia.

QUESTION 4:   *Has this people constituted a majority throughout its history?* In response, the Chinese in China have always been the majority. The Kurdish people as well (within their own national geographic boundaries) were the majority until Turkish occupation in the sixteenth century. In contrast, for over eighteen hundred years, until the creation of the modern Jewish state in 1948, Jews were always the minority.

QUESTION 5:   *Have dissimilar physical characteristics designated these peoples as outsiders?* Concerning the Chinese this is certainly the case. The Kurds, too, are distinctively Middle Eastern in appearance. In contrast, European and American Jews are more physically similar to their Gentile neighbors than they are to Mideastern Jews.

In short, once the above criteria are taken into consideration, the longevity phenomenon takes on an exclusively Jewish character. The celebrated American author, Mark Twain, in his essay "Concerning the Jews," marveled, as well, at this phenomenon:

> If the statistics are right, the Jews constitute but one quarter of one percent of the human race. It suggests a nebulous dim

puff of star dust lost in the blaze of the Milky Way. Properly, the Jew ought hardly to be heard of, but he is heard of, has always been heard of. He is as prominent on the planet as any other people, and his importance is extravagantly out of proportion to the smallness of his bulk.

His contributions to the world's list of great names in literature, science, art, music, finance, medicine, and abstruse learning are also very out of proportion to the weakness of his numbers. He has made a marvelous fight in this world in all ages, and has done it with his hands tied behind him. He could be vain of himself and be excused for it. The Egyptians, the Babylonians and the Persians rose, filled the planet with sound and splendour; then faded to dream-stuff and passed away; the Greeks and the Romans followed and made a vast noise, and they are gone; other peoples have sprung up and held their torch high for a time but it burned out, and they sit in twilight now, or have vanished.

The Jew saw them all, survived them all, and is now what he always was, exhibiting no decadence, no infirmities of age, no weakening of his parts, no slowing of his energies, no dulling of his alert and aggressive mind. All things are mortal but the Jew; all other forces pass, but he remains. What is the secret of his immortality?[5]

Since Mr. Twain's essay, hundreds of thousands of Jews were massacred in Russia (in the early twentieth century), and the Nazis succeeded in annihilating a third of the Jewish people. The twentieth century brought with it, as well, the creation of the third Jewish Commonwealth after eighteen hundred years of dispersion. At its inception the tiny Jewish state, composed primarily of refugees, succeeded in repelling the combined forces of five Arab states whose numbers and armaments vastly exceeded the fledgling Jewish force. The Jewish state would be required to fight another four wars over the next 35 years, while its unrelenting but defeated adversaries (with their vast lands, riches, manpower, and military equipment) continue to call for its *total liquidation*. What would Mr. Twain say today?

Moreover, from 1901 to 1981 (a period of Jewish carnage

and crises in Russia, Germany, Eastern Europe, and the Middle East), the number of Jews to become Nobel Prize recipients was *25 times* greater than their world proportion.[6] In addition, and despite the fact that the vast majority of American Jews came to America *no earlier* than the turn of the twentieth century (and, at present, comprise less than 3% of the American population), in 1970 (before the saturation of Jewish babyboomers) they accounted for 9% of all American physicians and 20% of American lawyers.[7] In universities their percentages were even more disproportionate. In 1971 they comprised 22.4% of all medical university faculty members, and 24.9% of all law faculties.[8] The Jewish people turned out a plethora of intellectual and humanitarian giants during the same period. Giants such as Albert Sabin, Jonas Salk, Sigmund Freud, Alfred Adler, Victor Frankl, Albert Einstein, Robert Oppenheimer, Edward Teller etc., and all after Mr. Twain had written his essay on the inexplicable Jewish phenomenon!

Anomaly No. 2

A second aspect which distinguishes the oppression of Jews from that of other discriminated against groups (e.g., Blacks, American Indians, etc.) and likewise is overlooked by historians and social scientists, concerns the origins of this discrimination. Historically, most other oppressed groups never had a choice to be otherwise. They were never given the chance to assimilate as equals. For example, Blacks, when taken from Africa, were never given the option to be like their white Christian or Arab Muslim captors. For them slavery was the only "option."

In contrast, Jews always had the opportunity to become one with the majority. In certain lands this opportunity was abrogated (e.g., Nazi Germany), but even there the possibility of total assimilation had at one time existed. Not only had Jews the chance to assimilate, but the assimilation of Jews was often a priority of the ruling power. It was always *after the fact*, when

Jews refused to *totally* relinquish their Jewish identity, that discrimination and persecution ensued.

Hence, by failing to distinguish between the anti-Jewish process and other anti-minority group processes we are, indeed, learning about the barbarous history of mankind, but little concerning anti-Jewish activity. In fact, by lumping the anti-Jewish process with others (as most scholars do) we are, in effect, leading the serious student astray. By failing to discriminate between the anti-Jewish process and others, we are, *at best*, describing only the superficial symptoms of group prejudice.

Anomaly No. 3

The third aspect which follows from the first (and therefore writers who fail to speak of the first will not speak of the third) concerns the *one* particular form of Judaism that has maintained itself throughout millennia. Though historically there have been different sects of Judaism (e.g., Sadducees, Nazarenes, Karaites, etc.), only one group (i.e., Oral-Law Judaism, which has been called in different eras Pharisaical, Rabbinic, and Orthodox Judaism) has consistently, throughout history, in divergent lands and cultures, kept the spark of Judaism alive.

Whereas other Jewish groups, throughout history, claimed to be the more progressive or true form of Judaism, whose destiny it was to replace the "antiquated" or "corrupt" Oral Law tradition, their claim was never realized. When a particular period in history ended, so did these various Jewish sects. The only group to survive, through every age and culture, was the Judaism which claimed that its detailed interpretation of the Bible was, in addition to the Bible, handed down to Moses from God. The other groups never claimed that their interpretation of Scripture was transmitted uninterruptedly from Moses to their respective era, but claimed (in the negative) that the Oral Law tradition (as propounded in the Talmud) was man-made. The corollary of their claim was evident; if the

Sages could make up their own interpretations and details, why should others be prevented from doing the same? Irrespective of their claims, the Oral Law tradition led the Jewish people in every era and culture, whereas the others disappeared (as a distinct Jewish religion).

This point becomes important when Jewish continuity plays a major factor in interpreting the anti-Jewish phenomenon. It demonstrates that Judaism's anomalous longevity is inextricably related to Oral Law (Orthodox) Judaism, which unlike other minority groups under similar circumstances, has miraculously preserved itself.

The Oral Law

In light of the relationship between Oral Law Judaism and Jewish longevity, a summary describing its origins and legislation is presented in the following. Although most people are familiar with the Bible, its Oral Law interpretation is little known among modern American Jewry, and even less so in the non-Jewish world.

According to the Talmud, which is the embodiment of the Oral Law, "the Holy One, Blessed be He, did not establish His covenant with Israel except by virtue of the Oral Law."[9]

Support for the claim that there was a concomitant body of legislation inseparable from the Written Law (that is, the Bible) comes from the fact that it is impossible to make tangible pragmatic sense of the Written Law without some accompanying interpretation. More specifically, there are terms in the Bible which are undefined. For example, the term "work" in Sabbatical law[10] or the term "slaughtering" in the dietary laws[11] are undefined, and *only* through a supplementary body of law can these concepts be practically applied. In addition, there are basic legal concepts and institutions, the existence of which is assumed by the Bible, but are not defined. For example, without previously specifying the formal institution of marriage and divorce, the Bible states that a husband cannot remarry the wife he has divorced if in the meantime she has been married to another man.[12] Only through the Oral Law are these Biblically assumed concepts explained.

The Talmud relates the story of a non-Jew who approached the two leading scholars of the time (Hillel and Shamai, the heads of the Jewish Supreme Court some 2,025 years ago) and asked of one: "How many Divine bodies of legislation are there?" He replied, "Two, the Written Law and the Oral Law." The non-Jew retorted, "The Written Law I believe in but the Oral Law I don't believe in, convert me on the condition that I accept only the Written Law." The non-Jew was led out. He then approached the second scholar and made the same request; the scholar began teaching him the Hebrew alphabet. The next day when he returned the scholar began teaching him the alphabet in reverse order. The man exclaimed, "But yesterday you taught me the opposite!" The scholar replied, "You now realize that you must rely on authority even for this [that is, even for understanding the letters of the alphabet], then rely on me, as well, with respect to the Oral Law"[13] (i.e., there must be a reliance upon authority before anything can be learned).

According to the philosopher, physician, and talmudist Moses Maimonides (1135-1204), the Oral Law (as its name indicates) was passed down orally from generation to generation by the leading scholars and their educational institutions for over 1,400 years (circa 1250 B.C.E. to 200 C.E.). The public redaction of the Oral Law, which became known as the Talmud (and comprises both the Mishna and Gemara) began in the days of Rabbi Yehuda HaNasi (circa 200 C.E.) in the Land of Israel, and was eventually completed in Babylonia (500 C.E.). The Jewish leaders, with their myriads of student-scholars, collected, edited, sorted, debated, and redacted the ocean of Oral Law literature for 300 years. In addition to Sinaitic legislation (i.e., laws given to Moses by God) the Talmud is replete with rabbinic legislation which, in most cases, are protectives or amendments, enacted to safeguard Sinaitic law. The Talmud, as well, is a conglomerate of philosophy, history, science, anecdotes, and even humor.

Emphasis placed on the *ethical quality* of Oral Law

teachers, and not on their quality of teaching alone, is a primary feature of Oral Law Judaism.[14] It is also a reason why it was originally prohibited to be redacted.[15] Its redaction enables any scholar, whatever his bias, to present himself as an interpreter and teacher. Conversely, when the Law is handed down orally, it is unlikely that it would be accepted from anyone whose character is such as to make his tradition unreliable.[16]

IV / Why the Jewish People Rejected Jesus and Christian Theology

Though truth be taken as scandal,
it is better to permit the scandal
than to abandon truth.
(Pope Gregory the Great)

This chapter is not a call to assail Christianity (for, as explained in chapter V, various authoritative Jewish sources see Christianity as a positive phenomenon *for non-Jews*), but to offer a brief explanation of Judaism's seemingly stiff-necked denial of Christian doctrine.

If this was left unexplained, both Christians and Jews alike may unfortunately believe that it was Jewish arrogance, ignorance, or sin that precipitated the Jews' rejection of Jesus and the Christian Church (as opposed to all other nationalities, throughout Christendom, who readily embraced the Christian faith). In other words, this chapter demonstrates that the Jews' "failure" to convert to Christianity (thereby maintaining their *separate identity* which, for millenia thereafter, would evoke untold persecution) was not without reason.

Before proceeding, however, an important point which bears emphasis and is oftentimes forgotten (or, for that matter, unknown) is that Judaism did not deviate from Christianity, but rather Christianity from Judaism. In other words, traditional Judaism was never a deviant sect of Christianity, but inversely, Christianity was, at its inception, a sect of the then 1200-year Jewish tradition. This fact must be noted when attempting to understand Christian theology, for it implies that the early and latter-day Christian proponents had substantive historical and empirical justification for breaking with Judaism. However, the following examples speak otherwise!

Why Do Jews Refuse to Accept Jesus as the Son of God?

The Old Testament states that there is only one indivisible God. For example, in Deuteronomy: "The Lord He is God, there is none beside Him."[1] The concept of the trinity is foreign to the Jew, for according to Judaism, God is unique unto Himself: "The Lord, He is God in heaven above and upon the earth below; there is none else."[2] It seems that Jesus himself accepted God's oneness, for in Matthew it states: "And he (Jesus) said unto him, 'Why callest thou me good? There is none good but one, that is God.'"[3] In the Jewish mind, at least, a mortal man, one who was naturally born and who died on a cross, could not be conceptualized as an immortal, indivisible God. In other words, the concept of infinity or indivisibleness cannot be ascribed to God if He is in manly form or a trinity. Moreover, in Numbers[4] it reads: "God is not a man."[5]

Why Did the Jews Refuse to Accept Jesus as the Messiah?

To the Jewish mind, if Jesus was the Messiah he would have fulfilled the Messianic prophecies mentioned in the Bible. For example, the Messiah is to bring about universal peace and tranquility: "And they shall beat their swords into plowshares, and their spears into pruning hooks; nation shall not lift up sword against nation; neither shall they learn war any more."[6] The Messiah is depicted as bringing about universal respect for God, and leading the peoples of the world in God's ways.[7] He is to cause an ingathering of the Jewish exiles,[8] and to bring about the reconstruction of the Temple in Jerusalem.[9] In addition, these accomplishments are to take place in his own lifetime.[10] Jesus did not accomplish any of these.

In order to deal with these problems, Christianity claims that Jesus will reappear in a "second coming." However, there is no reference to a second coming anywhere in the Old Testament. Jesus himself promised that he would succeed in his own time period: "Verily I say to you that there be some of them who stand here, which shall not taste of death until they have seen the Kingdom of God come with power";[11] "Verily I say to you that this generation shall not pass, till all these things be done."[12] However, they were not done.[13]

Jesus and Jewish Law

According to the Old Testament, a prophet is to observe Jewish law and to inspire others to do likewise.[14] However, Jesus considered himself above the law as is stated in Matthew: "For the Son of Man is master even of the Sabbath."[15] Jesus transgressed the laws of the Sabbath (part of the Ten Commandments) and ridiculed the Jewish scholars, who, in both Biblical and Talmudic literature, are accorded great respect. According to traditional Judaism, anyone who denies or makes light of God's law cannot be His Messiah or His Prophet.[16]

Jesus and Jewish Popular Support

Jesus lived during a time of great oppression. The Jewish people, in light of their harsh treatment at the hands of Rome, anxiously awaited the one who would save them from their torment (i.e., the Messiah). The Jewish scholars at that time were of the highest caliber, possessing a thorough knowledge of the accomplishments and character traits that would distinguish the Messiah, and would seemingly have accepted him had they reason to believe he had indeed come. Yet, the scholars of the time rejected Jesus's claim. The leaders saw and experienced Jesus in person and found him wanting. On the other hand, another Jew, Paul of Tarsus (who, in essence, founded the distinct Christian religion) never knew Jesus personally. Therefore, the serious Jewish and Christian student must come to terms with why the scholars, who had every reason to desire the Messiah, rejected Jesus.[17]

The Virgin Birth

Christian missionaries cite the Old Testament[18] as "proof" that Mary's "virgin birth" was prophesized hundreds of years prior. They translate the verse as: "Behold the *virgin* is with child, and she will bear a son, and his name will be called Immanuel." However, if one studies the verse in its original Hebrew, one sees that the mistranslated term virgin in Hebrew is *almah*. In Hebrew, the term *almah* means no more than young woman. More specifically, the Hebrew word for virgin is *betulah*, as mentioned in Leviticus![19]

Bethlehem and the Messiah

Missionaries cite the Biblical verse in Micha[20] as "further proof" that Jesus was the Messiah. The verse reads: "But you, Bethlehem Ephrata, though thou art little among the thousands of Judah, out of you shall come forth to me that is to be ruler in Israel." In essence, all the verse is saying is that the Messiah will come from the lineage of King David, who was born in Bethlehem. Moreover, one cannot claim that Jesus came from King David, for in Judaism, family (tribal) lineage follows the father, and according to Christianity Jesus had no earthly father.[21]

The Suffering Servant

Christian missionaries bring "proof" from Isaiah[22] which refers to God's suffering servant. They say this refers to Jesus, who suffered on the cross. However, the term "servant," when used elsewhere in the prophet Isaiah, denotes the Jewish people collectively. The Jewish people have, in fact, suffered through-out history. Moreover, further on in the same passage it reads: "He shall see his seed, he shall prolong his days." However, Jesus died childless at the age of thirty-three![23]

If Christianity is the Religion of Love and Grace, Why Have Christians, Historically, Been So Cruel, Particularly towards Jews?

In discussing the Crusades (which began in 1096), many non-Jewish history books choose to omit the fact that thousands of Jews were offered the cross or the sword. Because they refused to convert, thousands of Jews were slaughtered throughout France and Germany. The Church promised the Crusaders eternal bliss for killing Jewish infidels. In 1215, at the Fourth Lateran Council, Pope Innocent III decreed that Jews wear something identifiable. They were forced to wear yellow circular forms, pointed hats, and similar items when in public. In Medieval Spain, during the "Holy" Inquisition, heinous tortures were implemented to elicit confessions that the accused were observing Jewish practices.[24]

Jews who accepted Christianity were closely watched, and following any Jewish activity, tortures were implemented. If the accused confessed or was judged guilty, he or she, most often, would be burned alive at the stake. However, if the individual repented, Christian "mercy" would permit strangulation before burning.[25]

This was done with the consent of the Church. The Jewish people, therefore, have historically asked: Can anyone who understands history presume that the belief in Jesus makes one authentically kind and gentle?

Christian apologists say that these Christians acted in a very unchristian-like manner. However, they did it in the name of Jesus. They believed it the thing that Jesus would like, and this was then the accepted interpretation of Christianity. If today's Church feels it was a misrepresentation, then the question is — who is the official arbiter of Christian truth?[26]

Sin and Atonement

From the Biblical passages in Isaiah[27] and Ecclesiastes,[28] Christian missionaries deduce that man is condemned to sin. Man must sin, and therefore he needs something through which he can gain eternal salvation. That something is blood, specifically, the blood of Jesus. The reason for this, they claim, is that according to the Old Testament one needs blood to achieve atonement.[29] Therefore without the blood of Jesus, there can be no remission of sin and no forgiveness.[30]

However, the Bible states elsewhere: "The fathers shall not die for the children; neither shall the children die for the fathers; every man shall die for his own sin."[31] In other words, each individual is responsible for his or her own actions, and one's blood cannot absolve the sins of others. Moreover, the Bible does not state that blood is the sole means of atonement. A closer reading of the chapters on sacrificial worship shows that *animal* blood is prescribed for only a small category of transgressions.

There is one mode of atonement, however, mentioned repeatedly in the Bible. It is sincere repentance.[32] *In Judaism, the most important part of atonement is always concrete action and penitence.*

In addition, nowhere in the Old Testament is human blood allowed for atonement. This is a pagan concept. Jews never offered a human sacrifice with the consent of any Jewish court.

The idea of a god dying to atone for the sins of others is a pagan idea. In the book *The Golden Bough,* the author points out that the accumulated sins of an entire people were, at times, placed upon their dying god.[33] His supreme sacrifice was believed to save his followers the horror of eternal death.

The Jewish King and Messiah

In the Old Testament it reads:

Behold, the days come, saith the Lord, that I will raise unto David a righteous branch, and a king shall reign and prosper, and shall execute judgment and justice in the earth.... Therefore, behold, the days come, saith the Lord, that they shall no more say, The Lord lives Who brought the children of Israel out of the land of Egypt, but, the Lord lives who brought up and led the seed of the house of Israel out of the north country, and from all countries which I have driven them, and they shall dwell in their own land.[34]

This passage, which according to missionaries, refers to Jesus, was never fulfilled. In fact, shortly after Jesus's death, the Second Temple was destroyed, and its people exiled. To claim that the passage refers to a second coming is to admit there is no proof. Any passage which fails to prove that Jesus, in his first coming, was the true Messiah is objectively meaningless.[35]

The burden of proof rests on the person or group which wishes to make a change in the status quo. They are the ones who must demonstrate the legitimacy of their claims, and they must do so via solid evidence.[36]

Humility Before Greatness

In the Old Testament it reads: "The stone which the builders refused is become the head stone of the corner."[37] Missionaries explain this verse as referring to Jesus who, as the refused Jewish stone, became the basis for Christianity.

However, when examining the text closely, it becomes clear that the verse is part of a prayer of thanks and not prophecy. Secondly, using the missionaries' own reasoning, one could claim the verse refers to Adolf Hitler, for he too, at first, was refused power (and was, in fact, put in jail) and thereafter became the *head stone* for much of the world. Or it could refer to King David himself, the author of this psalm, who originally was refused (even) an interview for the position of king.[38] In brief, the verse does not point exclusively to Jesus, and its context excludes it from prophecy altogether.[39]

Christian Martyrdom and Truth

Some Christians believe that Christianity must be true, for if not, they reason, why would early Christians willingly face the lions rather than renounce their faith? Something must have convinced them, and whatever it was, it should be good enough for Christians today.[40]

However, this argument views history in a vacuum. For example, the early Muslims, in the seventh century (as well as today) were willing to give up their lives for their beliefs. Jews as well, throughout millennia, sacrificed their lives and the lives of their children rather than relinquish their beliefs and life-style. In other words, the willingness to give up one's life cannot not validate a theological truth.[41]

Should God Not Have Abrogated the Law before the Entire Jewish Nation?

As described in the book of Exodus, the entire Jewish nation was present when God gave the Law to the Jewish people at Mount Sinai. Now if Christianity is correct, and Jews need no longer obey Old Testament law, then it would be only fair for God to abrogate the (original) laws in a similar fashion. Would it not be absurd for the President of the United States to proclaim new legislation on national television and then, a few years later, let his press secretary (quietly) tell a few people that the law need no longer be obeyed? In other words, there was no indication in the Jewish world, at least, that the Law had been revoked.[42]

Paul vs. Jesus

In Matthew, Jesus said:

Think not that I am come to destroy the law, or the prophets: I am not come to destroy, but to fulfill. Whosoever therefore shall break one of these least commandments, and shall teach men so, he shall be called the least in the kingdom of heaven; but whosoever that shall do and teach them, the same shall be called great in the kingdom of heaven.[43]

This is the famous Sermon on the Mount, and throughout the discourse Jesus nowhere advocated disobedience to Torah law. Thus, in Matthew,[44] when Jesus was accused of violating the Sabbath (*Saturday*), he did not say that one is free to transgress the Sabbath. Rather, he tried to show that his behavior was consistent with Jewish law.

Paul, however, changed all this. Paul was unsuccessful in convincing Jews, so he went to the Gentiles. However, as the Book of Acts points out, he was about to meet failure once again.[45] Paul, then, effected a dramatic change in doctrine, and followers of the new faith were thereafter freed from Jewish law.[46]

In contrast, *all* Old Testament prophets obeyed Jewish law and advocated its obedience. In fact, the last prophet of the Old Testament, *in the last passage*,[47] exhorted the Jewish people thus: "Remember ye the law of Moses My servant which I commanded unto him in Horeb for all Israel, with the statutes and judgments."[48]

Mediation through Jesus

A basic tenet of Christianity is that of Mediation. This means that man cannot approach God except through Jesus.[49] Jesus himself proclaimed this doctrine when he said: "I am the way, the truth, and the life, no man cometh unto the Father but by me."[50]

However, this doctrine seems to contradict the opening statement of the Ten Commandments: "I am the Lord your God, Who brought you out of the Land of Egypt, from the house of slavery. You shall have no other gods beside Me."[51]

Judaism contends that one's relationship to God is not dependent on any mediating power. God is understood as infinite and omniscient. To imply He needs a mediator is to deny His infinite wisdom and omnipotence.[52]

Concrete Behavior and Observance

From the Jewish perspective, it is not enough to believe in God. Faith alone is inadequate; God is depicted as demanding concrete behaviors as well — more specifically, the observance of His commandments (mitzvot). God is portrayed as demanding "discipline, loyalty, and practice," not pious statements and ceremonies.[53]

Jews and Prophecy

Missionaries claim that Jesus fulfilled the prophecy of being a prophet like Moses, for in the book of Deuteronomy it reads: "I will raise them up a prophet among their brethren, like unto you [Moses],"[54] and in John[55] and the book of Acts[56] this verse is interpreted as referring to Jesus, which gives Jesus, therefore, the right to contradict Mosaic law.[57]

However, this is a superficial reading of the Old Testament, for in another place it states: "And there shall not arise a prophet in Israel like unto Moses."[58]

God Himself attested to Moses: "And God said to Moses: Behold, I come to you in a thick cloud, that the people may hear when I speak with you, and may believe in you forever."[59] At Mount Sinai, God attested to the prophecy of Moses by speaking to him in the presence of millions. He did not do similarly for Jesus.[60]

The Crucifixion

Missionaries claim that Jesus fulfilled the prophecy that the Messiah would be killed by crucifixion. They quote the Old Testament verse, which when correctly translated, reads: "For dogs have encompassed me, a company of evildoers have enclosed me, *like a lion,* they are at my hands and feet."[61] "Like a lion" in Hebrew is *KeAri.* However, Christian interpreters changed the spelling of the word from *KeAri* to *Kari.* If one then ignores the laws of Hebrew grammar, one can make it read: "He gouged me." Then, as in the King James Version (of the Bible), the verse may read: "they pierced my hands and feet!"[62]

Without belaboring the point, it should be mentioned that Christians make many other claims that are equally amenable to Jewish interpretation. In conclusion, the above presentation was made in order that the intelligent Christian and Jew alike will understand that Judaism's rejection of Jesus and Christianity was not based on arrogance, ignorance, or twisted theology!

V/ The Primary Cause of Anti-Jewish Hostility

They have said, "Come and let
us wipe them out as a nation;
That the name of Israel be
remembered no more."
(Psalms 83:4)

The advent of the Jewish nation began with one man, Abraham the *Ivri* (the Hebrew), in the seventeenth century B.C.E.[1] The Midrash (Judaism's non-legalistic teachings) explains that the word *Ivri* means "on the other side," where the idol worshipping population, at that time, was (figuratively) on one side, and Abraham, through his philosophical genius and ethical behavior, stood on the other.[2] Abraham suffered both persecution[3] and exile[4] because of his spiritual convictions and lifestyle.

Abraham was the first recorded iconoclast. His intrepid ridicule of the government and idol worship of ancient Mesopotamia endangered his material security and physical existence. The Midrash relates that when Abraham attained the age of twenty, his father spoke to him and his brother Haran:

> "I ask you, my sons, to sell these idols for me." Haran executed his father's wish, but if anyone came to buy an idol

from Abraham he would ask, "How old are you?" "Thirty years," the man said. Abraham then replied, "You are thirty years of age, and yet you would worship this idol I made but today?" After the man departed Abraham took two idols, put a rope around their necks, and with their faces turned downward, dragged them on the ground crying aloud: "Who will buy an idol wherein there is no profit? It has a mouth but it cannot speak; eyes, but it cannot see; feet, but it cannot walk; ears, but it cannot hear."

As he went through the streets, he met an old woman who approached him with the purpose of buying an idol, good and big, to be worshipped and loved. "Old woman, old woman," said Abraham, "I know no profit therein, either in the big ones or in the little ones, either unto themselves or unto others. And, what has become of the big image you bought from my brother Haran?" "Thieves," she replied, "came in the night and stole it while I was in the bath." "If it be thus," said Abraham, "how can you pay homage to an idol that cannot save itself from thieves, let alone save others like yourself?"[5]

A further Midrash states that Abraham took a hatchet and broke all his father's gods, and when finished, placed the hatchet in the hand of the biggest god. Terah his father, having heard the crash of the hatchet on the stone, ran to the room, and arrived at the moment of Abraham's departure. He asked "What is this mischief you have done to my gods?" Abraham answered: "I set savory meat before them, and when I came before them, that they might eat, they stretched out their hands before the biggest one had put forth his hand. Hence the big one, enraged, took the hatchet and broke them all, and behold, the hatchet is yet in his hands, as you see it now."

Terah turned to Abraham, and said: "You speak only lies! Is there spirit, soul, or power in these gods to do all that you have told me? Are they not wood and stone, and have I not myself made them? It is you that placed the hatchet in the hand of the big god." Abraham then replied: "How, then, can you serve these idols in whom there is no power? Can these idols in which you trust save you? Can they hear your prayers when you call to them?" After speaking, he jumped up, took the hatchet from the big idol and smashed it.[6]

The king, at the time, was the powerful Nimrod. Nimrod was considered a god. When Abraham was brought before Nimrod, in light of his heretical ideas and behavior, he requested of Nimrod to change the course of the sun as proof of his divinity. When Abraham's request was refused, he declared the king an imposter.[7]

Initially, Nimrod peaceably attempted to attract Abraham to the "true" faith, and went to great lengths to convince him of his misplaced beliefs. Nimrod tried to show him the benefits of adopting the Mesopotamian peoples' beliefs and general customs. He even arranged a seven-day festival for Abraham's benefit, at which his nobility were bidden to appear in their robes of state, their gold and silver apparel. By such display of wealth and power Nimrod expected to attract Abraham and bring him back to the religion of the masses. He desired Abraham to see his greatness and wealth, the glory of his dominion, and the multitude of his princes and attendants. However, Abraham refused to come.[8]

According to the Midrash, fear then gripped the king, for more and more of his people were attracted to Abraham's "heretical" teachings. The king's power and influence were threatened. Therefore, in order to estrange Abraham from his idiosyncratic philosophy and behavior, he was cast into prison, and in order to uproot any remaining rebelliousness, he was denied food and drink.[9] When these strategies eventually failed, Abraham was condemned to death.[10]

Nimrod's plans proved unsuccessful, but the vicissitudes of Abraham's life would become the prototypic path on which his progeny, over the following 3,700 years, would tread. Abraham eventually escaped the wrath of Nimrod, and at the command of God, as recorded in the book of Genesis, made his way to the land of Canaan (that is, ancient and present day Israel).

Abraham bequeathed this revolutionary philosophy and lifestyle (with its concomitant responsibilities) to his son Isaac, and sent Ishmael away at the urging of his wife Sarah, *which was afterwards justified by God.*[11] Isaac passed the tradition on to the younger of his two sons, Jacob (whose name was later changed to Israel), who then passed it down to his twelve sons, the Twelve Tribes of Israel.

The Egyptian Sojourn

Because of sibling rivalry, Jacob's sons sold their brother Joseph into slavery, in which state he was transported to Egypt.[12] Joseph became great in Egypt and attained the status of second in command.[13] He single-handedly saved the people of Egypt and other surrounding peoples from starvation, and simultaneously procured enormous wealth for Pharaoh.[14] In light of the great famine, which had also swept the Land of Canaan, Jacob and his family journeyed to Egypt at the urgings of his son. Initially, Pharaoh quite graciously granted to Jacob and his sons the best of Egypt, the fertile land of Goshen, to dwell in as free men.[15]

In Egypt, Jacob's family grew by leaps and bounds,[16] and within a short period of time developed into the Hebrew nation. Within eighty years after the Hebrews had entered Egypt with the passing of Joseph and his brothers,[17] they began adopting for themselves Egyptian customs (that is, they began to assimilate).[18] The Midrash relates that the Hebrews became ardent cosmopolitans, and that their presence was conspicuous at the great cultural events of the day.[19]

According to the historian Josephus, the industrious and successful nature of the Hebrew people made them the envy of Egypt.[20] Likewise, according to the Midrash, their remarkable rate of increase, coupled with feats of heroism, placed them in a highly visible and prominent position.[21] Although the Hebrews were rapidly assimilating and becoming highly integral features of Egyptian society (the most sophisticated society at the time), the Midrash tells of two distinctive Hebrew behaviors which, perforce, prevented total assimilation, (1) they retained their Hebrew names, and (2) they retained their Hebrew language.[22] Moreover, their belief system, originating from the Patriarch Abraham, was contrary to anything Egyptian.[23] This clash of religious cultures is seen in the following anecdote, as narrated in the Midrash:

> Now the two representatives of the children of Israel stepped before Pharaoh, and said, "The God of the Hebrews has met with us; let us go, we pray thee, three days' journey into the wilderness! But Pharaoh answered, stating: "What is the name of your God? Of what does His strength consist, and His power? How many countries, how many provinces, and how many cities has He under His dominion? In how many military campaigns was He victorious? How many lands has He made subject to Himself? How many cities has He captured?" Whereto Moses and Aaron replied: "His strength and His power fill the whole world....The heaven is His throne, and the earth His footstool...He nourishes and sustains the whole world, from the horns of the ram to the eggs of the vermin. Daily He causes men to die, and daily He calls men into Life!
>
> Pharoah answered, and said: "I have created myself, and if you say that He causes dew and rain to descend, I have [created] the Nile, the river that has its source under the tree of life, and the ground impregnated by its waters bears fruit so huge that it takes two asses to carry it, and is palatable beyond description, for it has three hundred different tastes!"[24]

The circumstances understandably created a *psychologically threatened* Pharaoh and government. The Hebrew populace was growing in size, success, and prestige, while proudly and stubbornly remaining (to some extent) distinctively non-Egyptian. And Pharaoh and his Egyptian nobility would not tolerate a distinct and competing Hebrew population in their midst. In the minds of Pharaoh and his dignitaries the Hebrew "epidemic" had to be curtailed, and if the Hebrews would not relinquish their "less progressive" and "obsolete" cultural traditions then other, more potent methods would be implemented.

82

Pharaoh was suddenly struck by a seeming paranoia (a common theme running throughout Jewish history), "Lest they multiply and endanger the land."[25] He then said: "Let us deal wisely with them."[26] The Talmud explains that Pharaoh requested their help in building his storehouse cities.[27] The Children of Israel fell into the trap and worked diligently[28] for the system which their forefather Joseph had originally instituted.[29] Gradually, the Hebrew people were pressed into involuntary servitude.

To the dismay of Egypt, the Jewish people began to increase in proportion to the oppression.[30] The Egyptian plan to uproot the Hebrews' stubborn national identity via slavery proved unsuccessful. The Hebrew tradition, initiated by Abraham and predicated on ethical monotheism with its ultimate fulfillment realized in the Land of Canaan as promised to Abraham,[31] was too strong a bond for even Egyptian bondage to sever.

Egypt then implemented its second stage of attack, physical backbreaking labor.[32] If national identity could not be eradicated via forced labor, then bone-crushing measures were to be implemented in order to subdue the Hebrews' spirit, creating, in effect, national misfits. This second stage of attack was also unsuccessful, and consequently Pharoah decreed the murder of all male infants at the time of delivery.[33] When the Hebrew midwives refused to carry out Pharaoh's command, he decreed that every newborn male be cast into the river.[34] *Pharoah's three-level strategy of oppression: (1) discrimination and subjugation, (2) spirit crushing physical persecution, and (3) extermination, was to be the prototype for all subsequent anti-Jewish activity throughout history.*

There are other similarities between Egyptian anti-Jewish hostility and those that followed. For example, Jews in Egypt were highly successful before their oppression. One of their founding fathers (Joseph) was second only to Pharaoh[35] and revered by the Egyptian populace.[36] Similarly, when Joseph's father (Jacob) died, all of Egypt mourned for seventy days.[37] Pharoah himself gave the Hebrews the finest land in Egypt, and offered them positions of prestige and power.[38] During the first eighty years of their sojourn, the Hebrews were highly successful, and only afterwards were bitterly oppressed. In other lands as well, Jews would, at first, succeed (when given the slightest opportunity) only to be eventually oppressed.

If the Hebrews would have completely assimilated into Egyptian society (as small groups, when given the opportunity, consistently do), or had they not been so successful, Egyptian oppression would logically not have been so spiteful, or may never have occurred. In essence, the threat of a successful and dynamic non-Egyptian population burgeoning in the midst of Egypt appears to be the cause of Pharaoh's paranoia. As will be seen, an ongoing theme, characterized by a successful entry into mainstream society without a concomitant disassociation from Judaism, has proved highly threatening to non-Jewish powers throughout history.

It is important to iterate at this point the difference between Jewish oppression and the oppression of other groups. Other targeted minorities, throughout history, were often depicted (by the ruling power), from the start, as inferior. The Jews, in contrast, were always prime targets for assimilation and only *after* they remained "stiff-necked" and refused to totally comply, did discrimination and persecution ensue. What began as a self-imposed desire to be separate, but equal, turned into a universally accepted antipathy toward Jews. It is, therefore, not difficult to understand why the persecution of Jews throughout history has transcended in scope and intensity the persecution of other minority groups. Discrimination and persecution of other groups was most often based on the majority population's superiority complex vis-à-vis the subjugants. Genuine hate and animosity was unusual while the subjugants "knew their place," and dared not overstep their "liberties." In such a state, these groups were easily tolerated (and, oftentimes, affectionately).

However, the circumscribing of Jewish liberties was always after the fact. Only after Jews, en masse, obstinately refused to become totally Egyptian, Persian, Grecian, Roman, etc. did curtailment of freedom ensue. Accordingly, they could not be subjugated without hostility (from the ruling power), for they themselves, by refusing to totally assimilate, inadvertently mocked the society and ruling power.

Persian Anti-Jewish Hostility

The Jewish homeland was eventually conquered by the great Babylonian empire, and with the destruction of the First Temple (in Jerusalem) in 423 B.C.E.,* the Jews were deported en masse to Babylonia.[39] After Babylonia fell to the mighty Media-Persian empire, the conquered Jews, living in the now conquered land, continued to remain voluntarily distinct. This self-imposed distinctiveness brought upon them an attempted genocide, more heinous than the one attempted by Pharaoh in Egypt.

This voluntary separatism was used against them by the infamous Persian prime minister Haman. In short, Haman claimed that by refusing to adopt the ways of the empire, the Jews were undermining the king's authority, and were therefore to be utterly annihilated.[40] The Talmud relates the king's predisposition to Haman's plan,[41] and an edict was thereupon promulgated.[42]

From what we know of the period it appears that the Jews were conspicuously successful in ancient Persia as they were, initially, in Egypt. For example, the leader of the Jews (Mordecai) was an official in the king's court[43] who, patriotically, had saved the king from assassination.[44] In addition, a Jewess (Esther) was the Queen.[45] Furthermore, from the Talmud[46] and Midrash[47] alike, it appears that the Jewish Elders were oftentimes consulted on issues of prime importance.

Total assimilation and integration as a rule follows societal success. The Jews, as well, began adopting non-Jewish mores and customs. For example, the Midrash relates that at the

---

* This date is derived from *Seder Olam* which, with the Talmud, is considered the most authoritative source of Jewish chronology.

king's banquet tens of thousands of Jews intoxicated themselves, and committed immoralities not unlike their more indigenous counterparts.[48] In addition, the traditional Jewish
belief system (as originated by Abraham more than one thousand years prior) was gradually deteriorating.[49]

Notwithstanding the above, the Jews still maintained their
distinctive Jewish character and national identity. This separatism is seen by Haman's denunciation of the Jews, which he
presented before the king:

> Haman appeared before King Achashverosh [Xerxes] claiming:
> "There is a certain people, the Jews, scattered abroad and
> dispersed among the peoples in all the provinces of the
> kingdom. They are proud and presumptuous.... Their reli-
> gion is diverse from the religion of every other people,and
> their laws from the laws of every other land.... Our religion
> finds no favor with them.... They do not give us their daugh-
> ters unto wives, nor do they take our daughters for wives....
>
> "The seventh day they celebrate as their Sabbath...and
> their women pollute the waters with ritual baths....On the
> eighth day after the birth of sons, they circumcise them
> mercilessly, saying, 'this shall distinguish us from all the
> other nations.' At the end of thirty days, and sometimes
> twenty-nine, they celebrate the beginning of the month. In
> the month of Nissan they observe the holiday of Passover.
> They put all the leaven in their homes out of sight saying,
> 'This is the day whereon our fathers were redeemed from
> Egypt.'
>
> "In Sivan, they celebrate the holiday of Shavuot. They
> ascend to the roofs of their meeting places and throw down
> apples, which are picked up by those below, with the words,
> 'As these apples are gathered up, so may we be gathered
> together from our dispersion.' They say they observe this
> festival, because on these days the Torah was revealed to
> their ancestors on Mount Sinai. "On the ninth day of the
> same month they slaughter cattle, geese, and poultry, they
> eat and drink and indulge in dainties, they, their wives, their
> sons and daughters. But the tenth day of the same month
> they call the Great Fast and all of them fast.

"On the fifteenth of the same month they celebrate the Feast of Tabernacles. They cover the roofs of their houses with foliage, they resort to our parks, where they cut down palm branches for their festal wreaths, pluck the fruit of the Etrog, and cause havoc among the willows of the brook, by breaking down the hedges in their quest after Hoshanot saying: 'As does the King in the triumphal procession, so do we....' This is Sukkot, as they call it, and while it lasts, they do none of the king's service, for, they maintain, all work is forbidden them on these days.

"In this way they waste the king's year with indolence and tomfoolery, only in order to avoid doing the king's service...."[50]

As in Egypt, Jewish success coupled with Jewish distinctiveness posed a grave psychological threat to this type of regime. In other lands as well, leaders and governments of this strain would be unable to tolerate a successful, yet distinct, Jewish minority — more specifically, a people who refuse to serve other gods.

After the king promoted Haman to second in command, the order was issued that all who saw him were to prostrate themselves. Of the king's court only Mordecai (the leader of the Jews) refused to obey.[51] And as recorded in the Book of Esther, this "presumptuous" act, on the part of Mordecai, was traumatic for the newly appointed Prime Minister,[52] and attempted genocide was the not too illogical consequence.

However, genocide was not the first strategy implemented. Prior to Haman's bitter clash with Mordecai, the king attempted to erase Jewish separatism via peaceful methods. For example, when the king prepared a banquet for all his citizens, he urged the Jewish population to attend. And in order not to offend their religious sensitivities, he had their food and drink prepared in strict accordance with Jewish law. Accordingly, he put Mordecai in charge of preparations.[53]

Moreover, during the festivities the king followed the Jewish, rather than Persian, manner of drinking. In Persia, the custom prevailed that every banquet participant would finish a large beaker of wine, exceeding his or her drinking capacity, though the individual lost reason. However, at this banquet the Jewish custom prevailed.[54]

The Midrash states that the king was so sure of his success that he said to his Jewish guests, "Will your God be able to match this banquet in the future world?" Whereupon the Jews replied: "The banquet God will prepare for the righteous in the world to come is that of which it is written, 'No eye has seen it but God's; He will accomplish it for them that wait upon Him.' If God were then to offer us a banquet like yours, O King, we would then be able to say, such as this we ate at the table of King Achashverosh!"[55]

However, peaceful methods were not the only methods used to erase Jewish separatism. For example, the Persian Queen Vashti (who reigned before Esther) had her own methods of uprooting Jewish distinctiveness. She would force Jewish maidens to spin and weave on the Sabbath day (something prohibited by Jewish law), and would force them to appear naked.[56]

After these various strategies failed to break the Jewish national and religious character, the following decree of genocide was issued:

This herein is written by me, the great officer of the king, his second in rank, the first among the grandees, and one of the seven princes, and the most distinguished among the nobles of the realm. I, in agreement with the rulers of the provinces, the princes of the king, the chiefs and the lords, the Eastern kings and the satraps, all being of the same counsel and opinion, using the same expressions and the same language, write you at the order of King Achashverosh this writing sealed with his signet, so that it may not be sent back, concerning the great eagle Israel. The great eagle had stretched out his pinions over the whole world; neither bird not beast could withstand him. But there came the great lion Nebuchadnezzar, and dealt the great eagle a stinging blow. His pinions snapped, his feathers were plucked out, and his feet were hacked off. The whole world has enjoyed rest, cheer, and tranquility since the moment the eagle was chased from his eyrie until this day. Now we notice that he is using all efforts to secure wings. He is permitting his feathers to grow, with the intention of covering us and the whole world, as he did to our forefathers. At the insistence of King Achashverosh, where all magnates of the king are assembled, we are writing you our joint advice, as follows: Set snares for the eagle, and capture him before he renews his strength, and soars back to his eyrie. We advise you to tear out his plumage, break his wings, give his flesh to the fowl of heaven, split his eggs lying in his nest, and crush his young, so that his memorial may vanish from the world. Our counsel is not like Pharaoh's; he sought to destroy only the men of Israel; to the women he did no harm. It is not like unto the plan of Esau, who wanted to slay his brother Jacob and keep his children as slaves. It is not like unto the tactics of Amalek, who pursued Israel and smote the hindmost and feeble, but left the strong unscathed. It is not like unto the policy of Nebuchadnezzar, who carried them away into exile, and settled them near his own throne. And it is not like the way of Sennacherib, who assigned a land for the Jews as fair as their own had been. We, recognizing clearly what the situation is, have resolved to slay the Jews, annihilate them, young and old, that their name and memorial be no more, and their posterity be cut off forever.[57]

The official edict issued by the king ran thus:

To this day they are among us, and though they are under our hand, we are of no account in their eyes. Their religion and their laws are different from the religion and laws of all other nations. Their sons do not marry our daughters, our gods they do not worship, they have no regard for our honor, and they refuse to bend the knee before us. Calling themselves freemen, they will not do our service and our commands they heed not.

Therefore the grandees, the princes, and the satraps have been assembled before us, we have taken counsel together, and we have resolved an irrevocable resolution, according to the laws of the Medes and Persians, to extirpate the Jews from among the inhabitants of the earth. We have sent the edict to the hundred and twenty-seven provinces of my empire, to slay them, their sons, their wives, and their little children, on the thirteenth day of the month of Adar — none is to escape."[58]

Fortunately for the Jews, Haman's plan backfired, and Mordecai, following Haman's demise, succeeded him as Prime Minister![59] As in Egypt, the Jews' refusal to assimilate infuriated the ruling power. When attempts to break the Jewish spirit by estranging them from their traditions proved unsuccessful, the only recourse (for these pathological-type despots) was annihilation. Consequently, however, the Jewish people continued to persevere in their already "antiquated" traditions, and in their relationship to the land promised them forever by God.[60] In contrast, the Persian empire was dissolved along with its indigenous type of religion(s), form of government, and societal mores.

Before proceeding, the rationale for extending the discussion on pre-Grecian forms of anti-Jewish hostility bears mention: (1) Most serious works on anti-Jewish hostility pay little (to no) attention to the anti-Jewish (Hebrew) climates in ancient Mesopotamia, Egypt, or Persia, but begin with ancient Greece or Rome. It was, therefore, deemed necessary to emphasize the longitudinal scope of this cancerous and repetitive anti-social phenomenon, and (2) By demonstrating that the phenomenon is as old as the nation itself, one perceives an extraordinary continuity, which is based on the intimidating nature of Jewish separatism.

Greek Anti-Jewish Hostility

After the Babylonian-Persian exile, the Jews were granted permission to return to their land and rebuild their Temple. However, in 332 B.C.E. Alexander (the Great) of Macedonia with his 40,000 soldiers attacked and defeated the larger Persian army, and conquered the land previously governed by Persia, including the Land of Israel (known then as Judea) with its indigenous Jewish population.[61] Alexander showed favor to the Jews, allowing them to continue their autonomous rule, and even extending their borders, adding to it three zones that had previously belonged to the Samaritans.[62]

Alexander's ambitions were cultural as well as military. He expected the segments of his newly founded empire to mingle and evolve a common civilization modeled after the progressive Hellenistic culture. The dissemination and influence of the Hellenistic spirit brought in its wake libraries, scientific research, and technological advancement.[63] However, as time elapsed, this progressive spirit degenerated into an intensification of idol worship, with its concomitant corruption of morals.[64]

For 150 years Greek civilization and Jewish culture were able to coexist, but with the advent of Antiochus Epiphanes (175 B.C.E.) the relationship became badly strained. Antiochus believed himself divine, and ordered all peoples under his rule to erect statues of him in their temples, and prostrate themselves before his image. He imposed Grecian culture, and would not tolerate Jewish obstinacy. He eventually decreed that *Judaism* be abolished in toto.[65] He called for cessation of the service in the Temple, and in its place set up pagan temples throughout the country. He then commanded that the Jerusalem Temple be converted into a pagan house of worship.[66] The observance of the Sabbath and Festivals, the dietary laws, circumcision, the laws of family purity, were all forcefully prohibited. All copies of the Torah (Bible) were to be burned, and anyone found possessing them would be executed. Even to profess one's Jewishness was punishable by death.[67]

This form of oppression was different from the attempted Persian genocide. In Persia, the Jewish body was targeted, while under Greek rule the Jewish spirit was to be dismembered. Nevertheless, according to the Egyptian archetype, both Persian and Greek forms of anti-Jewish hostility followed a common pattern. It began with an attempt to foster total assimilation. When Jewish separatism was maintained (in some manner or form) it was then relentlessly attacked. Accordingly, both the Persian and Greek empires (like their

91

predecessor in Egypt) enacted oppressive legislation in their attempt to deal with the stubborn Jewish phenomenon. And both forms of oppression (i.e., of body and of spirit) were used one thousand years prior in ancient Egypt.

Consequently, however, Antiochus (like his predecessors) was unsuccessful in uprooting the Jewish spirit or collective body. Mattisyahu the Hasmonean, with his five sons, led a group of militarily undisciplined zealots against the vastly superior Greek-Syrian army and miraculously prevailed.

Roman Anti-Jewish Hostility

During the next hundred years the Land of Israel (Judea) was ruled by a sovereign Jewish government,[68] but concurrently the Roman Eagle was conquering the already divided Grecian empire. In 63 B.C.E. the Roman general Pompey was invited by the Jews to intervene in their civil war. Unfortunately for the Jews, Pompey did not leave, but conquered the land in a battle which exacted tens of thousands of Jewish lives.[69] Once again the sovereign state of Judea was reduced to an autonomous vassal state, but this time under the auspices of mighty Rome.

Theoretically, the Jewish people should have been able to live peaceably under Roman rule despite economic hardships and loss of national sovereignty, as they did, for a time, under both Persian and Grecian rule.[70] Although possible, the Jewish spirit vying for independence proved itself (again) too "threatening."[71] Rome made many attempts to integrate Judea into its vast empire, but each attempt to erase Jewish national identity was countered by an equally strong Jewish resistance.

When Rome realized that Jewish separatism was not to be easily uprooted via peaceful methods, more forceful tactics were implemented. Accordingly, the Roman proconsul Gabinus abolished the spiritual core of the land which was the Sanhedrin (that is, the Jewish Supreme Court). He reasoned that by stripping the court of its powers the people would be lost, and hence become as docile as the other conquered nations.[72] However the strategy was unsuccessful, for the driving force of Judaism (that is, the Oral Law tradition) which propelled and directed the High Court was continually being propagated by the Jewish scholars.

The years between 60 B.C.E and 70 C.E. proved a perilous period in Jewish history. The Romans were unrelenting in their efforts to subjugate the minds and bodies of the conquered, but the Jews were equally as obstinate. This set the stage for fierce and vicious battles between the two nations in which literally hundreds of thousands of Jews were slaughtered,[73] and reached its climax in the destruction of the Second Temple (70 C.E.). In addition to the multitudes slain, many others were taken captive. Tens of thousands were sold into slavery, sent to toil in ships and mines, or presented as gifts to non-Jewish cities adjacent to Judea to fight against wild animals in their amphitheaters. Cities and villages were burnt and destroyed, either in the course of the war or afterwards, as acts of Roman revenge and intimidation.[74] The tortures inflicted on the Jews to compel them to transgress their traditional law reached an "apex of barbarity."[75] Not contented with these brutalities, the Romans sought out Jewish families said to be descended from the house of King David, in order to eradicate any hope for the restoration of the Davidic Kingdom.[76]

The Jews' refusal to succumb and assimilate was poignantly depicted by the historian Josephus some 1,900 years ago. He wrote:

> They have a passion for liberty that is almost unconquerable, since they are convinced that God alone is their leader and master. They think little of submitting to death in unusual forms and permitting vengeance to fall on kinsmen and friends, if only they may avoid calling any man master.[77]

Similarly in another place he states:

> For it is no new thing for our captives . . . to be seen to endure racks and death of all kinds upon the theaters, that they may not be obliged to say one word against our laws and the

records that contain them; whereas there are none at all among the Greeks who would undergo the least harm on that account.*

And the ancient historian Hecateus described the phenomenon thus:

> When they [the Jews] are stripped on account of this and have torments inflicted upon them, and they are brought to the most terrible kinds of death, they meet them in an extraordinary manner, beyond all other people, and will not renounce the religion of their forefathers.**

As uncanny as it may seem, the Jews' already protracted appearance in the annals of history was far from over. Although various Jewish sects, which had broken from Oral Law (Pharisaical) Judaism, were now abandoned, the Jewish scholars were diligently reestablishing Jewish communal life in the Land of Israel, but this time outside of Jerusalem in Yavneh. Unfortunately for the Romans, the scholars reawakened the people's spirit for national independence as well. During the ensuing sixty years (70 C.E. to 130 C.E.) the Jews, once again, began buying up and cultivating the land of Judea. They began flocking back to Jerusalem in the hope of rebuilding their holy Temple, though its construction would now be under the jurisdiction of the emperor Hadrian. Hadrian, however, abandoned his original plan of rebuilding Jerusalem as a Jewish city, but continued its construction as a pagan Roman city.[78]

Within this sixty year interval, the Jewish people consolidated their resources, and under Simeon bar Kosiba succeeded in liberating the whole of Judea, which for a short three year period, once again, came under independent Jewish rule.[79] But, as before, the Roman empire prevailed, destroying this time hundreds of Judean settlements. Hundreds of thousands of

---

*   Josephus. *Contra Apion* (I,8).
**   Hecateus. Cited in A. Miller, *Rejoice O Youth*, pp. 128-29.

94

Jews were slaughtered, and according to the Talmud, on the ninth of Av (the summer of 135 C.E.), the anniversary of the destruction of both the First and Second Temples in Jerusalem, the last stronghold (Betar) was captured.[80] The Romans, determined not to repeat the same mistake, massacred large Jewish populations, laid the land waste, sent multitudes of Jews off to slave markets, and under Hadrian, launched an all-out war forbidding the study and observance of Jewish law. Jews were forbidden to live in Jerusalem, and in order to blot out all reference to the land of Israel, changed its name to *Syria Palaestina* (thereafter known as Palestine).

The great and mighty Roman empire eventually faded from history, and its indigenous and conquered populations adopted (or were forced to adopt) new political leadership, foreign ideologies, novel individual and group mores, and untried innovative religions. Ironically, however, its fierce opponent, the nation of Israel, continued as a distinct civilization (as if nothing had happened). Another remarkable phenomenon was that the Land of Israel (Syria Palaestina), after being laid waste by Rome, was to remain a wasteland for the next 1,750 years, and was never to become a sovereign or even autonomous political entity till the creation of the modern Jewish State of Israel in 1948.

Though Jewish suffering at the hands of Rome was more intense than before experienced, Roman persecution did not deviate, in kind, from the Egyptian anti-Jewish paradigm discussed above. Again, the irrepressible desire to uproot Jewish distinctiveness became the catalyst aimed at destroying Jewish national identity and the Jewish (religious) spirit. Despite the fact that hundreds of thousands of Jews were slain in battle or savagely massacred, Rome's objective was never the eradication of the Jewish people (as in Persia). Rather, the brutal methods were implemented only to break the Jewish national character and spirit.

For the next 1,800 years (that is, from 135 C.E. to the establishment of the modern Jewish state in 1948) Jews, together with their religious traditions, wandered literally around the globe. For example, in the third century (C.E.) they were expelled from Carthage (North Africa), in the fifth century from Alexandria (Egypt), in the sixth from provinces in France, and in the seventh from the Visigothic empire. In the ninth century they were expelled from Italy, in the eleventh from Mayence (Germany), in the twelfth from France, the thirteenth from England, the fourteenth from France, Switzerland, Hungary, Germany, and in the fifteenth from Austria, Spain, Lithuania, Portugal, and Germany. In the sixteenth and seventeenth centuries Jewish populations were expelled from Bohemia, Austria, Papal States, the Netherlands, the Ukraine, Lithuania, and Oran (North Africa). In the eighteenth and nineteenth centuries they were expelled from Russia, Warsaw (Poland), and Galatz (Romania). And in the twentieth century, all Jews living in Nazi-controlled lands were relocated, clearing the way for the implementation of Hitler's "Final Solution."[81]

Christian Anti-Jewish Hostility

The next epoch of anti-Jewish hostility, which lasted for 1,500 years (from approximately 400 C.E. to 1900) was probably the most unfortunate and unforgettable oppression the Jews had experienced heretofore. Unfortunate, because the non-Jewish world never had a chance to objectively observe and understand Jewish tradition. Unforgettable, because the group carrying out this oppression was an outgrowth of Judaism itself, and when all auxiliary manifestations (which came about only after the foundations were set) are removed, may be called a form of Judaism, not too distinct, historically, from other Jewish sects of the past. However, whereas the other Jewish sects died out, Christianity became a non-Jewish religion.

This new religion centered on the person of Jesus. Jesus, however, was not a Christian but a Jew. It appears, historically, that Jesus had no intention of ever breaking with Judaism, and that he would have been profoundly shocked to know that his works and teachings would be used to justify the rejection of Judaism, and the persecution of its people.[82] For instance, in the book of Matthew the following passage is attributed to Jesus:

> Think not that I am come to destroy the Law, or the prophets: I am not come to destroy, but to fulfill. For verily I say unto you, Till heaven and earth pass, one jot or one tittle shall in no wise pass from the Law, till all be fulfilled.[83]

Jesus did break with the scholars in his interpretation of the Law, but was, at worst, a revolutionary force within, not against, Judaism. This is further seen in Matthew: "I am not sent but unto the lost sheep of the house of Israel."[84] Similarly the Apostles, the group of disciples chosen by Jesus to preach his gospel, were Jewish, and their message (in the beginning at least) was specifically for the Jews. Only after the Jewish people, in general, refused to accept this brand of Judaism (that is, they did not consider Jesus the Messiah) did the Apostles (particularly Paul) venture out to preach among the non-Jews. Other movements in Judaism had sprung up over the centuries (particularly during the Greek and Roman persecutions), but none had succeeded in swaying Jewish popular opinion (for any length of time) from the scholarly Oral Law tradition.

However, when confronted with Jewish resistance, the Jewish-Christian movement, unlike the others, turned to the non-Jews, but their relationship to Judaism was far from severed. Initially, the founding fathers of Christianity (i.e., the Apostles) were split on the desired relationship to mainstream Judaism, and two schools of thought (i.e., the Petrine and Pauline doctrines) competed to become the official dogma of the up and coming Catholic Church.[85] The accepted argument is that the Petrine (as advanced by Peter) school of thought advocated a Judaized Christianity where both Jew and Gentile would be obligated to observe the Law, whereas the Pauline doctrine, which eventually prevailed, called for a complete disassociation from the Law.

Though this has been the accepted argument for millennia,

it has been called into question by John G. Gager, who in his book, *The Origins of Anti-Semitism*, brings substantive support to justify the claim that the Pauline doctrine was significantly doctored by later Church Fathers. In essence, in order to wean the people from any Judaizing influence, the Church Fathers recreated a Paul totally antagonistic to Pharisaical (Oral Law) Judaism.[86] Gager concludes that Paul's intent was, most probably, to propagate the message of Torah (based on the Oral Law) for Jews and Christianity for Gentiles, but that the possibility of any positive Judaization on the new religion was too threatening (for later Church Fathers), and demanded total eradication.

According to Gager, both Petrine and Pauline doctrines, which lay at the foundation of true Christianity, as propagated by Jesus and his Apostles, were not inherently anti-Jewish, but ironically philo-Jewish in their relationship to Jewish Law (Peter) and Jewish distinctiveness (Paul). Historically, only after the Apostles, when Christianity, in the second and third centuries, began severing itself from Judaism, did harsh intolerance of Judaism and the Jewish people commence.[87] The early Church Fathers, while trying to consolidate Christianity and formulate an official dogma, viewed the Judaizing influence as too threatening. This was especially true all the while a dynamic Jewish people, following their own traditions, continued to exist.[88] To sever Jewish tradition from Christianity meant to uproot Christianity, but to accord it legitimacy meant to shed doubt on the Church's role as the "New Israel." The only alternative was to claim that the Church had replaced the Old Israel, because of the latter's "grievous sins," and particularly the abomination of deicide.[89] According to the Church, only through conversion could Jews redeem themselves in this world and the next. In effect, it was this disassociation (from Judaism) which supplied the rationale for the ensuing discrimination, persecution, and massacre of Jews in the name of Christianity.

Before proceeding, it is important to note Judaism's view of Christianity, for this point is not often made, and when discussed is oftentimes misleading. The Church's culpability for the oppression of Jews from the fourth century onward is sometimes mitigated by relating individual and local Jewish hostility towards Christians, during the first and second centuries. This approach is misleading, for the Jewish persecution of "Christians" (which is infinitesimally insignificant in comparison to the latter's persecution of Jews) was never aimed at the Church or its congregants. This was, rather, the result of infighting among *Jews themselves* as to which movement *in Judaism* was to prevail. This was not an uncommon occurrence (particularly during that critical period) where, historically, other Jewish movements (e.g., Hellenists, Sadducees, Essenes, etc.) who claimed parity or even the right to succeed the "antiquated" Oral Law tradition, went to battle (both figuratively and literally) against the scholars and their adherents, and which, at times, had bloody consequences.

However, traditional Judaism's view of Christianity as a legitimate religious creed for non-Jews is documented. Not only is the Oral tradition tolerant of other monotheistic faiths, but it states explicitly that all non-Jews who obey the seven general commandments (e.g., prohibition against killing, stealing, etc.) have a portion in the world to come.[90] In addition, various Talmudic scholars throughout history (e.g., Moses Nachmanides) have openly taught that Christianity (the very religion in whose name the Jewish people have endured untold oppression) is a permissible religion for non-Jews, and may be conceived of as a positive phenomenon "in fulfillment of God's ultimate purpose."[91]

Paradoxically, the above Pauline doctrine (as reevaluated by Gager) is consistent (that is, Judaism for Jews alongside a Gentile population embued with the Christian spirit) with traditional Judaism. This compatibility however was never actualized, and only the stark differences based on the "despicable" Jewish character in concert with the Jewish "heinous" lifestyle governed the relationship.

The pattern of Christian anti-Jewish hostility again reflects the pattern of oppression mentioned above in relation to

Egypt, Persia, Greece, and Rome, and only by virtue of its intensity and extensiveness qualifies as something historically distinct. The themes of anti-Jewish hostility discussed above are, as well, present here:

1. The Jews refuse to assimilate (i.e., convert) into the ever-growing Christian empire.
2. The Church is psychologically threatened and reacts accordingly.
3. This reaction takes two of the three forms mentioned above:
   A. An attempt to uproot any positive national identity via ghettoization or expulsion.
   B. An attempt to break the distinctive Jewish spirit via bookburning (specifically the Talmud), forced conversions, and physical persecution.
4. Traditional Judaism continues to flower (in the intellectual and spiritual sense).

According to Grosser and Halperin, during the early Christian period (325-500 C.E.), after Christianity had become the pre-dominant religion of Rome:

1. Christians were forbidden to interact with Jews.
2. State policy restricted the political and civil rights of Jews.
3. Jews were forbidden to live in Jerusalem.
4. Marriage between a Jew and Gentile was punishable by death.
5. Forced conversions were carried out.
6. Sporadic Christian mobs would attack Jewish quarters and synagogues.[92]

The Dark Ages (500-1000 C.E.) ushered in a new era of anti-Jewish hostility. In light of political instability in Europe, the Church became the major unifying and stabilizing force. Jewish settlements, at the time, existed throughout Christendom in virtually every province and city. Although Jews were declared enemies of the state (for refusing to convert to Christianity), the hostility was more an elitist phenomenon with an absence of popular anti-Jewish sentiment. Support for this came from the repetitive royal and Church decrees, commanding the faithful and lower clergy to refrain from interacting and maintaining friendly relations with Jews.[93]

It is interesting to note the gradual development of Christian anti-Jewish hostility at this point, for it mirrors the above Egyptian paradigm. During the early Christian period (325-500 C.E.) activity was limited to discrimination in which Jewish national identity was threatened. The Land of Israel and Jerusalem were off limits to the Jewish masses, and while residing in foreign lands their civil, economic, political, and even marital rights were restricted. Subsequently, however, the Jews' refusal to convert brought in its wake further oppression, where the goal was no longer to break the Jew's national pride, but rather to destroy his Talmudic spirit, rendering him susceptible to Christian influence. Forced conversions, book burnings, child-nappings, and prohibitions against the observance of the Law were the more salient forms of persecution.

Accordingly, when this plan failed, the body of the Jew became endangered. Though there appears to be little in the way of direct decrees issuing from the Church to annihilate Jews, the random torture and slaughter of literally hundreds of thousands of Jews during the Crusades (1000-1348), the Black Death (the Bubonic Plague, 1348-1357), the Inquisition (1366-1500), and the Eastern European pogroms (during the seventeenth and eighteenth centuries), all in the name of Christianity,[94] appear to belie the Church's declared goal of spreading Christianity throughout the Jewish world.

Muslim Anti-Jewish Hostility

Islam was the second major religion to spring forth from Judaism,[95] but unlike Christianity, its founder was not a Jew, and it was not originally a Jewish sect. Islam also had a universal mission to save the world, but in contrast to Christianity, it was armed with the sword of the "state" almost at its inception.[96]

With the advent of Islam in the seventh century C.E., there was a large Jewish population in Medina, where the first Muslim community was founded.[97] Muhammad, the founder of Islam, was greatly influenced by Jewish practices and ideas.[98] In fact, Moses is mentioned in the Quran (i.e., the sacred text of Islam) over one hundred times and may be considered its predominant figure.[99] Muhammad accordingly declared: "Yet before it, was the Book of Moses for a model and a mercy; and this is a Book [i.e., the Quran] confirming."[100]

Muhammad adopted the Jews' founding father Abraham as his new faith's founding patriarch, but in disregard for Hebrew Scripture (from which he based his new religion) inserted Ishmael as one of the Hebrew patriarchs,[101] and traced his own geneology through Ishmael to Abraham. Muhammad granted *theological legitimacy* to Christianity as well, and though he denied the divinity of Jesus, did consider Jesus the last of the Hebrew prophets, while claiming himself the messenger of God and "the Seal of the Prophets." While accepting most narratives of the Hebrew Bible, Muhammad accused the Jews of deleting Biblical predictions of his eventful coming.[102]

According to the scholar Abraham Katsh:

> Muhammad never intended to establish Islam as a new religion. He considered himself the rightful custodian of the Book sent by Allah (God) to "confirm" the Scriptures. It is for this reason that in the beginning he saw no difference between Judaism and Christianity and believed that both Jews and Christians would welcome him. It is only later, when he realized that he could never gain support from either of them, that he presented Islam as a new Faith.[103]

For example, in the early days of Islam, Muhammad's followers prayed in the direction of Jerusalem, and observed the most solemn Jewish holiday, Yom Kippur. Only when Muhammad concluded that the Jews were unwilling to accept him as their prophet did he substitute Mecca for Jerusalem, and the Fast of Ramadan for Yom Kippur.[104] (It is important to note, however, that while Judaism was never intolerant of Islam as a viable faith for non-Jews, it did reject Islam as a substitute for its millennia-old tradition.)

The consequences in rejecting Islam were inevitable. No group could validate Muhammad's claims as could the Jews, and no group could so seriously undermine the new creed as could the Jewish nation. As a result, Muhammad turned against them. His hostile reactions were then recorded in the Quran, granting pious Muslims, throughout history, divinely-based antipathy towards Jews.[105] In response to the Jews' refusal to convert, Jewish communities in the area of Medina were attacked and either slaughtered or forced to migrate. The Jews living north of Kaibher were besieged by the Army of Islam, and after Muhammad's death were expelled, purging northern Arabia of all "infidels."[106]

Although there were periodic physical persecutions, mass expulsions, and massacres of Jews in the name of Islam,[107] the focus of Muslim anti-Jewish hostility was more of political subjugation, social humiliation, and decreed religious inferiority.[108] In essence, Islam's anti-Jewish activity targeted, almost exclusively, Jewish independence (nationalism).

Jews were allowed to physically exist in "Muslim lands" as "people of the book" as opposed to pagans who would have to choose Islam or the sword. Officially (though not always in practice), Jews were granted religious freedom, thus allowing them to continue their traditions. Islam did not feel pressured to attack the Jewish spirit via religious persecution, or to annihilate the Jewish collective body. Islam only required that Jews be relegated to positions of inferiority vis-à-vis Muslims.

Official Islamic legislation, which delineated the restriction of liberties and conditions of life for Jews, was promulgated in the seventh-century *Covenant of Omar* (named after Muhammad's second successor), which if transgressed was punishable by death. According to the Covenant, Jews were compelled to wear a distinctive costume with a ribbon and a yellow piece of cloth as a badge; they were not permitted to perform their religious practices in public, or to own a horse; they were forbidden to drink wine in public; and they were required to bury their dead without allowing their grief to be heard by Muslims. Islam's law decreed the lightest of penalties for killing a non-Muslim, and the testimony of a non-Muslim against a Muslim was considered invalid. As payment for being allowed to live, the non-Muslim paid a special head and property tax. These and other restrictions of the Covenant remained in force for centuries, and were implemented with varying degrees of cruelty depending upon the particular Muslim ruler.[109]

Islam's guiding principle concerning treatment of Jews (and Christians) was that Islam dominates and is not to be dominated. Once non-Muslims forfeited their civil liberties, they were allowed some degree of freedom and expression. However, when the Jews would receive equal status in "Muslim territory," and needless to say, when they would forge their own independent state, the Jewish "threat" would be intolerable!

This, in fact, occurred in the twentieth century. The "demeaned subjects" had the impudence to claim independence over "Muslim land." As Yehoshafat Harkabi, a leading scholar of the contemporary Arab world put it: "A Jewish state is incompatible with the view of Jews as humiliated or wretched."[110] As long as the Jews were subjugated in "Muslim lands," Islam could claim (via extensive rationalization) superiority as the true faith which had displaced the older monotheistic creeds. *However, with the advent of Israel as an independent Jewish state, the foundations of Islam were shaken.* The "inferior" somehow prevailed, casting doubt on Islam's superiority, and with each successive victory the dissonance intensified.

Accordingly, it was not utilitarian strategy, manipulated to foster Muslim unity, that Khomeini, in his book, *Confronting Israel*, proclaimed:

> Oh brothers! Let us not regard this holy and sacrificial war as a war between Arabs and Israel. Let us regard it as a war of all Moslems together against Jews and their leaders.[111]

The similarities between Muslim anti-Jewish hostility and its antecedents are clear. Judaism and the Jewish people were a serious threat to Islam from its inception. At the outset, Jews stubbornly refused to accept the majority religion. In addition, the type of anti-Jewish hostility that emerged was one of the three forms delineated above, where strict limitations on civil liberties and a total negation of Jewish statehood (that is, nationalism) were diligently enforced. Though physical attacks have been constant since the early part of the twentieth century, these attacks are not targeted at the Jewish collective body, but rather at Jewish statehood which is anathema to any God-fearing Muslim.

Another common trend is Jewish tenacity. Though it appears anticlimactic when compared with Jewish tenacity prior to Islam, the remarkable perseverance of the Jews can, as well, be seen here. It is particularly noticeable when compared to the Christian communities of the Mideast. As mentioned above, Muslim ferocity vis-a-vis non-Muslims applied also to Christians. However, where Jewish communities in "Muslim lands" often flourished (in spiritual terms), most Christian communities never even survived. This is often lost sight of when favorably comparing Muslim anti-Jewish activity with hostile Christian activity. However, the conversion to Islam of nearly every pre-Islamic Christian community in the Muslim world, bears testimony to what the Jews actually endured.[112]

Russian and Communist Anti-Jewish Hostility

In both Europe and America, with the advent of the industrial revolution, a promising economic order via capitalism and socialism, all pervaded by a spirit of enlightened liberalism, the nineteenth and twentieth centuries were to be a positive turning point for mankind. Unfortunately for the Jewish people, it turned in the wrong direction. For the Jew, the nineteenth, and particularly the twentieth century would bring with it discrimination, persecution, and massacre on a scale heretofore never experienced.

Almost from the beginning of Russia's history, a tradition of autocracy and devotion to Eastern Orthodox Christianity shaped a policy of suspicion toward European influence, and specifically toward Judaism.[113] This distrust was heightened to the point of paranoia when Poland was partitioned in the late eighteenth century. Russia then became governor of the largest body of Jews in the world. Simultaneous with their admission into the Russian empire, Jews were restricted to live in the "Pale of Settlement."[114] Even within the Pale, Jews suffered economic restrictions, extra taxes, and other hardships. For example, in 1808, the Czar, Alexander I, issued an edict calling for the expulsion of Jews from all villages, and consequently one-half million Jews were driven, like cattle, into the cities, and left in the open squares to starve and freeze.[115]

Alexander's successor, Nicholas I, introduced hundreds of disabling laws curbing Jewish activities and went further than his predecessors who, for the most part, only stripped the Jews of their civil liberties to live, own land, and work where and as they pleased. Nicholas I, determined to complete the Russification of the Jews, attacked the Jewish spirit by conscripting Jewish youths of twelve to an extended military service of twenty-five years (the twenty-five year stint commenced once the boy turned eighteen). Jewish youth were brought to the farthest outposts of the empire, to be beaten and tortured in an effort to "persuade" them to convert to Russian (Christian) Orthodoxy.[116] When Nicholas failed to break the Jewish spirit (i.e., Jews were not converting) he turned his attention to Jewish education. He decreed that Jewish children go to special Jewish schools where Talmud was not to be taught, and where Judaism, in general, was taught according to Russian Orthodoxy.[117] Nicholas eventually abolished these schools, for conversion was not being achieved.

A third type of Russian anti-Jewish activity was initiated in 1881, when the Czar, Alexander III, under the influence of his chief advisor Pobedonstsev, formulated his "anti-revolutionary program," with Russian Jewry as its target. The Jewish problem was to be solved simply; one-third was to emigrate, one-third was to die, and one-third was to convert.[118] On Easter of 1881 the massacres commenced, and over a twenty-five year period (1881-1906) thousands of Jews were murdered while tens of thousands were left maimed and destitute.[119]

In 1915 Grand Duke Sergei, commander-in-chief of Russia's military, ordered the relocation of 600,000 Jews to interior Russia. Approximately 100,000 died from exposure or starvation during its implementation.[120] In 1917, during the Russian Revolution, massacres of Jews were organized and carried out by the Ukranians and the Russian Whites. In the Ukraine 200,000 Jews were slaughtered, and 300,000 children were left homeless and orphaned. During the revolution and ensuing civil war Jewish populations were accused by both sides as being members of the opposing force, and were accordingly tortured. During this period it was considered a mercy to be killed outright, rather than to be tortured to death. Parents were forced to watch the torture of their children, and children of their parents. Jewish women were subjected to obscene acts and mutilation before being granted the privilege to die.[121]

It was within this historical context that the Russian people collectively "converted" to Marxism and set out like their predecessors, to convert and save the world. Paradoxically, the "pious" Russian populace metamorphosed almost overnight from devout religionists to progressive communists (i.e., the transition from Eastern Orthodoxy to Communism, over a relatively short period of time, did not appear overly taxing), while the Jews, on the other hand, remained distinctively Jewish.

One major adjustment, however, was that pre-revolutionary Russia would only attack Jews residing within its borders, while Communist Russia would strike at Jews and Judaism everywhere. With the adoption of Marxism, the Russian government no longer feared the indignation and repulsion of the Western world. They were now universalists, furthering the ideals of one of the century's leading thinkers, and this ideology just happened to be inherently anti-Jewish.

Karl Marx, whose father had him baptized at the age of six in order that he not have to suffer anti-Jewish oppression,[122] became the new "legitimizing" force, aimed at uprooting and destroying the Jewish "cancer." Karl Marx, who himself descended from a long list of distinguished rabbis argued that the Jew not be emancipated until he abandon his "exclusive religion, morality, and customs."[123]

Marx theorized that the role of economics was the key determinant in the development of mankind. He argued that world peace and happiness would be achieved once man restructured the economic order. And in composing passages like the following, he bequeathed "legitimacy" to the suppression and oppression of Jews and Judaism everywhere. For example, he wrote:

> It is from its own entrails that civil society ceaselessly engenders the Jew....
>
> Money is the jealous god of Israel, beside which no other god may exist....
>
> The chimerical nationality of the Jew is the nationality of the trader, and above all of the financier....
>
> As soon as society succeeds in abolishing the empirical essence of Judaism — huckstering and its conditions — the Jew becomes impossible, because his consciousness no longer has an object.[124]

Marxist nations today (particularly the Soviet Union) attack the Jewish people via the three aforementioned strategies. They attempt to break Jewish nationalism by defining Zionism as "a reactionary movement...which denies the class struggle and strives to isolate the Jewish working masses from the general struggle of the proletariat."[125] Their highly sophisticated propaganda apparatus consistently associates Zionism with Nazism, and often refers to the Jewish State as Hitlerian.[126] In addition, requests by Soviet Jews to immigrate to Israel are fraught with hardships ranging from losing one's job, to an extended prison term, to exile to Siberia.

Concomitantly, the Soviets have attempted to destroy the Jewish spirit. Synagogues are seized and converted into Communist Youth Clubs. Rabbis and religious teachers are imprisoned. All forms of Jewish education are barred, and the teaching of Hebrew is outlawed.[127] Their attempt to annihilate the Jewish collective body, however, is more subtle. They do so by providing untold amounts of organizational and military training together with sophisticated military hardware to Israel's most hostile adversaries (while these adversaries openly call for the total liquidation of the Jewish State).

After describing both Muslim and Marxist sources of anti-Jewish hostility, it is interesting to note an overt historical oversight. Following from the above analysis, it should have been clear that an effort to create a third Jewish Commonwealth in the Mideast would be met by zealous opposition from both Muslim and Marxist camps. If a stateless Jewish people was intimidating, how much more so while living independently in their own land. Though the consequences should have been foreseen, they were not. In fact, Theodore Herzl, the father of modern Jewish nationalism, together with his successors, repeatedly proclaimed that the creation of a third Jewish Commonwealth was the only effective response to anti-Jewish hostility.[128]

German Nazi Anti-Jewish Hostility

Theoretically, the juxtaposition of Soviet leftist ideology with Nazi right-wing fanatacism appears absurd. Is it logically possible (barring wartime alliances) for two radical movements which are ideologically at opposite ends of the spectrum, and accordingly anathema to one another, to claim as their most natural enemy the same seemingly innocuous Jewish people? More ridiculous it seems, is that each movement projects on the Jews the guise of the other. Soviet leftists often refer to Jews as Nazi collaborators and Israel as a Hitlerian state,[129] while Nazis did (and still do) refer to Jews everywhere as Communists.[130]

In short, this contradiction in doctrine is, at best, superficial. Just as the Russian psychological and spiritual incapacity to tolerate Judaism predates Communism, so too, did Hitler's pathological hostility towards Jews predate Nazi right-wing ideology. Both movements merely bequeathed to their adherents an ideological base from which to "justify" the discrimination and persecution of Jews.

Hitler's paranoia towards Jews was blatant from the start. Hitler's Nazism was not an independent movement which gradually incorporated anti-Jewish dogma. Rather, the foundation of Hitler's Nazism was specifically Aryan superiority *over the Jew* and the threat of the "Jewish peril." For example, as early as the 1920s Hitler called for the total elimination of the Jews who, in his words, were "contaminating the Aryan race."[131]

In *Mein Kampf*, which Hitler wrote while in prison in 1923-1924, he blamed the defeat of Germany in World War I on those "Marxist leaders" (i.e., the Jews), and stated that had "twelve or fifteen thousand of these Jews, who were corrupting the nation, been forced to submit to poison gas," the millions of deaths at the front "would not have been in vain."[132] In Hitler's twisted mind, Jew-hatred came first and afterwards, Nazi racial ideology. For example, neither the Japanese nor the Arabs were denigrated by the so-called racist Nazis (indeed, both were Nazi allies). According to Hitler, the racial impurities disseminated by Jews were their subversive value system and alien ideas. As he put it, "the Jews speak German, but they think Jewish."[133]

In essence, the "racial" war of Hitler was focused almost exclusively on the Jew. Most everything Hitler did in the political arena centered around the Jews. Hitler's first political speech as well as his last will and testament contained explicit charges against the Jewish people. Even the swastika represented for Hitler the battle between the "pure" Germanic race and the "inferior" Jew. In writing about the Nazi flag, he explained that the swastika symbolized "the mission to struggle for the victory of the Aryan man, and at the same time the victory of the idea of creative work, which is eternally anti-Semitic and always will be anti-Semitic."[134] Albert Speer, one of Hitler's ministers, wrote in *Spandau: The Secret Diaries*, that

Hitler was capable of tossing off quite calmly, between the soup and the vegetable course, "I want to annihilate Jews!"[135]

Fantastic as it may seem, Hitler did not attack Jews to achieve power, but was driven to power in order to annihilate Jews.[136] For example, late in the war when the Nazis were being defeated, German troops were taken from Allied fronts in order to continue the mass murder of Jews. In 1944, when the Germans required every train to evacuate Greece, not one train was diverted from those transporting Jews to death camps. And, while addressing the German people for the last time in 1945, Hitler proclaimed:

> Above all I charge the leaders of the nation and those under them to scrupulous observance of the laws of race and to the merciless opposition to the universal poisoner of all peoples, international Jewry.[137]

The insanity of Hitler, abetted by a pervasive anti-Jewish world prejudice,[138] set the stage for the unprecedented massacre of six million civilian Jews, in a war which consumed over fifty million people!

In conclusion, Hitler himself enunciated best his ultimate purpose:

> It is true we are barbarians; that is an honored title to us. I free humanity from the shackles of the soul, from the degrading suffering caused by the false vision called conscience and ethics. The Jews have inflicted two wounds on mankind: circumcision on its body and "conscience" on its soul. They are Jewish inventions. The war for domination of the world is waged only between the two of us, between these two camps alone; the Germans and the Jews. Everything else is but deception.[139]

Hitler's paranoia could find no respite until all Jews were annihilated. In the end, however, the Hitlerian monster was destroyed, while his crippled and maimed "arch adversary" lived on to create an independent Jewish state after eighteen hundred years of wandering!

VI / The Primary Dynamics

As the title indicates, this chapter attempts to further explain the above historical process. Nonetheless, the analysis in chapter V goes two steps further than most others. First, it explains how consistent themes throughout history cover all major periods of anti-Jewish hostility, and secondly, it describes the anti-Jewish process as existing from the inception of Jewish nationhood. However, at least two questions still demand explication. They are:

1. What are the psycho-social dynamics underlying the above historical process?
2. What is the significance of the three target areas (i.e., Nationalism, Jewish Spirit, and Collective Body) that powerful movements throughout history have so fervently attempted to eradicate?

The Primary Dynamics

Psycho-Social Dynamics

As described in chapters III and V, the *primary* catalyst of anti-Jewish hostility is the intimidating nature of *Jewish distinctiveness*, and the psychological threat it poses to both national and international movements, whose objective to dominate runs counter to and collides with Jewish separatism. To win the world over to their way of thinking, these movements were psychologically pressured to crush all forms of Jewish resistance.

The Jewish nation, with its ancient ideology and lifestyle, was unlike the other nations and refused to disappear (in fact, most often, it prospered on an intellectual, spiritual, and/or material level). While the Jewish presence existed, the declared supremacy of these anti-Jewish movements was brought into question, and absolute authority was (psychologically) withheld. Therefore, to create a sense of political and/or spiritual security (and unity) these authoritarian-type movements attempted to eliminate the source of Jewish separatism.

Jewish separatism as the source of anti-Jewish hostility is supported by the work of the distinguished social scientist, Muzafer Sherif. Professor Sherif contends that the primary cause of *intergroup conflict* is *not* "displacement of individual aggressive tendencies, individual ignorance, individual observation, or experience with members of the despised group"; rather, it is the primary consequence of fierce *competition* among groups, in which only *differences* (rather than similarities) dictate and direct the relationship.[1]

In his work, based on experimentation with intergroup processes, he concluded:

> ...intergroup conflict has shown that neither cultural, physical, nor economic differences are necessary for the rise of intergroup conflict, hostile attitudes, or stereotyped images of out-groups. Nor are maladjusted, neurotic, or unstable tendencies necessary conditions for the appearance of intergroup prejudice and stereotypes.
>
> The *sufficient condition* for the rise of hostile and aggres-

sive deeds...is the existence of two groups competing for goals that only one group can attain, to the dismay and frustration of the other group.[2]

The Jewish competitive threat was that the Jews could have merged with the dominant culture, but refused to totally disavow their Jewish identity. This refusal created intergroup competition, which brought in its wake untold cruelty.

The interpretation is incomplete, however, for group differences, however contradictory, need not lead to intergroup hostility. For example, ideological opposites like the Soviet Union and the United States were allies during World War II. Accordingly, the racist Nazis allied themselves with the "inferior" Japanese and Arabs. Why was it different with the Jews?

In discussing intergroup cooperation, Professor Sherif refers to what he calls *superordinate goals*. Superordinate goals are "goals that are compelling for the groups involved, but cannot be achieved by a single group, through its own efforts and resources." According to Professor Sherif, when groups believe that their collective good will be realized through cooperation and goodwill, then peaceful coexistence is possible. In other words, vast differences are, at worst, tolerated when the attainment of goals requires reciprocity among groups.

In the words of Professor Sherif, intergroup

cooperation and harmony is possible...when there is initially a motivational base encompassing members of all groups caught in conflict. Such a motivational base is provided when the conflicting groups and their respective members are directed towards superordinate goals, clearly perceived and requiring joint efforts for attainment....[3]

If Professor Sherif's analysis is correct, why have Jews failed to build, on the basis of similarities and necessity, an infrastructure of peaceful coexistence? Why have only differences been accentuated? Have not Jews, throughout history, benefited the many nations in areas as diverse as art, science, commerce, and politics? Could not their productivity be used to create, at worst, a tolerant intergroup atmosphere? How much more so, when Judaism itself demands tolerance, civil obedience, and prayer for the ruling government irrespective of time and place. In other words, if Professor Sherif's theory is correct, then why have Jews so often been depicted as "strangers from a strange land," instead of fellow countrymen?

As depicted in chapter V, it was specifically the Gentile *leaders* who demanded the eradication of Jews and/or Judaism (despite the potential advantages). Why were these leaders so compelled to uproot the Jewish presence?

In examining history, the psychodynamic factor becomes apparent. Jewish distinctiveness (as a "competitive threat") was psychologically too intimidating for these authoritarian-type leaders to bear. The drive to dominate (in both the physical and spiritual sense) precluded accommodation. In effect, Jewish distinctiveness precluded any relationship based on "superordinate goals."

Regarding the "authoritarian-type" personality, the noted psychotherapist Erich Fromm writes:

> The most important feature to be mentioned is the attitude towards power. For the authoritarian character, there exists, so to speak, two sexes: the powerful ones and the powerless ones. His love, admiration and readiness for submission are automatically aroused by power, whether of a person or an institution.[4]

Abraham Maslow describes the world view of the authoritarian personality as such:

> Like other psychologically insecure people, the authoritarian person lives in a world which may be conceived to be pictured by him as a sort of jungle in which man's hand is necessarily against every other man, in which the whole world is conceived of as dangerous, threatening, or at least challenging, and in which human beings are conceived of as primarily selfish or evil or stupid. To carry the analogy further, this jungle is peopled with animals, who either eat or are eaten, who are either to be feared or despised. One's safety lies in one's own strength and this strength consists primarily in the power to dominate.[5]

T.W. Adorno explains the relationship between the authoritarian personality and the Jews thus:

> ...they are highly projective and suspicious. An affinity to psychosis cannot be overlooked: they are "paranoid." To them, prejudice is all-important: it is a means to escape acute mental disease by collectivization, and by building up a pseudoreality against which their aggressiveness can be directed without any overt violation of the "reality principle." Stereotypy is decisive; it works as a kind of social corroboration of their projective formulae, and is therefore institutionalized to a degree often approaching religious beliefs.... In order to confirm to each other their pseudoreality, they are likely to form sects, often with some panacea of "nature," which corresponds to their projective notion of the Jew as eternally bad and spoiling the purity of the natural. Ideas of conspiracy play a large role: They do not hesitate to attribute to the Jews a quest for world domination, and they are likely to swear by the Elders of Zion.[6]

To admit frailty and imperfection is unbearable. Their frustration is best displaced on some out-group whose "heretical" nature poses a fateful threat. Attacking Jews and Judaism is rationalized as something positive, and fosters unity and power. Jews are portrayed as undermining society itself. In order to bring the world over to their way of thinking, they are driven to *crush* all resistance. However, the Jewish nation, unlike others, does not significantly change or disappear. As long as the Jewish presence exists, their supremacy is questioned and total domination (perforce) withheld. In effect, to totally dominate, the subjugation or elimination of Jews is mandatory!

The Three Areas of Focus

The primary attack against the Jewish nation was never against the Jews per se, but against their stubbornness (to totally assimilate) and the *sources* thereof. Attacks against Jews were attempts to uproot (1) the Jewish people's relationship to their land (i.e., Jewish nationalism), (2) the Jewish people's relationship to their law, and/or (3) the Jewish collective body. Historical anti-Jewish movements were (psychologically) pressured to eradicate the Jewish presence by attacking one or more of these perceived sources.

Jewish nationalism was usually attacked first. When this failed, the Jewish spirit was attacked (via book-burning, prohibitions against following Jewish laws, and physical persecution). As the Jewish entity remained (more or less) intact, annihilation became the logical and "final solution."

Why did subjugation result in spiritual and physical oppression? Why did expulsion and physical annihilation often follow suit? In essence, what is the significance of the three target areas that tyrannical movements throughout history have so assiduously tried to destroy?

If Jewish separatism lay at the core of anti-Jewish hostility, then any attack against the Jews was an attack against those components most responsible for creating and maintaining this separateness. More specifically, the above three components, representing the Jews' relationship to their God (as demonstrated below) have literally preserved this "hateful" Jewish nature. In effect, anti-Jewish powers have attacked these components, not to annihilate Jews, but to eradicate the "intolerable" attachment it represents.

When a relationship was perceived between the Jewish people and their God, conflict and tension resulted. The means of dealing with this threat was to destroy the mechanisms responsible. The first strategy (usually) employed was to suppress Jewish independence. This was accomplished by expelling the Jews from the Land of Israel, by prohibiting their return, and by denying them the civil liberties granted to others (until they renounced Jewish nationalism). By denying Jews equal civil liberties they were, in effect, relegated to vassal status, far removed from independent nationalists, and a seemingly easy prey to assimilate. When this failed, the Jewish spirit was targeted via pillaging, childnapping, torture, and prohibitions against the study and observance of Jewish law. When this failed to erase Jewish separateness, physical annihilation was the final solution.

Following therefrom, the following paragraphs explain, via traditional Jewish sources, the significance of (1) Jewish nationalism, (2) Jewish spirit, and (3) the Jewish collective body, which authoritarian leaders throughout history have attempted to destroy.

Jewish Nationalism

The following represents the relationship between the Land of Israel and the people of Israel. This is usually the first of the three attachments (components) anti-Jewish movements attempt to destroy.

1. Nearly two-thirds of the Oral Law, as embodied in the Talmud, deals with the Land of Israel.[7]

2. A leading Talmudic scholar of the thirteenth century, Moses Nachmanides, wrote in his *Hosafot to Sefer Hamitzvot*:

> The commandment is that we should inherit the land given by God, exalted be He, to our forefathers Abraham, Isaac and Jacob, and that we should neither let it fall to any of the other nations nor let it grow into a wasteland....This is a positive commandment for all time unto eternity. It is obligatory on each and every one of us, even in times of exile and dispersion, as evident from many places in the Talmud.[8]

3. Accordingly, in the Old Testament it states: "For the Lord has chosen Zion [i.e., a name used by the Hebrew Prophets some 2,700 years ago in reference to the Land of Israel or Jerusalem]; He has desired it for His habitation."[9]

4. "A land [the Land of Israel] which the Lord thy God cares for; the eyes of the Lord thy God are always upon it."[10]

5. If I forget thee, O Jerusalem,
   Let my right hand forget her cunning.
   If I do not remember thee,
   Let my tongue cleave to the roof of my mouth;
   If I do not set Jerusalem
   Above my highest joy.[11]

6. "Every Jew who lives in the Land of Israel is similar to one who has a God, and one who dwells elsewhere is similar to one who hasn't,[12] as it is written:[13] 'To give to you [the Jewish people] the Land of Canaan, to be for you God.'"

7. According to the Talmud, even after one dies it is important to be buried in the Land of Israel because of its holiness. To be buried in the Land of Israel is analogous to being buried under the altar of the Temple in Jerusalem.[14]

8. The commentary on the Biblical books of Numbers and Deuteronomy, the *Sifri*, composed in the third century C.E., relates:

> The story of Rabbi Yehuda son of Betayra, Matya son of Cheresh, and Rabbi Chanina son of the brother of Rabbi Yehoshua and Rabbi Yonatan who ventured outside the Land of Israel. They reached the Paltom and remembered the land. They picked up their eyes, cried bitterly and tore their clothing [as a sign of mourning] and recited the verse "when God excises the nations to which you are coming, and drives them away before you, you shall expel them and live therein."[15] They immediately returned, reciting: "Living in the Land of Israel is equal to all the commandments of the Torah."[16]

The architects of the Talmud, the Amoraim, who lived during the third to sixth century of the Common Era, expressed their affection thus:

> Rabbi Abba would kiss the cliffs of Akko [a city on the northern coast of Israel]. Rabbi Chanina would repair its roads.... Rabbi Chiyya the son of Gamda would roll himself in its dust, for the Bible states:[17] "Thy servants take pleasure in her stones, and love her dust!"[18]

9. The Jewish people's active relationship to the land, over a period of eighteen hundred years (135 C.E. to 1948) while in exile, bears testimony to this attachment. Whether they lived in neighboring Persia, or in warm Italy or Spain, whether they found homes in cold Eastern Europe, found their way to North America, or came to live in the southern hemisphere where the

seasons are reversed, the Jews celebrated the Land of Israel's seasonal change. They prayed for dew in May and for rain in October. On Passover, they celebrated their liberation from Egyptian bondage, the beginning of Jewish nationalism in the Promised Land. They prayed three times daily facing the land, and requested in each prayer to be brought back to the land with all the Jewish exiles. After eating bread they prayed for the rebuilding of Jerusalem, and during weddings as well as deaths made explicit mention of their exile, their hope, and their belief in their eventual return.

10. In conclusion, Israel today is the only country inhabited by the same nation, with the same religious culture and language, that lived there some thirty-two hundred years prior (despite two exiles, where the latter lasted eighteen hundred years).

The Jewish Spirit

The following represents the "threat" posed by the Jewish people's attachment to their Torah (used here to denote both the Written and Oral Law).

1. According to the Talmud, God's purpose in creation required that Israel accept the Torah. If not, all creation would lose its reason for being and would cease to exist.[19]

2. The Torah is considered the only means through which the Jew can fulfill God's purpose in creation.[20]

3. The immediate benefit of following the Torah is spiritual, bringing a person closer to God.[21] Each law is nourishment for the soul, strengthening it, and increasing a person's spiritual fortitude.[22]

4. The many laws associated with daily life are to teach the Jewish people self-discipline.[23] The Talmud asserts: "When Israel is occupied with the study and practice of Torah they master their desires, and are not mastered by them."[24] Similarly in Numbers it states: "You shall remember all God's commandments and keep them, and not stray after your heart or after your eyes, by which you are led astray."[25]

120

5. Torah law acts as a survival mechanism, enabling the Jewish people to survive through even the harshest of persecutions,[26] while a single generation's lapse leads to major spiritual debilitation.[27]

6. According to the Talmud, the Torah sets limits through which a Jew can fulfill God's purpose while living in a materialistic world. Through the Torah, the Jew learns to be part of the world, and at the same time, dedicated to the spiritual.[28]

7. The following narrative is found in the Midrash:

> God said to the people of Israel, "*If you accept My Torah and observe My laws,* I will give you a thing most precious." "And what," asked Israel, "is that precious thing?" God replied, "The world to come."[29]

Similarly, when Moses entreated God to enter the land of Canaan, the following reply was given: "My son Moses, much honor has been stored up for you in the future world ... which I have created for every pious man, that through love of Me devoted himself to the [study and fulfillment of the] Torah."[30]

8. The following Midrashic conversation, between the non-Jewish prophet Bilaam and the non-Jewish nations of the world, relates: The nations asked Bilaam: "Why did God command Israel, and not us, to bring sacrifices?" He replied: "The purpose of sacrifices is to establish peace; but peace without Torah is impossible, and the Israelites accepted the Torah."[31]

9. According to the Talmud, the Revelation of the Torah (at Mount Sinai) was final, and would never be abrogated or altered by any succeeding prophet.[32]

10. When God instructed Moses to teach the Torah to Israel, Moses asked that it be written down in full. God replied:

> Gladly I would give them the whole in writing, but I know that the nations of the world will, at a later date, read the Torah translated into Greek [the Septuagint] and will say: "We are the true Israel, we are the chosen children of God." Then I shall say to the nations: "You claim to be My chosen

children, but are you not aware that My chosen children are those who received My oral teachings as well?"....God then said to the Jewish people: "Before you accepted the Torah, you were like all other nations, but for the Torah's sake alone I have lifted you above all others. Even your king, Moses, owes the distinction he enjoys in this world and in the world to come to the Torah alone."[33]

11. The Midrash relates the following dialogue between God and Moses: Moses said: "Lord of the world, if we had worshipped the stars and planets, the Midianites would not have hated us, they hate us only because of the Torah that You have given us."[34]

Similarly, when the Persian prime minister Haman delivered his indictment of the Jews, the angel Michael spoke to God saying: "Lord of the world, You know that the Jews are not accused of idolatry, nor of immoral conduct, nor of shedding blood. They are accused only of observing Your Torah." God then placated Michael by saying: "As thou livest, I have never completely abandoned them. I will not abandon them."[35]

The Jewish Collective Body

With the dissolution of Jewish nationalism and Torah spirit badly maimed, enemies of the Jewish people (e.g., Hitler, Marxist proponents, etc.) are still unable to find respite. They remain intimidated by the nominal Jewish presence. However, unlike the above two components, the only way to sever the relationship between God and the Jewish collective body is through physical annihilation. Examples of this attachment are:

1. "Israel is holy to the Lord; the first fruits of His increase."[36]

2. According to the Jerusalem Talmud, the Jewish people are to represent God's presence in the world.[37]

3. In Isaiah, the Jewish people are depicted as having a

mission to bear witness to God's existence: "You are my witnesses...and My servant whom I have chosen."[38]

4. "I have put My words in thy mouth, and I have covered thee in the shadow of My hand, that I may plant the heavens and lay the foundation of the earth, and say to Zion, Thou art My people."[39]

5. The Jewish people are portrayed as having the mission of proclaiming God's teachings to the world (the objective is not, however, to proselytize) as is portrayed in Isaiah: "I, God, have called you in righteousness...and have set you up as a covenant of the people, for a light to the nations."[40]

6. The Jews are described as the means through which God's essence becomes more revealed in the world. As is written:[41] "[to] give strength to God is the duty of Israel His pride."[42]

7. "...you shall be My treasure from among the nations, for all the earth is Mine; and you shall be to Me a kingdom of priests and a holy nation."[43]

8. "Thou hast avouched the Lord this day to be thy God, and to walk in His ways,... and the Lord has avouched thee this day to be a people for His own possession, as He promised thee,... and that thou mayst be a holy people to the Lord thy God, as He has spoken."[44]

9. In the Midrash, "Rabbi Shimon bar Yochai said: God said to the people of Israel, 'I am God of the entire world, but I did not designate My name on any nation but you. I am not called the God of all the nations, but only the God of Israel."[45]

Similarly, the Zohar, which is the primary classic of Jewish mysticism, attributed to the school of Rabbi Shimon bar Yochai (circa 120 C.E.), reads: "And the people of Israel are holy, pleasant is their portion in this world and the next, for God did not give them over to any other power but He Himself holds them for His special portion."[46] Likewise in the book of Deuteronomy: "God's portion is His people,"[47] and in Psalms "For the Lord has chosen Jacob to Himself."[48]

10. "I am God your Lord who has separated you out from

among all the nations."[49] "You shall be holy to Me, for I, God, am holy, and I have separated you from among the nations to be Mine."[50]

11. "You are a nation consecrated to God your Lord. God your Lord chose you to be His special people among all the nations on the face of the earth. It was not because you had greater numbers than all the other nations that God embraced you; you are among the smallest of all the nations. It was because of God's love for you, and because of the oath He made to your forefathers."[51]

Chosen People

The concept of "chosen people" has negative connotations, for it smacks of racism with its ugly manifestations. However, the Jewish concept of "chosen" is different in thought and deed from that of others. Therefore, in light of the concept's unseemly connotations, the *Jewish meaning* requires clarification.

In short, the Jewish meaning of "chosen" has more to do with obligations than benefits. According to the Bible, man was created to emulate God's righteousness on earth. Originally, all mankind was chosen for this task but early man failed, and allowed corruption and violence to predominate over justice and kindness. Thereafter, punishment for failure was to be on a national rather than universal scale. As the Bible relates, God chose one nation to act as a model, whose purpose was to demonstrate, in practice, the desired society.[52]

The people chosen for this task were the descendants of Abraham, Isaac, and Jacob. Abraham's covenant with God guaranteed that his descendants would receive Divine favor provided they followed God's teachings. The covenant required that Jews meet obligations not required of others. They were expected to maintain a higher level of morality, and their self-control and devotion to a spiritual end would be severely tested. If the Jewish nation did not live up to the standards set by the Written and Oral Law, they would cause a

124

lessening of God in the eyes of mankind, and would be held accountable.[53]

As is evident, the traditional Jewish concept of "chosen" is radically different from that of others. The term "chosen," concerning other groups, connotes superiority, freedom to act with impugnity, exclusive salvation, and/or the right to dominate. In Judaism, rights are replaced by obligations.

VII / The Secondary Cause

*If a lie is repeated often enough,
it will come to be perceived
as truth.*

(Josef Goebbels, Nazi Propaganda
Minister)

Chapter V delineated the recurring process of anti-Jewish hostility. However, the pattern, as yet, falls short, for it describes only the Primary cause, without explaining how or why the common people, the masses, have turned so violently against the Jews.

In response, attacks against Jews have historically been provoked by misinformation and slander about Jews and Judaism alike. The Primary catalyst remains the Jewish "threat," but the dissemination of lies is needed to push the masses into action. Slander about Jews and Judaism is then the *Secondary cause* of anti-Jewish hostility affecting the masses.

"Threatened" Gentile leaders have succeeded in fostering animosity towards Jews through the tactic of slander. The propagation of misinformation, misconceptions, and outright lies has precipitated anti-Jewish activity throughout history. Through the spreading of lies, demogogues have directed the

126

masses' frustration towards Jews and Judaism. And the continuous bombardment of anti-Jewish slander, throughout millennia, has set the stage for subsequent slander and its believability.

It may be difficult, however, for some people to accept the premise that truth can be so totally twisted. On a common sense level, it sounds absurd that large populations throughout history have believed that "up is down and down is up" in regards to Jews and Judaism. Therefore, to make the upcoming presentation more palatable, the slander heaped on another target group (the United States of America) is briefly described.

In his address to the Assembly of Captive European Nations, Constantine Visoianu, Former Minister of Foreign Affairs of Rumania asserted:

> The United States is one of the rare guiltless powers. America has set free territories that were under its jurisdiction; it has assisted in the liberation of many nations; it has helped almost every country you can name to save its independence and to restore its economy. In one way or another the United States has displayed a generosity that is without parallel in history.
>
> Now let us look at Soviet Russia. That country has set at nought every treaty it has ever signed; it has violated every principle of international law; it has never ceased working by subversive means to overturn the political order and to destroy the independence of other countries; it has, most notably of all, subjugated by force nine countries of Europe, each of which has an impressive record of freedom and independence. It can be asserted without hesitation that Soviet Russia's aggressions are unmatched both in number and in scope.
>
> *And yet the United States is criticized and suspected throughout the greater part of the world, whereas Soviet Russia has become the champion — if you please — of anti-imperialism and anti-colonialism, and the defender of the independence of states!*[1]

Accordingly, from 1960 to 1980 the Soviet propaganda apparatus (which is rigorously deployed throughout the world) *religiously disseminated "information" which accused the United States of exploiting the developing world, promoting the Cold War, opposing Strategic Arms Limitation Talks (SALT), etc.*[2] The United States, not unlike the Jewish people throughout history, is not the Soviets' scapegoat but rather the Soviets' formidable adversary. America, in fact, represents the last real threat standing between Soviet Russia and world domination. It is within this context, that a brief (non-exhaustive) historical overview of Jewish slander begins.

Ancient Egyptian Anti-Jewish Teachings

Consistent with the analysis in chapter III, the propagation of misinformation is already seen in ancient Egypt. Only eighty years before Pharaoh, King of Egypt, began offering his "reasons" for enslaving the Jews,[3] did Joseph single-handedly save Egypt from ruination. Furthermore, the Hebrew people formed an integral part of cosmopolitan Egypt,[4] and their patriotism, in behalf of Egypt the fatherland, is recorded.[5] However, despite the above scenario, Pharaoh, emperor of the most powerful and cultured nation during that time period, declared:

> Behold, the people of the children of Israel are too many and too mighty for us; come let us deal wisely with them, lest they multiply, and it come to pass, that, when there happens any war, they will join our enemies, and fight against us.[6]

Though little more is known of ancient Egyptian anti-Hebrew propaganda, the above verses imply that without Pharaoh's incitings (of a Jewish threat in the midst of Egypt), the masses would have been less prone to subsequent anti-Jewish activity. Pharaoh required the *Big-Lie*, something to successfully play on the emotions and fears of the general populace. He did so by fabricating the Hebrews' anti-Egyptian leaning, with its logical consequence in time of war. In essence, the

Jewish people were portrayed as a powerful and inimical force, undermining Egypt's collective well-being and sovereignty.

Ancient Persian Anti-Jewish Teachings

Haman (the prime minister of ancient Persia), with the explicit intent to annihilate world Jewry, persuaded the Persian King (Achashverosh/Xerxes) with the following argument, as recorded in the Midrash.

> There is a certain people, the Jews, scattered abroad and dispersed among the peoples in all the provinces of the kingdom. They are proud and haughty.... When they see us, they spit out before us.... When we levy them for the king's service, they jump over the wall and hide to escape. If we try to arrest them, they turn to us and glare with their eyes, grind their teeth, and so intimidate us that we become virtually helpless.... If one of them is obligated to work for the king, he wastes the entire day. If they want to buy or sell with us they say, "This is a day for doing business." But if we request the same from them they say, "We cannot do business today."...
>
> On the first day of their New Year they go to their meeting places, read out of their books, translate pieces from the writings of their Prophets while cursing our king and execrating our government.... On the tenth day of the same month...they torture their children without mercy, forcing them to abstain from food.... They again go to their synagogues, read their books, translate from the writings of their Prophets, and curse our king and government by saying, "May this empire be wiped off from the face of the earth."...They pray that the king may die, and his rule be made to cease.... On the twenty-first day of the same month they again go to their meeting places to pray, read from their books, and make circles with their willow branches while jumping and skipping, so that there is no telling whether they are cursing or blessing us....[7]

Haman's vilification of the Jews was thereupon accepted.[8] The king then issued his edict which read:

To all the peoples, nations, and races; peace be with you. This is to tell you that the Persian prime minister, Haman the Amalekite, the son of great ancestors made a small request of me, saying, "Among us dwells a people, the most despicable of all, who have been a stumbling block throughout history. They are exceedingly haughty, and they know our weaknesses and shortcomings."

Therefore,...we have taken counsel, and have decided upon an irrevocable resolution, according to the laws of the Medes and Persians, to eradicate the Jews from among the inhabitants of the earth. We have sent the edict to all provinces of my empire, to slaughter them, their wives and their children on the thirteenth day of the month of Adar, none is to escape.[9]

Greek Anti-Jewish Teachings

Hecateus of Abdera, a Greek historian of the early third century B.C.E., in explaining Jewish origins stated that Moses "in remembrance of the exile of his people, instituted for them a misanthropic and inhospitable way of life."[10] Manetho, a Hellenist-Egyptian priest and historian, embellished the story by describing how the Jews, who in "actuality" were Egyptian lepers and diseased, were expelled by the Egyptian king and led by Moses, who taught them impudently "not to adore the gods."[11] The themes of leprous origins and misanthropy were rarely absent from Greek and Roman anti-Jewish literature.[12] Following his predecessors, Democritus, in his *On the Jews*, claimed that Jews adore the golden head of an ass, and according to the historian Suidas, charged that "every seven years they capture a stranger, lead him to their Temple, and immolate him by cutting his flesh into small pieces."[13] The infamous "ritual murder" libel was born which (in various forms), was to be used against the early Christians, and again against the Jews from the twelfth century onward.[14]

Apion, who transposed the story, reduced the interval of human sacrifice to once a year, and proved himself a most effective propaganda agent for the self-proclaimed divinity

Antiochus Epiphanes. By explaining to his people the "barbaric" Jewish ceremonies, Epiphanes would be blameless for profaning the Temple, and for his unbridled slaughter of Jews.[15]

Seeking out strategies to vilify Jews and Judaism, the Greek-Syrian government concocted stories and motifs which "proved" the "animalistic" nature of the Jewish people and their rites. Apion, as spokesperson for Hellenistic anti-Jewish rhetoric, explained in the following the nature of "Jewish ceremony":

> ...Antiochus [Epiphanes the king] found in the [Jerusalem] Temple a couch, in which a man was reclining, with a table before him laden with a banquet of fish of the sea, beasts of the earth, and birds of the air, at which the poor fellow was gazing in stupefaction. The king's entry was instantly hailed by him with adoration as about to procure him profound relief; falling at the king's knees, he stretched out his right hand and implored him to set him free. The king reassured him and bade him tell who he was, why he was living there, and what was the meaning of his abundant fare. Thereupon, with sighs and tears, the man, in a pitiful tone, told the tale of his distress. He said he was a Greek and that, while traveling about the province for his livelihood, was suddenly kidnapped by men of a foreign race and conveyed to the Temple; there he was shut up and seen by no one, but was fattened on feasts of the most lavish description. At first, these attentions deceived him and caused him pleasure, suspicion followed, and then consternation. Finally, on consulting the attendants who waited upon him, he heard of the unutterable law of the Jews, for the sake of which he was being fed. The practice was repeated annually at a fixed season. They would kidnap a Greek foreigner, fatten him up for a year, and then convey him to a wood, where they slew him, sacrificed his body with their customary ritual, partook of his flesh, and while immolating the Greek, swore an oath of hostility to the Greeks. The remains of their victim were then thrown into a pit.[16]

Since Hellenistic culture considered itself the true standard for enlightened behavior, the Jews' refusal to assimilate on the grounds that Greek gods were false and their ceremonies hedonistic was a cultural affront of no small measure. The insult was not to be taken lightly, and elaborate propaganda used to deprecate both Jews and Judaism was rigorously employed. For example, in Alexandria Egypt (a bastion of Greek culture during that period) a literary tradition of anti-Jewish polemics was established. It was claimed, for example, that Jews had been a base and disease-ridden people who had integrated with the Egyptian slave population. Their exodus from Egypt was explained as forced by the Egyptians themselves, who drove them out in order to rid themselves of a leprous element. The Sabbath was no more an honorable commemoration, but rather part of the "dirt-ridden" Jewish condition. The Jews, in fleeing from Egypt could travel only six days at a time because they were "afflicted with syphilis," and the Sabbath allegedly reflected this.[17]

Roman Anti-Jewish Teachings

According to Flannery, Roman fabrications can be traced back to Cicero in 59 B.C.E. Occasion to vent his hostility was presented in a trial for the defense of the Roman official Flaccus, who had despoiled the Jewish treasury. "Their kind of religion and rites," Cicero claimed, "has nothing in common with the splendor of the empire, the gravity of our name, and the institutions of our ancestors...and, conquered and enslaved, how little the immortal gods care for them."[18]

Further slander was expressed by the Roman historian Tacitus. According to this "celebrated" historian, Jews descended from lepers expelled from Egypt, and followed a band of wild asses out of the desert. From these repugnant origins Jewish rites were derived. According to Tacitus, Jews worship the ass, which is "consecrated in Jewish temples." They abstain from pork in remembrance of their leprosy. Their use of unleavened bread on Passover symbolizes the food they stole in Egypt, their Sabbath represents the day on which they escaped,

132

and to which, in their indolence, they became attached. Their other institutions are "sinister, shameful, and have survived only because of their perversity." Among the Jews themselves, said Tacitus, "nothing is illicit, the first instructions they [the Jewish children] are given is to disdain the gods, objure the fatherland, forget their parents, brothers, and children."[19] They "reveal a stubborn attachment to one another...which contrasts with their implacable hatred for the rest of mankind."[20] It is interesting to note that as Christianity became more and more differentiated from Judaism in the second and third centuries, they too were accused by Roman writers of ritual murder, infanticide, sexual perversion, worshipping the ass, and cannibalism.[21]

The Roman intelligentsia provided ample "justification" for attacking the "perfidious" Jews with their "loathsome" beliefs and lifestyle. For example, Quintilian called the Jews a "pernicious nation" and their faith a "superstition."[22] To Martial, circumcision and the Sabbath were tantamount to everything despicable.[23] And Jewish education, according to Juvenal, was described thus:

> The Jewish child has been taught to adore nothing but the clouds and the divinity of the sky, and make no distinction between human and porcine flesh....Brought up in contempt of Roman laws; he learns, observes, and reveres only the Judaic law and all that Moses taught in a mysterious book: not to show the way to a traveler who does not practice the same rites, nor point out a well to the uncircumcised. And all this came about because his father passed each seventh day in idleness, taking no part in the duties of life.[24]

Rutilius Namatianus, a Roman poet, wrote similarly:

> An unsociable animal this Jew, to whom all human nourishment is repugnant....We [the Roman nation] answered him with injuries deserving his ignoble race, his shameless nation that practices circumcision and is the root of every imbecility....[25]

Namatianus attacked other Jewish institutions, and concludes

133

his polemic by denouncing the "curse" Judaism "inflicted" on mankind, Christianity.[26]

Christian Anti-Jewish Teachings

Christian anti-Jewish slander, consistent with chapter V, does not necessarily lay at the foundation of Christianity. The Church's brutal vilification of Jews came about only after Jesus and his (Jewish) Apostles established their foundations. Only after Christianity severed its close relationship with Judaism did Pontius Pilate, known throughout history for his ruthlessness, become vindicated in his execution of Jesus.[27] Accordingly, early Gospels do not single out the Jews in general as at fault for the crucifixion, but the last in the series of Gospels to be written down does, and turns out to be the most anti-Jewish and pro-Roman of the Gospels.[28] Hence, Pontius Pilate is sympathetically portrayed as deferring to Jewish pressure, a deference he failed to exhibit in his other dealings with the Jews.[29] Thereafter, the Jew as "Christ-killer" (until he or she converts) became the progenitor for the countless ritual murder, desecration of the Host, and Jew as devil charges.

Once the Church became dominant, in the fourth century, attitudes towards Jews became increasingly deprecating. The most complete expression of Christian slander in its "century of victory" came from St. John Chrysostom. It was this type of mind-set which would dictate Christianity's relationship to Judaism throughout the following millennium.

According to St. John, Jews are "inveterate murderers, destroyers, men possessed by the devil.... They have surpassed the ferocity of wild beasts, for they murder their offspring and immolate them to the devil." Their synagogue, said Chrysostom, is "the domicile of the devil," their rites "criminal," and their religion a "disease." Jews were depicted as degenerate because of their "odious assassination of Christ..." and God's "vengeance is without end; Jews will always remain without Temple or nation."[30]

The Catholic Church, *in 1965*, put to rest much of this

slander with its statement on the Jews, issued by the Second Vatican Ecumenical Council.[31] Vatican II, after over eighteen hundred years, broke the long-standing theme of Jewish collective and eternal complicity in the crucifixion of Jesus!

Lest one believe that Christian anti-Jewish rhetoric was an exclusively Catholic phenomenon, a summary of Protestant slander bears mention. Martin Luther, the founder of Protestantism, began his reformation with seeming pro-Jewish concern, but turned against them once he discerned their obstinate nature.

In the beginning, Luther was highly critical of the Church's historical anti-Jewish policies. He believed, *like others,* that if he courted the Jews, they would adopt his new reformed Christianity. In fact, in his essay entitled, "Jesus Christ Was Born a Jew" he wrote:

> They (the papists) have dealt with the Jews as if they were dogs rather than human beings.... If the Apostles, who also were Jews, had dealt with us Gentiles as we Gentiles deal with the Jews there would never have been a Christian among the Gentiles.... We in our turn ought to treat the Jews in a brotherly manner in order that we might convert some of them...we are but Gentiles, while the Jews are of the lineage of Christ. We are aliens and in-laws; they are blood relatives, cousins and brothers of our Lord.[32]

However, when the Jews refused to convert, and worse, when some of Luther's disciples began displaying Judaizing tendencies, he turned savagely against them. His later writings were so venomous that latter-day Nazis often cited them. In *Mein Kampf*, Hitler called Luther one of the three great German patriarchs together with Frederick the Great and Richard Wagner. Luther, consequently, renewed many of the old anti-Jewish libels. In his later writings, he labeled Jews "poisoners," "ritual murderers," and "parasites" preying on Christian society who were worse than the devil. They were, according to Luther, the embodiment of the anti-Christ himself, and were doomed to eternal hell.[33]

In his pamphlet entitled *Concerning the Jews and Their Lies*, he outlined the actions to be taken against them. They were:

1. Burn All Synagogues
2. Destroy Jewish Dwellings
3. Confiscate Jewish Holy Books
4. Forbid Rabbis to Teach Torah
5. Confiscate Jewish Property
6. Force Jews into Physical Labor, and
7. Expel the Jews from All Christian Dominated Provinces.[34]

Muslim Anti-Jewish Teachings

Unlike Christianity, the negative stereotype of the Jew in Islamic literature is as old as the religion itself. One need go no further than the Quran (i.e., Islam's sacred texts believed to contain the revelations made by Allah to Muhammad) to understand Islam's stereotype of the Jew.

For example, Muhammad charged the Jews with deliberately omitting the prophecies of his coming:

> And when a Book came unto them from God, confirming the Scriptures which were with them, although they had prayed for assistance against those who believed not, yet when that came unto them which they knew to be from God, they would not believe therein: *therefore the curse of God shall be on the infidels.*[35]
>
> People of the Book! Why do you disbelieve in God's signs, which you yourselves witness? People of the Book! Why do you confound the truth with vanity, and conceal the truth and that wittingly?[36]
>
> People of the Book, now there has come to you a Messenger [i.e., Muhammad], making clear to you many things you have been concealing of the Book, and effacing many things.[37]

In other places Muhammad spoke unabashedly about the "vile disbelieving" Jews, who "...brought on themselves indignation on indignation; and the unbelievers shall suffer an ignominious punishment."[38]

> They are smitten with vileness wheresoever they are found; unless they obtain security by entering into a treaty with God [i.e., convert to Islam]...and they draw on themselves indignation from God, and they are afflicted with poverty. This they suffer, because they disbelieved the signs of God, and slew the prophets unjustly; this because they are rebellious, and transgressed.[39]

"Thou shall surely find the most violent of all men in enmity against the true believers [i.e., the Muslims] to be the Jews and the idolaters."[40]

Muhammad declared that Jews, like their Christian counterparts, were not true monotheists. He supported the charge by claiming that Jews believe the prophet Ezra to be the son of God. "The Jews say: 'Ezra is the son of God'...God assail them! How they are perverted!"[41]

Accordingly, all "God-fearing people" were exhorted to keep a distance from the "evil" Jews and Christians:

> O believers, take not Jews and Christians as friends; they are friends of each other. Whoso of you makes them his friend is one of them. God guides not the people of the evildoers.[42]

The Jews' alleged hopes were also described by Muhammad: "Those unbelievers of the People of the Book and the idolaters wish not that any good should be sent down upon you from your Lord."[43]

For not believing in Muhammad, the Jewish people were depicted as diseased and corrupt:

> As for the unbelievers...they would trick God and the believers....In their hearts is a sickness, and God has increased their sickness...for that they have cried lies....Truly, they are the workers of corruption.[44]
>
> Fettered are their hands, and they are cursed for what they have said....As often as they light a fire for war, God

will extinguish it. They hasten about the earth to do corruption there.[45]

The Jews were portrayed as the enemy of God Himself.

Surely God is an enemy to the unbelievers. And we have sent down unto thee signs, clear signs, and none disbelieve in them except the ungodly.... Them that were given the Book reject the Book of God behind their backs, as though they knew not, and they follow what the Satan recited over Solomon's kingdom.[46]

According to the Quran, Jews were to suffer eternal damnation for refusing to relinquish their ancient beliefs:

And the unbelievers, who cried lies to our signs — they shall be the inhabitants of Hell.[47]
Those are they whose hearts God desired not to purify; for them is degradation in this world; and in the world to come awaits them a mighty chastisement.[48]
Abasement shall be pitched on them... they will be laden with the burden of God's anger, and poverty shall be pitched on them; that, because they disbelieved in God's signs.[49]
Had God not prescribed dispersal for them, He would have chastised them in this world; and there awaits them in the world to come the chastisement of the fire.[50]
The unbelievers of the People of the Book and the idolaters shall be in the Fire of Gehenna [Hell], therein dwelling forever; those are the worst of creatures.[51]

Following therefrom, the relationship between the above declarations and more contemporary anti-Jewish, anti-Israel rhetoric, by leading Arab-Muslim leaders, is transparent. For example:

I declare a holy war, my Moslem brothers! Murder the Jews, murder them all! (*Haj Amim al Husseini, Mufti of Jerusalem, 1948*).[52]
The Arab nation should sacrifice up to 10 million of their 50 million people, if necessary to wipe out Israel.... Israel to the Arab world is like a cancer to the human body, and the

only way of remedy is to uproot it, just like a cancer (*Saud ibn Abdul Aziz, King of Saudi Arabia, 1954*).[53]

The existence of Israel is an error which must be rectified. This is our opportunity to wipe out the ignominy which has been with us since 1948. Our goal is clear — to wipe Israel off the map (*President Abdel Rahman Aref of Iraq, 1967*).[54]

All countries should wage war against the Zionists, who are there to destroy all human organizations and to destroy civilization and the work which good people are trying to do (*King Faisal of Saudi Arabia, 1972*).[55]

Perhaps the worst result of the shameful visit [to Jerusalem] is that the "faithful" president [Sadat] was mixed up in interpreting the word of God....He praised the Jews in a manner that is contradictory to the Quran....The late King Faisal [of Saudi Arabia] said he had reviewed the Quran from the beginning to the end and could not find one single sentence praising the Jews....Does Sadat know more about the interpretation of the Quran than King Faisal?

Let us tell Sadat to go to hell in order to restore Arab solidarity, stronger than ever (*Syrian Minister of Defence, Mustafa Tlas, 1978*).[56]

Jerusalem's occupation is a deep wound bleeding in our hearts and souls....We are determined to recover it and continue to pursue its recovery together with our beloved land Palestine. This, however, cannot be achieved by talking about it or by talking about peace, but through patience and sound planning and by efforts and jihad [holy war], and above all through unity of the word and the closing of ranks (*King Khalid of Saudi Arabia, 1980*).[57]

The removal of the Israeli occupation from our occupied land, Palestine, is the first and basic condition for just peace....The Islamic nation and just believers in any religion or creed will not accept the situation of the land of the Prophet's [i.e., Muhammad] flight to heaven and the cradle of prophets and divine message being the captive of Zionist occupation (*King Hussein of Jordan*).[58]

In conclusion, the words of Dr. Maarouf al-Dawalibi, counselor to the Saudi royal court, and Saudi Arabia's delegate to the *1984 United Nation's* Geneva conference on *religious tolerance* bear mention. At the conference Dr. Dawalibi explained: "The Talmud says that if a Jew does not drink every year the blood of a non-Jewish man, then he will be damned for eternity." The Talmud further states, he said, that "the whole world is the property of Israel, and the wealth, the blood and the souls of non-Israelis...are theirs."[59]

Russian and Communist Anti-Jewish Teachings

The father of Marxist ideology and modern Communism was Karl Heinrich Marx (1818-1883). Marx's father converted to Christianity before Karl's birth in order to retain his law practice (forbidden to Jews under Prussian law), and baptized his children in order that they not have to suffer from anti-Jewish legislation.[60] The anti-Jewish rhetoric sowed by the "great emancipator" was to be used to "justify" the oppression and denunciation of Jews and Judaism everywhere.

On the Jewish Question Marx wrote:

Let us consider the real Jew: not the Sabbath Jew...but the everyday Jew.

Let us not seek the secret of the Jew in his religion, but let us seek the secret of the religion in the real Jew.

What is the profane basis of Judaism: Practical need, self-interest. What is the worldly cult of the Jew? Huckstering. What is his worldly god? Money.

Very well: then in emancipating itself from huckstering and money, and thus from real and practical Judaism, our age would emancipate itself....

We discern in Judaism, therefore, a universal antisocial element of the present time, whose historical development, zealously aided in its harmful aspects by the Jews, has now attained its culminating point, a point at which it must necessarily begin to disintegrate.

In the final analysis, the emancipation of the Jews is the emancipation of mankind from Judaism....[61]

The primary source of anti-Jewish propaganda today comes from the Soviet Union. It is said that the Soviet Union expends more energy in disseminating anti-Jewish/Israel propaganda than it does in disseminating anti-American propaganda.[62] In his book, *The Creeping Counter-Revolution*, the Soviet propagandist Vladimir Begun (1974) writes:

> If we view the Torah from the standpoint of modern civilization and progressive Communist morality, it proves to be an unsurpassed textbook of bloodthirstiness and hypocrisy, treachery, perfidy and licentiousness — of every vile human quality.[63]

Similarly, the Soviet intellectual Yevegeny Yeuseev (1971), in his book *Facism under the Blue Star*, writes:

> There really exists on earth a huge and powerful empire of Zionist financiers and industrialists.... If we tried to depict it with the usual means of pictorial art, it would obviously look like a sticky spider's web enmeshing a good half of the globe; at its center swarm bloodsucking spiders, lying in wait for their prey.[64]

And, Lev Korneev, one of the more prolific Soviet propagandists, claims that of the alleged 165 military-industrial monopolies that control Western Imperialism, 158 (no more, no less) are owned and controlled by Jews.[65]

Lest the reader believe that Russian anti-Jewish slander began with the Russian Revolution, it is important to note other libels circulated by Russian governments of the past. For example, the infamous government-instigated anti-Jewish pogroms (1881-1906), which destroyed hundreds of Jewish communities,[66] were legitimized in light of Jewish "exploitation" and for the killing of Jesus.[67]

In addition, *The Protocols of the Elders of Zion*, the forgery of the century, was the handiwork of Czarist Russia.[68] *The Protocols* first appeared in 1905, printed by the government press, and was said to comprise extracts from the 1897 World Zionist Congress in Basel, which dealt with Jewish plans to conquer the world that dated back to King Solomon in 929 B.C.E. *The Protocols* were an alleged series of lectures on plans to subjugate the world and establish a Jewish world state (this alleged conspiracy was similar to its medieval predecessor, where Jews were held responsible for the Black Death [Bubonic Plague] in their "attempt" to destroy all of Christendom). Despite *The Protocols'* exposure as a crude forgery it received excited attention throughout Europe and beyond, and reached its peak of influence in Nazi Germany.[69]

In conclusion, during the Russian Revolution of 1917 and subsequent civil war, over 250,000 Jewish civilians were massacred. They were primarily slaughtered by the Ukranians and Russian Whites, who were convinced of the Jews' *Communist nature*.[70]

Nazi Anti-Jewish Teachings

The foundation for most Nazi-German slander can be found in Hitler's *Mein Kampf*, which he wrote years earlier in prison. The book was an attempt to put forth his ideas in the form of an autobiography, ideological doctrine, and party manual in one. The following are selected excerpts:

> The effect of Jewry will be racial tuberculosis of nations.[71]
> If the Jews were alone in this world, they would stifle in filth and offal.[72]

Concerning democracy, Hitler maintained, "only the Jew can praise an institution which is as dirty and false as he himself."[73]

"The Jewish doctrine of Marxism," Hitler wrote, rejects "the aristocratic principle of Nature." The goal of *Marxism* "is and remains the destruction of all non-Jewish national states." Marxism, Hitler believed, "systematically plans to hand the world over to the Jews."[74]

Accordingly, he declared:

> It is the inexorable Jew who struggles for his domination over nations. No nation can remove this hand from its throat

except by the sword. Only the assembled and concentrated might of a national passion rearing up in its strength, can defy the international enslavement of peoples. Such a process is and remains a bloody one....

The Jew would really devour the people of the earth, would become their master....

The international world Jew slowly but surely strangles us....

The Jew destroys the racial foundations of our existence and thus destroys our people for all time....[75]

Hence today I believe that I am acting in accordance with the will of the Almighty Creator: by defending myself against the Jew, I am fighting for the work of the Lord.[76]

On April 15, 1945, after six million had been systematically annihilated, Hitler gave his final "military" assessment:

For the last time our mortal enemies the *Jewish Bolsheviks* have launched their massive forces to the attack. Their aim is to reduce Germany to ruins and to exterminate our people.[77]

Hitler's psychopathology filtered even into children's nursery rhymes. For example, a book of nursery rhymes, published during the Nazi regime, had on its first page in bold type: THE FATHER OF THE JEWS IS THE DEVIL.[78] In addition, two years after Hitler took office, *The Protocols of the Elders of Zion* was required reading in all German schools. It was not surprising that in 1935 in Nuremberg, one million children swore "eternal enmity" towards the Jewish people.[79]

The efficacy of Nazi propaganda can be seen in the following school essay written in 1935, and reprinted in the German newspaper *Der Stürmer*. The student's class was assigned to write on the subject "The Jews Are Our Misfortune." He wrote:

Unfortunately many people today still say, "God created the Jews too. That is why you must respect them also." We say however, "Vermin are also animals, but we still destroy them."...The Jews have a wicked book of laws. It is called the Talmud. The Jews look on us as animals as well and treat us accordingly. They use cunning tricks to take away our wealth....

In Gelsenkirchen the Jew Gruenberg sold us rotten meat. His book of laws allows him to do that. The Jews have plotted revolts and incited war. They have led Russia into misery. In Germany they gave the Communist Party money and paid their thugs. We were at death's door. Then Adolf Hitler came. Now the Jews are abroad and stir up trouble against us. But we do not waver and we follow the *Fuehrer*. We do not buy anything from the Jew. Every penny we give them kills one of our own people.

Heil Hitler.[80]

VIII / Present Day Anti-Jewish Slander

*History teaches us that
man learns nothing from history.*
(Hegel)

Though the Western world (both Christians and Jews alike) likes to believe that public slander against Jews is no longer a serious problem, a new wave of propaganda, affecting much of the world today, is in vogue and may have dire consequences. However, this time the allegations are not directed against a vulnerable minority group, and this time the group is not (usually) portrayed as craftily attempting to undermine society. Today the allegations are directed against a powerful majority population (the Jews of Israel), a group portrayed by Communist and Arab-Muslim propagandists alike, as savagely and imperialistically subduing and attempting to eradicate an entire Palestinian nation.

A primary platform for disseminating this propaganda is, none other, the beacon of "fraternity" itself, the United Nations.[1] Israel's former ambassador to the United Nations, Yehuda Blum, while addressing the United Nations general assembly, proclaimed:

In this building [the U.N.], Southern Yemen, East Germany, or Afghanistan are democracies. In this building, Libya, Vietnam, and Iraq are peace-loving states. In this building, Cuba is a non-aligned country. In this building, the Soviet Union is the leader of an alleged peace camp, and any challenge in this regard is always refuted by the representatives of Budapest, Prague, Kabul, and Warsaw, who can testify to the Soviet Union's peaceful intentions. In this building, the Arab aggressors who are ganging up on my country since its establishment as an independent state, and who openly profess their desire to see it disappear from the face of the earth — are proclaimed as victims of aggression, and Israel, the target of their sinister design, is branded an aggressor.[2]

Daniel Patrick Moynihan, former U.S. ambassador to the United Nations, similarly wrote:

It would be tempting to see in this propaganda nothing more than bigotry of a quite traditional sort that can, sooner or later, be overcome. But the anti-Israel, anti-Zionist campaign is not uninformed bigotry, it is conscious politics. We are dealing here not with the primitive but with the sophisticated, with the world's most powerful propaganda apparatus — that of the Soviet Union and the dozens of governments which echo it. Further, this fact of world politics creates altogether new problems for those interested in the fate of democracies in the world, and of Israel in the Middle East. It is not merely that our adversaries have commenced an effort to destroy the legitimacy of a kindred democracy through the incessant repetition of the Zionist-racist lie. It is that others can come to believe it also. Americans among them.[3]

Another former U.S. ambassador to the United Nations, Jeane J. Kirkpatrick, declared:

The Holocaust did not begin with building gas chambers. It began with uttering evil words, with defamation. The United Nations, today, is following the same path by poisoning the atmosphere with hatred against Israel, Zionism, and Judaism.[4]

146

Present Day Anti-Jewish Slander

In brief, the more sophisticated Arab propaganda theme (disseminated in the West) goes something like the following:

At the onset of the British mandate of Palestine there were close to three-quarters of a million Arabs living in Palestine who had been on the land since time immemorial. The land of Palestine was a land flowing with milk and honey, adorned with beautiful mountains and luxurious valleys; the rocks producing excellent water; and no part empty of delight or profit. The Palestinian people were a socially, culturally, politically, and economically identifiable people. A people with an indissoluble bond to the land.

Zionism is not rooted in the history and culture of the Jews. It is a very recent movement. The advantage achieved by Zionism in Palestine resulted from the identification of the movement with Western imperialism, as it expanded and consolidated its dominance over the Afro-Asian world during the late nineteenth and early twentieth centuries.

What the Jews failed to buy, they expropriated when they announced the establishment of the State of Israel. The Arabs fled their homes and possessions for fear of death. Jewish terrorism was the prime motivating force behind the Arab exodus.[5]

This distorted version of history has been taken up and embellished by Third World leaders of all kinds, by the Chinese, by the Soviet Communist Bloc, by "progressive" Europeans and by United Nations officials. In the United States, elements of the left, "liberal" clergy, university students, and even alienated Israelis have been known to disseminate the above version of history.

A problem in exposing current propaganda is that while it is in vogue, any effort to uproot it is itself depicted as a fabrication, politically serving the other side. For example, to have convinced the European populace of the Middle Ages that Jews were not responsible for the Black Death would have been impossible. In Nazi Germany, to have explained to the German masses that Hitler's accusations were based on little more than the man's diseased mind would have been futile. Likewise, to explain the "Palestinian problem" in contradic-

147

tion to Arab and Soviet versions would appear to many (Jews included) as a second biased version of the same phenomena.

Unfortunately, historical accuracies only seem to surface after the issues lose political and social import. Historically for Jews, only *after* the destructive consequences have untruths been (publicly) exposed. In this author's opinion, the most accurate version of the Palestinian refugee problem reads something like the following:

> The land called Israel today was governed by its own inhabitants *only* during periods of Jewish sovereignty (i.e., there never was an independent or even autonomous Palestinian Arab nation). The Land of Israel was depopulated and laid waste by the Romans (second century C.E.), in which condition it remained, till mass Jewish immigration began in the latter part of the nineteenth century.
>
> Only *after* the Jews started cultivating and developing the land did Arabs immigrate, en masse, in order to find work. The Arab immigration process was fostered by the British government, which stringently upheld the Jewish quota (despite the fact that masses of Jews were being slaughtered in German-dominated territories), but were flagrantly negligent with regards to Arabs.
>
> Israel's independence was declared in 1948, and the infant state was immediately attacked by *five Arab states* in conjunction with the Arab population from within. Civilian Arabs were urged by their Muslim leaders (outside the land), to leave till victory was assured. After the predicted slaughter, they would return to gather the spoils. Only after the Jewish forces began to prevail, and panic overwhelmed the Arab population, did Arab leaders start exhorting their people to stay put. Two sources for Arab panic were: (1) their own propaganda concerning Jewish "savagery," which had been used in the past to incite Arabs against Jews, now worked against them, and (2) they knew their own forms of revenge, and failed to discern a different form of justice. Ironically, the fledgling Jewish government itself urged Arab populations to remain in their place (via radio and leaflets).
>
> The 600,000 Arabs that left the land were then *refused*

citizenship in all surrounding Arab lands except Jordan. They were instead placed in refugee camps (by their own people) where a bulk of them still remain today, *some forty years later!* The 160,000 Arabs who remained are full Israeli citizens today. In contrast, over the next several years some 800,000 Jewish refugees fled their homes and left their possessions in Arab lands. The Jewish refugees, however, were granted immediate Israeli citizenship.

The result of growing up in Arab refugee camps, with their "unique" educational system, financed in great part, by oil-rich Arab countries and Western "humanitarians," has been the establishment of the Palestinian Liberation Organization (PLO). The PLO is little more than an international terrorist organization, whose primary objective is the total liquidation of Israel.[6]

The consequences of adopting one of the above versions is more profound than most people think. Acceptance of the pro-Arab version, which bestows legitimacy on the Palestinian national movement and creates sympathy for the "Palestinian cause," while simultaneously condemning Israel's "racist" and "imperialistic" actions, is the "moral justification" required to support or ignore another Jewish slaughter.

In short, the American public's or government's abandonment of Israel on "moral" grounds (i.e., via the pro-Arab version) would lead to a world supported Arab attack against an isolated (both economically and militarily) Israeli people. An Arab victory would not necessarily mean a state for the "Palestinians," for both King Hussein of Jordan and the PLO have declared that *Jordan is Palestine and Palestine is Jordan*,[7] but it would mean the eradication of Israel as officially canonized in the *Palestinian National Covenant*. Even a position of indifference (based on the middle-of-the-road belief that a symmetry of truth and non-truth exists in both versions) would produce dire consequences. This neutrality would be pitting Israel against Arab money and Soviet armaments. The situation becomes more dire when one realizes the virtually unlimited monetary and military resources the Arab states have at their disposal.

Consistent with the pro-Arab version is the view that the Palestinian refugee plight lies at the heart of the more general Arab-Israeli conflict. This stance is regularly taken by Arab leaders.[8] The implication of this seemingly innocuous belief, is that the Arab states do not oppose the fact of Israel's existence, but that their hostility reflects the injustice done to their "Palestinian brethren." The corollary of this belief is that once the "Palestinians" have their own state, the Arabs will then recognize Israel's right to exist.

Historically, however, the Palestinian refugee plight *cannot* be the source of the conflict. For example, in 1937 the British government recommended a tripartite partition of western Palestine (*eastern Palestine* had already been severed by Britain in 1922, and today constitutes the Arab state of Jordan) which would have entailed the creation of a Jewish state, a larger Arab state, and a continued British Mandate over the Jerusalem-Bethlehem area, with a corridor to the sea. The Arabs, however, rejected this proposal. Correspondingly, five Arab states (in 1948), together with the Arab population from within, attempted to destroy the Jewish state *before there ever was a refugee problem.* Moreover, when the United Nations voted (in 1947) to partition (western) Palestine, giving both Jews and Arabs equal shares, the Arab world again rejected the opportunity. Furthermore, when the Arab state of Jordan had sovereignty over the West Bank from 1948 to 1967, *no attempt* was ever made to establish an independent Palestinian state. Jordan, in fact, annexed the West Bank, making it officially part of Jordan!

In addition, the proclamation that the Arabs have initiated four wars with Israel *on behalf of the refugees* is historical nonsense. For instance, from the start of the problem in 1948 to the present, no Arab nation, except one, has been willing to grant the refugees citizenship. This, despite the Arab's vast oil resources, their limited populations, and their total area comprising *640 times* more land than "imperialist" Israel. By refusing to absorb their Arab "brothers," they have, in effect, forced them to remain in their wretched camps. Jordan, the only country to grant the refugees citizenship, showed its "love" in 1970-1971. During that period, King Hussein's army slaughtered thousands of refugees and forced 20,000 others to flee.[9]

By way of contrast, the number of refugees throughout the world in 1982 totaled more than ten million, including over two million African refugees, one million Asians, and 2.6 million Afghans fleeing Pakistan. Yet the figure was significantly reduced from the number reported two years prior in 1980 where 12.6 million refugees, including six million Africans and two million Asians, were reported. As the United Nations High Commissioner for Refugees reported,… "communities, institutions, cities and nations have generously opened their doors to refugees."[10] The Arab states however, in dealing with their own people, were stark exceptions to the rule.

Similarly, the United States Committee for Refugees noted that more than a million Indochinese refugees were resettled between 1975 and 1981. The report made mention that among the African refugees, "substantial numbers…are 'settled in place.'" To be "settled in place" or "resettled in a third country" was considered by the United Nations a "durable solution" for the Indochinese and the Africans.[11] Moreover, unlike the Afghans, the Ethiopians, the Vietnamese, or the Cambodians, the Arab refugees went (mostly) to places only a few miles from where they left, to be placed in camps and used as political pawns against Israel.[12]

The ingenuity of Arab propaganda is that while the world believes the core issue to be the Palestinian plight (and is therefore caught up in attempts to force Israel's hand at making concessions), Arab responsibility never becomes an issue. In other words, the money and resources expended for what (the) vast majority of the world believes (or at least rationalizes) is a humanitarian endeavor, could be the basis for yet another Jewish holocaust.

At present, the United States is Israel's closest ally. Without American weaponry Israel seemingly would not be able to contend with its Arab neighbors and their allies. Though public and congressional support for Israel has been strong over

151

the last ten years,[13] Arab propaganda has made inroads via the mass media and among senior government officials. The American news media's latent "sympathy" for the "Arab cause" surfaced during Israel's 1982 incursion into Lebanon. During the three- to six-month interval following the incursion, the news media united in an unholy war aimed at condemning the State of Israel. Gross exaggerations of casualties, fatalities, and displaced persons were a common phenomenon during this period.[14]

An example of this type of news coverage was reported by Ilya Gerol, a correspondent for *The Citizen* daily newspaper of Ottawa, Canada. Mr. Gerol visited Lebanon a few months after the invasion. He wrote:

> With a group of other Western correspondents, I crossed the Israeli-Lebanese border expecting to see destroyed cities, burned villages and other signs of fierce battles. Like everybody in the Western world, we arrived there after watching daily reports from Lebanon via NBC, CBS, or ABC.
>
> NBC commentator John Chancellor, only a few days before my departure for the Middle East, was talking about the destroyed cities of Sidon and Tyre. The films of destroyed houses, falling bombs, the sounds of screams and fear were shocking indeed. Who would have doubted Chancellor's statements about tens of thousands of civilian victims and cities being in ruins during the first weeks of the Lebanon conflict?
>
> Those were my thoughts when I arrived in the city of Tyre. For the first few minutes after driving through the streets it looked as if we had missed our road and were maybe even in a different country.
>
> There was no destruction. The cafes were full of people, schools were operating, stores were open and Lebanese policemen regulated the traffic. We asked one policeman how to get to the mayor's office. "It's just around the corner," he said. "Not far from Television Alley."
>
> Later the mayor showed us "Television Alley" — the only street where several blocks had been destroyed by bombs. He said: "All 11 destroyed buildings were occupied by the PLO headquarters and offices."

The mayor was very busy. After our conversation, he had to accompany a new group of television crews to the same famous alley to film the "total destruction" of Tyre. I asked an ABC man: "How did you manage to make a picture of apocalyptic destruction out of only 11 ruined houses?"

"We just had to film them from different angles," was the answer.[15]

A further example of the media's a priori intent to condemn Israel was seen in its coverage of the Sabra and Shatilla refugee camp massacres. In early September 1982, 460 people (425 of them adult men) were killed by Lebanese Christian units. The nation's four leading dailies (i.e., the *Los Angeles Times*, the *New York Times*, the *Washington Post*, and the *Christian Science Monitor*) devoted nearly *eight thousand column-inches* of news copy to the massacres, *focusing on Israel* which, *at worst*, was only indirectly involved. Yet, the same four newspapers allocated only *six thousand column inches* of news space to the *combined coverage* of the *ten bloodiest massacres* of the past decade, in which a total of over *three million* men, women and children were put to death. In addition, the word *massacre* appeared at least ninety-nine times in headlines related to Sabra and Shatilla, while showing up in twenty-four headlines pertaining to the other ten massacres combined![16]

The media's most demonstrated bias, however, dealt with its failure to report Israel's invasion in its proper historical context. For instance, had Americans known of PLO bombings of civilian targets in northern Israel,[17] PLO terrorist attacks against Jews and non-Jews throughout the world,[18] the PLO's massive stockpiling of arms in southern Lebanon,[19] the PLO's official platform to liquidate the State of Israel,[20] the PLO's terrorizing of Lebanon from 1975 to 1982,[21] and the PLO's use of large civilian populations as human barricades against advancing Israelis,[22] public support for Israel most probably would not have dropped to a ten-year low.[23]

As the Arab leaders shifted (after the Six-Day War in 1967) from outraged proclamations calling for the total destruction of Israel to sympathetic rhetoric in behalf of their "Palestinian

153

brethren," the new approach granted "legitimacy" to those already opposed to the existence of a Jewish state and blurred understanding of the conflict in general.

The aspect of the above phenomena, however, unique to the present overall analysis, is that once again Jews are victimized by propaganda based on misconceptions. And once again, the majority of the world accepts this propaganda at face value. (This is corroborated by the United Nations' adoption, November, 1975, of the resolution proclaiming Zionism a form of "racism and racial discrimination." The vote was 72 to 35 with 32 abstentions.)

Objectives of the Study

Arab propaganda against the Jewish State has achieved a new level of sophistication and credibility today.[24] Pro-Jewish organizations have attempted to counter this propaganda. However, Arab accusations and Jewish recriminations are, in the long run, to Israel's disadvantage, for they create an image of mutual culpability which becomes increasingly difficult to diffuse.

A symmetry of blame in the context of a virtually inexhaustible supply of Arab petrodollars, continued Western dependence on Arab oil, and the threat of a nuclear war resulting from tension in the Middle East insidiously weakens American support for Israel. Unless Jewish organizations go on the *offensive*, support for Israel (in time of crisis) may dissipate rapidly.

To educate the public, it is first necessary to recognize what the public does and does not know. Money is allocated yearly to ascertain the public's perceptions and attitudes toward Israel (e.g., Gallup 1973-1983), but little to nothing is known of the public's true knowledge of the conflict. Therefore, the present study, as part of the author's 1985 doctoral dissertation from Loyala University of Chicago, measured the American public's awareness of the conflict, and then correlated this awareness with attitudes towards Israel.

154

A second objective was to address the relationship between attitudes toward Jews and attitudes toward Israel. This relationship has been advanced and argued against,[25] but hard data (to support or refute the relationship) are lacking.

The third objective concerned the news media. The contents in four magazines representing American, Arab, Jewish liberal, and Jewish religious (Orthodox) orientations were analyzed with regard to their portrayal of the Palestinian refugee problem. The effects these periodicals had on the American non-Jewish and non-Arab public were then compared.

Results

The study was based on an American *non-Jewish and non-Arab* random sample of *400 participants* (from Chicago proper). The participants (ages 25 and up) were interviewed by telephone.

A. The following demographics describe, in part, the study's sample.

Gender
Female = 53%
Male = 47%

Race
White = 57%
Black = 36%
Other = 7%

Religion
Catholic = 46%
Protestant = 39%
Other = 15%

Age
25 to 40 = 49%
41 to 54 = 32%
55 and over = 19%

Country of Citizenship
U.S.A. = 98%
Other = 2%

Born in U.S.
Yes = 92%
No = 8%

Last Year of Formal Education Completed

Grade 1 thru 11	= 13%
High School Degree	= 27%
Some College	= 26%
Bachelors Degree	= 16%
Some Graduate School	= 5%
Masters or Doctorate Degree	= 12%

Employed or Retired

Employed or Retired	= 82%
Unemployed	= 18%

B. The first analysis measured the public's awareness of the Arab-Israeli conflict. *Eight questions* were constructed. Response categories were *True* (T), *False* (F), or *Don't Know* (DK). This implies that by guesswork only, respondents should have scored on the average 50%.

The following represents the complete scale, with response breakdown for each item. The correct response for items 4, 7, and 8 is *True*, and *False* for the other five.

1. Palestine was an independent Palestinian State over the last 300 years until the creation of Israel. Is this true or false?

    True = 37%   False = 28%   Don't Know = 36%

2. From the time many Jews started arriving in Palestine in the late 1800s until the creation of Israel in 1948, thousands of Arabs were kicked out of the land by the Jewish settlers. Is this true or false?

    T = 35%   F = 32%   DK = 33%

3. Arab hostility toward Jews began with the start of Jewish nationalism in the late 1800s. Is this true or false?

    T = 25%   F = 36%   DK =40%

4. Middle-East Arab nations openly hostile to the State of Israel have spent over three times the amount of money in military equipment than Israel has. Is this true or false?

    T = 41%   F = 25%   DK = 34%

5. Over the last ten years, Saudi Arabia's voting record in the United Nations has shown a strong connection between itself and the United States. Is this true or false?

    T = 40%   F = 25%   DK = 36%

6. Israel's past actions have expanded its borders so that it now almost equals in size the area of all its Middle East enemies put together. Is this true or false?

    T = 23%   F = 48%   DK = 29%

7. Over the last ten years, Saudi Arabia has been openly dedicated to the destruction of Israel. Is this true or false?
    T·= 40%   F = 37%   DK = 24%
8. In 1948, Israel took control of less than one-fifth of the land identified by the League of Nations as Palestine. Is this true or false?
    T = 45%   F = 15%   DK = 41%

The frequency breakdown for the complete scale was:

N (Number of Participants) = 400
0 to 2 correct = 41%
3 to 4 correct = 38%
5 to 6 correct = 18%
7 to 8 correct = 3%

In brief, 79% of all participants scored 50% or lower. The results demonstrate that, despite the barrage of Middle East news coverage over the last several years, very little is actually known.

Based on the theory that misinformation correlates with attitudes,[26] the participants' knowledge of the Middle East was predicted to correlate significantly with their attitudes toward Israel. The results supported this hypothesis, which implies that attitudes toward Israel would be significantly enhanced if more were known of principal Middle East issues.

Though the complete scale correlated significantly with attitudes towards Israel, individually, only four of the items were significantly correlated. They were: item 1, item 2, item 3, and item 6.

The first significantly correlated item (no. 1) was:

Palestine was an independent Palestinian State over the last 300 years until the creation of Israel. Is this true or false?

Seventy-three percent of all respondents did not know the correct answer (if they would have guessed, approximately 23% more would have scored correctly). In fact, there *never* was a separate Palestinian Arab nation. Palestinian Arab nationalism is a post-World War I (British Mandate) phenomenon. In essence, only after 1948 (primarily in the refugee camps) was a distinct Arab-Palestinian "national character" created. Understanding present day Palestinian "nationalism" as a hostile response to an independent Jewish state, as opposed to a historical positive entity in and of itself, sheds light on the subject and should have (and according to the correlation does have) far-reaching consequences.

The second item (no. 2) was:

From the time many Jews started arriving in Palestine in the late 1800s until the creation of Israel in 1948, thousands of Arabs were kicked out of the land by the Jewish settlers. Is this true or false?

Sixty-eight percent answered incorrectly. Not only were Arabs not kicked out of the land, but according to British census figures (which failed to take into account the myriad of Arabs who, with the help of the British, succeeded in entering the land illegally[27]) the Arab population in Palestine during the British mandate period rose by 75.2% as compared with a 25% increase in relatively fertile Egypt. More interesting, however, was that the Arab increase was greatest in areas of intensive Jewish development. For example, the Arab population in Haifa increased by 216%, and in Jaffa and Jerusalem by 134% and 90% respectively. In contrast, where there was an absence of Jewish settlement, the Arab population increased substantially less. For example, in Nablus, Jenin, and Bethlehem increases over the same period were 42%, 40%, and 32% respectively.[28]

The third item (no. 3) was:

Arab hostility towards Jews began with the start of Jewish nationalism in the late 1800s. Is this true or false?

Sixty-four percent responded incorrectly. This inaccuracy is profound in light of the historical relationship between Arab-

Muslims and Jews as described in chapters V and VII.

The fourth significantly correlated item (no. 6), in which *fifty-two* of the participants answered incorrectly (though more answered correctly on this item than on any other), was:

Israel's past actions have expanded its borders so that it now almost equals in size the area of all its Middle East enemies put together. Is this true or false?

Taking into account Israel's more active and verbal enemies in the Middle East (e.g., Iraq, Jordan, Libya, Saudi Arabia, Syria and Iran) the present land ratio is more than 250 to 1, to the disadvantage of "imperialist" Israel. The importance of this datum is that despite relentless and detailed American news coverage concerning most every Israeli blemish, the ignorance of fact is pervasive.

In conclusion, the significance of the above findings should not be taken lightly. In times of crisis this propaganda (which may appear harmless at present) will be used to rationalize an abandonment of Israel. Unless Israeli, Jewish, or even non-Jewish organizations begin to educate the American public on basic Mideast issues, an American abandonment of Israel may someday, in the not too distant future, occur.

Effects of the Media

Democracy in the United States is based on the faith that an individual's best thinking will emerge if he/she is adequately informed of the facts. "Informed people will be more likely to decide on reasonably practical, just, and humanitarian policies because in the long run it is in their interest and their country's to do so."[29] If the purpose of disseminating news information is, in the words of the Federal Communications Commission, "the right of the public to be informed, rather than any right on the part of the government, any broadcasting license or any individual members of the public to broadcast his own particular views on the matter,"[30] then the transmission of factual, unbiased, and historically accurate news is paramount.

However, in regards to the media's coverage of Israel over the last few years, this standard has rarely been met. For example, in the case of Israel's incursion of Lebanon, non-factual news reports and biased opinions were circulated by the most respected and influential news media of today. In light of the last forty years of history, sympathetic stereotypic scenarios of the Arab plight, the "friendly moderate" Arab states, and the "belligerent" State of Israel are a distortion of facts at best.

Therefore, because of the role slanderous material and misinformation have played historically in both the cause and expression of anti-Jewish hostility, the content and perceptual effects of four news periodicals *during a time of international crisis* (here, the seven months following the initial Lebanese incursion) were examined. Periodicals representing American (*Time Magazine*), Arab (*Arab Perspectives*), Jewish-liberal (*The [Chicago] Sentinel*), and Jewish-religious (*The Jewish Press*) orientations were content analyzed with respect to their portrayal of the Arab-Palestinian refugee problem. The perceptual effects these periodicals had on the Chicago public were then compared.

The magazine representing America at large (based on national circulation), and the magazine representing Jewish liberal interests (the Jewish periodical most widely read by a random sample of over 800 Chicago Jews) were content analyzed for their portrayal of the Arab-Palestinian problem. Over 80% of their weekly issues, from June 1982 to January 1983, were reviewed. The other two periodicals were a pro-Arab monthly (recommended by the PLO office in Chicago), and a religious Jewish weekly (the most widely circulated English language Jewish newspaper in the world), which were similarly analyzed with minor modifications.

The results showed that the Jewish-religious periodical presented the Arab-Palestinian problem in a significantly more pro-Israel light than did the other three. It also produced a significantly more pro-Israel cognitive effect. No significant differences were found between the American, Arab, and Jewish-liberal magazines.

After content analysis, once paragraphs were categorized on a dichotomous pro-Israel vs. pro-Arab scale (concerning the Palestinian refugee plight), the *American* and *Jewish-liberal* magazines were found to be respectively *89* and *85* percent *pro-Arab*. The Arab magazine was *96* percent pro-Arab, and in contrast, the Jewish-religious periodical was *92* percent pro-Israel. These results imply that during times of international crisis and condemnation (as happened immediately following the Lebanese incursion) the general American and American-Jewish "liberal" media will support pro-Arab positions.

Reasons Why

In the following, five reasons are given to explain these rather strange results.

1. *Arab Monies:* Based on the Arabs' pocketbook power and their special relationship with large American corporations, it is not unprecedented to suggest that the major American news media are indirectly cooperating. For example, according to a 1974 report of the Senate Foreign Relations Subcommittee on Multinational Corporations, the ARAMCO consortium (Exxon, Mobil, Texaco, and SOCAL) attempted to block America's emergency airlift to Israel in 1973 during exceedingly desperate times (i.e., in the beginning of the Yom Kippur War). During the same war, these companies cooperated closely with Saudi Arabia to deny oil and fuel to the United States Navy.[31]

2. *Anti-Jewish Prejudice:* This prejudice could derive from many sources. The more salient are jealousy of American-Jewish success, negative past experiences with Jews (whether vicarious or real), and/or negative religious orientations towards Jews and Judaism.

3. *Physical Intimidation:* The question of how media

giants, who argue so vociferously and self-righteously for their prerogatives under the First Amendment, could collectively distort reality is indeed interesting. An understanding, however, of Middle East news, which sheds light on the above question, is furnished by Zeev Chafets, in his book *Double Vision*. He writes:

> During the past decade no region in the world has been more important to the United States than the Middle East.... And yet, despite the torrent of media coverage and commentary, surprisingly little is actually known about the region.[32]

This has a great deal to do with the fact that:

American journalists in some parts of the Arab world have been the victims not only of exclusion but of physical intimidation. The Syrians, the Palestine Liberation Organization, and to a lesser extent, some other Arab regimes have practiced terror as a tool of news management. They have subjected unfriendly reporters to threats, harassment, assault, and even murder.[33]

As John Kifner of the *New York Times* once wrote (in February, 1982): "To work here [in Beirut] as a journalist is to carry fear with you as faithfully as your notebook. It is the constant knowledge that there is nothing you can do to protect yourself, and nothing ever happened to any assassin. In this atmosphere a journalist must decide when, how, and even whether to record a story."[34]

The decision to practice self-censorship is often humiliating and many reporters justify it to themselves by rationalization. "Faced with undefined threats," says Mort Rosenblum, "reporters may inadvertently withhold sensitive information by convincing themselves that their perfectly reliable sources are not good enough."[35]

To work in Beirut one needed the help and sponsorship of the PLO. Bill Marmon put it this way: "The PLO was able to play on the willingness of journalists to meet it more than half way. Generally in the Arab world it is necessary, to an extent unknown in Israel or the West, to prove you are a friend, and you try to do this to the extent possible without totally sacrificing your integrity. I did it myself. Often you must have a patron. He's crucial, and sometimes that rela-

tionship comes at the expense of hard hitting journalism."
After a while, though, the pretense of friendship and sympathy can ripen into the real thing! There is a sort of contract
you make with organizations like the PLO — and they are
skillful at extracting a good price from the press. One way it's
done is through the "I'm a friend, you should talk to me"
kind of arrangement. You know, you tell the guy, I'm pro-
PLO and anti-Israel, that sort of thing. The problem is that
once you start that, some people really begin to believe it."[36]

If the press in Beirut was not fully reporting out of fear of
Arab reprisal, then Israel was being forced to fight the war
for Western public opinion with one hand tied behind its
back. People who knew little of the PLO's operations in
southern Lebanon or its connections with international terrorist groups or about the internal situation in Syria often
found Israel's concern about these matters "paranoid" and
its attempt to deal with them overreactive. Moreover, when
Israel tried to point out what was happening in Lebanon or
Syria, its arguments had little credibility — after all, people
reasoned, there were plenty of American and European
reporters in Beirut who would surely be aware of a Palestinian "mini-state" in south Lebanon if one existed, or of
large-scale massacres in Syria![37]

4. *Identification with the Left:* Jews are sufficiently aware
that they are not the only group reviled, but fewer are aware
that against only them has discrimination been officially sanc-
tioned by both the *reactionary right and radical left.*[38] The
following excerpt by Jack Newfield, in a leftist periodical *The
Village Voice*, speaks of the leftist trend towards Jews and
Israel. Correspondingly, it is this left-wing thrust which the
American and Jewish liberal news media, in general, identify
with.

> The thing that troubles me about a part of the American left
> doesn't have an official sociological name. It's more than
> anti-Zionism, and different from traditional anti-Semitism.
> Its impact is often in omissions — the injustice not men-
> tioned, the article not written, the petition not signed. It is
> often communicated in code words. But it is essentially a

series of dual standards. It is a dual standard for the human rights of Jews in certain countries. It is a dual standard that questions Israel's right to exist by denying to Zionism the same moral legitimacy that is granted to every other expression of nationalism in the world. And it is an amnesia of conscience about the creation of Israel, and about the Holocaust, symbolized by Noam Chomsky [a Jew himself] writing an introduction to an insane, anti-Semitic book that alleges the Holocaust is a Zionist hoax. And by Jesse Jackson saying he is sick and tired of hearing about the Holocaust.[39]

5. *Jewish Self-Hate:* A disproportionate number of Jews hold important and influential positions in the American news media today.[40] Therefore the question is asked "Why would Jews (in both the American and Jewish media) blatantly misrepresent their own people?" One answer to this question is found in Jean-Paul Sartre's *Anti-Semite and Jew,* in which Sartre speaks of the assimilated Jew. He writes:

> He [the assimilated Jew] has allowed himself to be persuaded by the anti-Semites, he is the first victim of their propaganda. He admits with them that, *if there is a Jew,* he must have the characteristics with which popular malevolence endows him, and his effort is to constitute himself a martyr, in the proper sense of the term, that is, to prove in his person that there are no Jews.[41]
>
> They have allowed themselves to be poisoned by the stereotype that others have of them, and they live in fear that their acts will correspond to this stereotype .... Thus many inauthentic Jews play at not being Jews ....[42]
>
> The Jew who encounters another Jew in the drawing room of a Christian is a little like a Frenchman who meets a compatriot abroad. Yet the Frenchman derives pleasure from asserting to the world that he is a Frenchman, whereas the Jew, even if he were the only Israelite in a non-Jewish company, would force himself not to feel that he was a Jew. When there is another Jew with him, he feels himself endangered before the others, and he who a moment before could not even see the ethnic characteristics of his son or his

nephew now looks at his coreligionist with the eyes of an anti-Semite, spying out with a mixture of fear and fatalism the objective signs of their common origin....

He is so afraid of the discoveries the Christians are going to make that he hastens to give them warning, he becomes himself an anti-Semite by impatience and for the sake of others. Each Jewish trait he detects is like a dagger thrust, for it seems to him that he finds it in himself, but out of reach, objective, incurable, and published to the world....[43]

...in anti-Semitism he [the Jew] denies his race in order to be no more than a pure individual, a man without blemish in the midst of other men.[44]

Jews and Israel

The final objective was to examine the relationship between attitudes towards Jews and attitudes towards Israel. In short, a *strong relationship* was detected. This supports the hypothesis that attitudes towards Israel are, in nature, Jew-focused and directed.

IX/The Tertiary (Third) Cause

*The hottest spots in Hell are
reserved for those who in times of
moral crises remain neutral.*
(Dante)

Though the *Primary* and *Secondary causes* of anti-Jewish hostility have been delineated, there remain at least two major problems. The first is based on common sense, while the second flows from scientific experimentation.

The first problem asks: How could the process of slander alone motivate large populations throughout history to pillage, torture, and murder literally millions of innocent men, women, and children? All of us, at times, become recipients of negative misinformation, but unrestrained violence is not perforce a direct consequence. The second problem is: How does the above overall analysis deal with the wealth of *hard data* which support the relationship between social-psychological disease (of the masses) and anti-Jewish prejudice? In other words, how does this author reply to others whose interpretations of anti-Jewish hostility (based on hard data) are different from the Primary and Secondary causes posited above?

For example, the *socio-cultural approach* to prejudice

(which includes anti-Jewish prejudice) emphasizes cultural causation. One theory of this type contends that prejudiced behavior is heightened during periods of changing social conditions. Rapid social change may be accompanied by a loss of predictability in life, accelerated disruption of social structure, and an abrupt diminution of preexisting social values. This disintegration of societal structure in times of social change is called *anomie*, and has been found to correlate significantly with negative attitudes towards Jews.[1]

Another approach used to describe the *Primary cause* of anti-Jewish hostility is the *situational approach*. This approach is different from the socio-cultural approach in that it deals with the current forces (as opposed to the development of those forces) impinging on the individual and society. Various social scientists have proposed that threats of economic, political, and/or military crises will reinforce anti-Jewish attitudes and behavior.[2] Bettelheim and Janowitz have interpreted this relationship as reflecting a regressive response which enables the individual to combat feelings threatening his or her emotional well-being.[3]

A more individual approach is the *psychodynamic approach*. These theory types contend that prejudicial attitudes and behavior (of the masses, in contrast to chapter VI which focused on the psychology of the leaders) reflect the individual's personality. A popular theory of this type is the frustration theory of prejudice (known also as the scapegoat theory). It posits that when the cause of frustration is either too intimidating or obscure, people may redirect their hostility against an available and identifiable group, which is unlikely or unable to fight back.[4]

A second *psychodynamic* variable found related to attitudes towards Jews is *sense of identity*.[5] Individuals who fail to achieve an effective personal identity may be prone to discriminatory behavior, in their attempt to establish a "solid" self-concept. Acts of aggression (whether verbal or physical) may temporarily block a diffusion of self, by projecting on others the unacceptable tendencies residing within oneself.[6] It may also reduce anxiety, by suggesting to the person or group that they are better than others.

An Integrating Interpretation

With due respect to the above theories, a parsimonious solution to the two problems above is made by (temporarily) leaving the theoretical realm of prejudice, and entering that of *aggression* — more specifically, *the drive theory of aggression* as defined by L. Berkowitz.[7] Berkowitz contends that various kinds of adverse situations (e.g., frustration, harsh physical conditions, or loss of face) serve to arouse and motivate the individual to engage in aggressively directed behavior. Experimentation over the last twenty years supports Berkowitz's claim that negative effect, from almost *any source*, can produce an aggressive drive.[8] Accordingly, individuals suffering emotional and/or social pain will be more prone to violence against others.

Berkowitz describes the characteristics associated with the individual or group under attack. He writes:

> My guess is that these characteristics involve associations with two types of events: with earlier painful incidents, or with prior reinforcements for aggression. Thus, a potential target will be attacked more strongly than it otherwise might have been to the extent that it is associated with adverse experiences, while other objects can intensify the violence that is performed if they are connected with positive reinforcement for aggression.[9]

Jews have historically fit Berkowitz's stimulus paradigm. In light of the vile misinformation historically disseminated about Jews, the non-Jew's perception of the Jew should be, at best, disturbing. Perceptions of the Jew as Jesus's murderer, exploiter of the masses, or heretic par-excellence are images that inevitably evoke negative affect. Moreover, the positive reinforcement of doing the "will of God" (plus the added bonus of pillage) has undoubtedly made the persecution of Jews appealing (i.e., to individuals suffering severe psychosocial pain).

168

The Tertiary (Third) Cause

It is therefore not surprising that the mass slaughter of Jews has often been precipitated by mass frustration and pain. For example, the *exploitation* of the *Ukrainian peasants* by the *Polish nobility* in the seventeenth century brought in its wake retaliation (against the Poles). However, during this period one-hundred to five-hundred thousand vulnerable and accessible Jews were savagely tortured and massacred.[10] Alternatively, the German people's *great frustration* after their defeat in World War I, with temporary *loss of national self-respect* accompanied by *economic disaster*, required only a substantive stimulus object (such as the Jews) upon which to aggress.

Following therefrom, the two problems mentioned above are resolved by positing a *Tertiary (Third) cause* of anti-Jewish hostility. The first of the two problems (which is: How could slander motivate large populations to acts of atrocity?) is resolved by positing mediating variables (i.e., Berkowitz's aggression-drive hypothesis), which explain how negative perceptions are manipulated to effect unrestrained aggression. The second problem (which asks: How do other theories of anti-Jewish hostility fit into the present overall analysis?) is equally interpretable. In effect, the aggression-type Tertiary (Third) cause involves the same variables posited by other theoretical approaches (e.g., socio-cultural, situational, psychodynamic), but unrelated (directly) to the Primary and Secondary causes of anti-Jewish hostility.

In other words, the more frustrated or in pain the individual or group is (for any number of socio-cultural, situational or psychodynamic reasons), the more tangibly affected they are by Big-Lie propaganda (the Secondary cause of anti-Jewish hostility), which is itself propagated by highly *threatened* demagogues (the Primary cause of anti-Jewish hostility). Chronologically, the anti-Jewish process is:

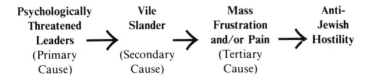

| Psychologically Threatened Leaders (Primary Cause) | → | Vile Slander (Secondary Cause) | → | Mass Frustration and/or Pain (Tertiary Cause) | → | Anti-Jewish Hostility |

Other theorists have unknowingly identified aggression-arousing variables, which only *indirectly* become part of the anti-Jewish process. These theorists have discovered little more than its *Tertiary cause.* Metaphorically, they may be described as blind men touching different parts of the elephant and explaining, on the basis of touch, what an elephant is. In effect, all are correct, and yet all are in error.

In conclusion, social scientists and historians who refrain from mentioning the relationship between psychosocial maladjustment/frustration and attitudes towards Jews are ignoring a tremendous amount of literature supporting this relationship.[11] However, those who focus *exclusively* on these relationships promote little more than pessimism. More specifically, if psychosocial maladjustment/frustration (as these theorists imply) were the primary cause of anti-Jewish hostility, then the only way to uproot the malady would be to eliminate international crises, mental illness, and overly frustrating experiences. In effect, if anti-Jewish hostility was dependent (primarily) on psychosocial malaise, the future for Jews would be grim indeed.

Potential Present-Day Tertiary Causes of Anti-Jewish Hostility

Four hundred adults from Chicago proper were randomly selected and interviewed as part of the author's 1985 doctoral dissertation in social psychology.[12] Participants were asked the same demographic and social-psychological questions, which were deemed potential present-day Tertiary causes of anti-Jewish hostility. The questions or sets of questions were scientifically constructed to measure the variables of:

1. ego strength
2. anomie
3. life satisfaction
4. purpose in life
5. fear of impending crisis
6. age

7. income
8. education
9. race
10. occupational status, and
11. gender

The variables were correlated with attitudes towards both Jews and Israel. Those variables which correlated significantly with attitudes towards Jews and/or Israel are discussed in the following.

Two variables found to correlate significantly with *Attitudes towards Jews* were the *Anomie Scale* and the *Abridged Purpose in Life Scale*. The Anomie Scale corresponds to the disintegration of societal structure in times of rapid social change. The heightened pace of American society, with its concomitant weakening of traditional values, in an atmosphere of "living for today," inevitably creates anomie, and can breed anti-Jewish aggression (all the while misinformation about Jews and/or Judaism runs unrestrained).

The Abridged Purpose in Life Scale represents the individual's lack of meaning and purpose in life. Though interpretation must be tempered by the instrument's low reliability coefficient (.56), an unpredictable (and less than encouraging) future can indeed produce "existential frustration," which could have dire consequences for Jews.

The Opinion-Fear Rating Scale (an instrument constructed to measure participants' apprehension and anticipation of impending crises) correlated significantly with *Attitudes towards Israel*. Perceptions of an impending catastrophe or crisis creates a sense of helplessness. In this state the individual may (1) stoically resign himself/herself to getting on with life despite the obstacles, (2) become depressed, or (3) strike out against a tangible and vulnerable entity, whose direct actions have little to do with the ongoing crisis.

A case in point was the hijacking by Arab terrorists of a T.W.A. airline (June 1985), with American citizens on board. The terrorists' primary demand was the release of 700 Arabs from Israeli detainee camps. The detainees were taken as prisoners, while Israel was in the process of (expeditiously) departing from Lebanon, to ward off further attacks. At the outset, the Israeli government made it clear that the detainees would be released once Israel had retreated, and once there was relative calm on the Israeli-Lebanese border. In fact, before the hijacking, Israel began releasing prisoners. Despite the above scenario, American public opinion towards Israel, when the hostages' fate was as yet undecided, dropped to an all-time low. Following therefrom, it does not require too much imagination to predict the American public's reaction to future Mideast outbreaks, where the crisis is of greater proportion.

Another significant factor is the general message, disseminated in the West, which claims that the Arab-Israeli conflict lies at the heart of Mideast instability. Allegedly, once the problem is resolved, *via territorial concessions by Israel*, there would be peace in the region (with its seemingly positive international ramifications). Blaming Israel for creating Mideast instability depicts Israel, at best, as international trouble-maker. Accordingly, this popular viewpoint may have been a factor in producing the above (statistically significant) relationship. However, as Benjamin Netanyahu, Israel's present ambassador to the U.N. explains, this perception fails to correspond with other realities in the region. He writes:

> In the last 30 years, virtually every Arab state has been at war or on the verge of war with at least one of its Arab neighbors....
> In North Africa, Libya has clashed with Egypt and Tunisia, threatened Sudan and financed efforts to topple other Arab regimes. Egypt under Nasser invaded Yemen and now trades threats with Qaddafi. Algeria has waged surrogate warfare against Morocco using the Polisario forces in the Sahara.
>
> In the Arabian peninsula, the two Yemens have been warring intermittently for years. Saudi Arabia, while trying to buy off all potential enemies in the Arab world, in turn seeks to dominate the smaller states of the Gulf and has pressed territorial claims against all of them. Kuwait frets over Saudi encroachment on its territory, but worries even

more about Iraq, which claims Kuwait in its entirety. And in the heart of the Middle East, Syria has attacked Jordan, jostles with Iraq and has made a shambles of Lebanon in seven years of ruthless occupation....

The Arab world is littered with broken agreements. At the first sign of a neighbor's vulnerability, aggression erupts against the potential victim, to be checked only by the perception or presence of countervailing power. Thus when Saadam Hussein of Iraq perceived post-revolutionary Iran as weak and ripe for plunder, he swiftly revoked the border agreement he had signed five years earlier with the Shah and invaded Iran's oil-rich provinces. As early as 1928, T. E. Lawrence characterized the Arab regimes as "tyrannies cemented with blood" and said that "it will be generations before any two Arab states join voluntarily." Fifty-five years later nothing has changed....

None of these conflicts has anything to do with Israel. None of this violence has Israel as its target. *Yet most of the discussions about achieving "peace" in the Middle East focus exclusively on the Arab-Israeli conflict* and ignore the pervasive violence that characterizes the Arab world.[13]

Demographics

In the following, the variables of *Race* and *Age* and their relationship to Attitudes towards Jews and/or Israel are discussed.

Race

The significant correlation between Race and Attitudes towards both Jews and Israel suggests that Whites, in general, are more pro-Jewish and pro-Israel than their Black counterparts.

Quinley and Glock interpret this relationship in economic terms. They cite the study that Blacks who had *dependent* economic contacts with Jews via patronizing Jewish-owned stores, working for Jewish employers, or having Jewish landlords, had more negative attitudes towards Jews than Blacks that did not. In other words, unequal-status contact may account for anti-Jewish prejudice among today's Blacks.[14]

To counter Black anti-Jewish attitudes it is important to know the source of this potentially hostile mind-set. Is it directed against Jews per se, or is it a reaction against White America in general? Black Americans may not be reacting to a Jewish landlord or boss, but rather to a White person in a seemingly superior position.

Selznick and Steinberg's findings imply that Blacks indeed see little difference between having a Jew or another White as an employer, store owner, or landlord (i.e., the prejudice is general and not Jewish-specific).[15] They found a strong relationship between Black respondents' positions on a White (non-Jewish) attitude scale and those on a Jewish attitude scale. In total, only four percent of Blacks were anti-Jewish and not anti-White, while another four percent were anti-White but not anti-Jewish.

Though the above may be comforting to some, it is disconcerting to others, for breaking Black animosity towards White America (and consequently towards Jews) is an unusually difficult (and possibly impossible) task. Furthermore, because Jews are a vulnerable minority group, they may one day become the target of Black anti-White aggression.

The Jews' situation vis-a-vis Blacks is curious in light of the fact that it was not Jews who enslaved them for hundreds of years in Christian and Muslim lands. In fact, it would be hard to find another group in America who has taken such an active role in the Civil Rights Movement, in the nourishment of the infant NAACP, and the Urban League as the Jewish people have.

In addition, if Blacks knew the relationship of modern Zionism to their own cause, vis-à-vis Arab subjugation of Blacks, their sympathies in the Middle East would most probably be reversed. For example, the founder of secular Zionism, Theodore Herzl, wrote in 1902 in his book *Old-New Land*:

>...There is still one other question arising out of the disaster
>of the nations which remains unsolved to this day, and

whose profound tragedy only a Jew can comprehend. This is the African question. Just call to mind all those terrible episodes of the slave trade, of human beings who, merely because they were Black, were stolen like cattle, taken prisoner, captured and sold. Their children grew up in strange lands, the objects of contempt and hostility because their complexions were different. I am not ashamed to say...that once I have witnessed the redemption of the Jews, my people, I wish also to assist in the redemption of the Africans.[16]

In contrast, it is interesting to note the Arabs' (historical) treatment of Blacks (with whom a significant number of Black Americans today identify). The following excerpts are taken from L. J. Davis's *Myths and Facts 1985*:

The Arabs, who ran the world's Black slave markets for centuries, continue to engage in the slave trade among themselves.

Recent incidents of chattel slavery have been cited in Saudi Arabia — which "abolished" it years ago — and in Mauritania, Kuwait, Yemen, Oman, Qatar, and Sudan, according to British correspondents and observers.

Britain's Anti-Slavery Society notes that slavery was legal in much of the Arab world until *1962* and that vestiges of the practice survive today.

In the case of Mauritania, however, the Anti-Slavery Society charges that slavery still flourishes openly to this day. In late 1981, the society accused the Arab League member of maintaining "at least 100,000 slaves and 300,000 semi-slaves." Although the Mauritanian government decreed the abolition of slavery in July 1980, the British anti-slavery group labelled the decree a maneuver to improve Mauritania's international standing.

Former Black Panther leader Eldridge Cleaver, who returned to the United States in 1975 from exile in Algeria, reported in *The Boston Herald* in January 1977, that "having lived intimately for several years among the Arabs, I know them to be amongst the most racist people on earth. This is particularly true of their attitude toward black people. ....Many Arab families that can afford it keep one or two

175

black slaves to do their menial labor. Sometimes they own an entire family. I have seen such slaves with my own eyes."[17]

Age

A significant correlation was also found between *Age* and *Attitudes towards Israel*. The relationship suggests that the older a person is, the more pro-Israel he or she is likely to be.

This relationship may be a function of the Arabs' public relations metamorphosis following their 1967 defeat. Their change in propaganda, which shifted from proclamations calling for the total annihilation of Israel to sympathetic rhetoric on behalf of their Palestinian "brethren" may be affecting the younger generation. It may affect them more because they know and viscerally perceive little of what was explicit before 1967, but only implicit thereafter, and therefore have been more easily influenced by Arab and Communist-backed propaganda. Young America has only perceived Israel in the role of "Goliath", while the older generation (irrespective of lack of fact) has itself witnessed the Holocaust and the subsequent miraculous birth of the Jewish state.

In 1977, Marvin Feuerwerger wrote:

> For much of today's younger Congress...the Holocaust is a vague memory and the creation of Israel is not recalled as a meaningful and vivid realization of an urgent Jewish need nor as the near-miraculous redemption of a persecuted people.[18]

He then quoted a former Administration official who stated:

> ...younger members...haven't experienced the Holocaust personally or seen the newsreels depicting the death camps or watched the Nuremberg trials. These members don't have a vivid image of the war, and they don't understand what the State of Israel means.[19]

The relationship may also reflect the emphasis and placement of Arab propaganda over the last twenty years, which has become increasingly powerful and sophisticated. Already in 1955, Eleanor Roosevelt noted: "Arab propaganda on American college campuses across the country is beyond the wildest imagination."[20]

In October 1964, a *Near East Report Special Survey* cautioned that:

> Arab propagandists have recognized the possibilities for affecting American public opinion at the college level. College newspapers resound with their pronouncements. College lecterns shake with the force of their oratory. As the Arab approach becomes more sophisticated, Arab distortions of history become more palatable to young Americans.[21]

In recent years, anti-Israel propagandists have made college campuses a still higher priority.[22] For example, when Harten Husseini (the PLO's deputy permanent observer to the United Nations) was interviewed by the *Saudi Report* in 1982, he was asked if he spoke on many college campuses. He said he had lectured "to some colleges." In truth, 17 of the 20 speeches Husseini delivered in the preceding six-month period had been on college campuses. In fact, 85 percent of Husseini's lectures from 1980 to 1984 were on American campuses, though college students comprise less than 1 percent of all Americans.[23]

X/The Resolution

> *The vast number of archaeo-*
> *logical discoveries in Israel*
> *have all tended to vindicate*
> *the pictures that are pres-*
> *ented in the [Old Testament]*
> *Bible. If therefore the Bible*
> *has been proven true concern-*
> *ing the past, we cannot look*
> *lightly at any prognostication*
> *it makes about the future.*
> (Chaim Herzog,
> President of Israel)

The anti-Jewish cancer culminated during World War II with the annihilation of six million. Immediately thereafter, the defamation and persecution of Jews was condemned by the vast majority of mankind. However, as few as forty years later, the respite from discrimination and persecution has ended. Jews today are targets of Communist and Muslim discrimination, harrassment, and terrorism. The United Nations has become a breeding ground for the dissemination of venomous anti-Jewish and anti-Israel slander, and in the West the reactionary Right and radical Left attack both Jews and Israel.

The Resolution

Twenty to forty years ago interpreters of anti-Jewish hostility described its primary source in terms of psychological maladjustment and/or social circumstances (which in the present analysis were deemed the *Tertiary causes* thereof). The problem with these types of theories is that they are inherently pessimistic. Pessimistic in the sense that anti-Jewish hostility is dependent on individual and social well-being, and if history is our guide, a world or nation free (for any extended period of time) from significant social and psychological malaise is an aberration. In fact, an argument may be made that despite the vast amounts of money and human energy devoted to societal distress over the past twenty-five years (particularly in America) collective and individual frustration has *not* subsided.

Alternatively, over the last twenty years the cognitive (phenomenological) approach has superseded the more pathological-type theories mentioned above in terms of credibility and professional support (and which, according to the present analysis, is the *Secondary* cause of anti-Jewish hostility). According to this approach, the solution is not some elusive strategy to prevent or alleviate universal illness (which would *presumably* curtail the anti-Jewish cancer in the process), but rather the concrete implementation of mass educational campaigns to *directly* combat *misperceptions* about Jews and Judaism. In other words, if hostility and prejudice towards Jews is (primarily) cognitive in nature, then a massive reeducation program, concerning Jews and Judaism, is the logical solution.

Unfortunately, these latter theorists (and experimenters) fail to see the inadequacy of their solution. In teaching about anti-Jewish hostility, they themselves failed to research the problem adequately. If they would have thoroughly investigated, they would have discovered that slander and misinformation about Jews, which historically has resulted in untold barbarities, was most always initiated and augmented by the totalitarian *leaders* then in power.

If these despot leaders had not been so preoccupied with condemning Jews and Judaism, anti-Jewish hostility would

179

have been relatively innocuous (e.g., the United States and Europe today). In effect, in *non*-anti-Jewish environments (that is, when the ruling power is not psychologically threatened), where the problem is of a relatively minor nature, a mass reeducation program can indeed (as many present-day theorists suggest) be implemented. However, in a *government backed* anti-Jewish environment (where this educational process would be of utmost necessity), any effort to educate the masses would be immediately blocked. *In other words, the places these programs would be most needed, are the very places they could never be actualized in practice!*

An Evolving Solution

According to the present analysis, the *Primary catalyst* of anti-Jewish hostility is the "threatening" nature of Jewish distinctiveness. The Jewish "threat" has been the source of the most severe persecution (both in terms of extensiveness and intensity) of any one group throughout history.

In light of this historical anti-Jewish process, the onus of change devolves on the Jews themselves (*expecting competitively threatened leaders or groups to refrain from discriminating or persecuting Jews for any extended period of time, is historically unprecedented and psychologically unrealistic*). From a *secular pragmatic perspective* (which is *not* the personal perspective of this author), in order to free themselves and posterity from further psychological and physical torment, *Jews must relinquish their distinctive Jewish identity!* Just as Jews, historically, have obstinately made every effort to salvage their distinctiveness (when logically speaking, no immutable difference was apparent), so must they now in the "enlightened" latter part of the twentieth century make every effort to disband and become one with the majority, like all other physically similar and culturally interactive groups (as discussed in chapter III).

The Jewish people in general (as visible to all) are not cognitively and psychologically inflexible. They are a dynamic, intellectual, *adaptable*, and even pace-setting minority, functioning exceptionally well (when given the freedom) in every culture wherein they reside. They quickly learn the laws, customs, language, dialect, and become almost indistinguishable in their gentile environment. Their intellect, similar physical characteristics, and adapatability should indeed greatly expedite the process of total assimilation. The Jewish culture could remain in the form of historical archives (as is the case with every great culture) where all humanity could unabashedly learn, if desired, from traditional Jewish culture without the unpleasant consequences of being different. According to this pragmatic approach, in order to live unmolested and without fear in the real world, Jews must collectively disband, and become one with the respective majority wherein they reside.

Although this strategy may seem outlandish to some, it is in essence currently being implemented. The process is seen worldwide. For example, there are roughly thirteen million Jews today. Approximately six million reside in the United States, where intermarriage is rampant; that is, anywhere from 40 to 60 percent of American Jews today are marrying non-Jews. Of these intermarriages, only a small minority convert to Judaism.

In Russia, where approximately two and one-half million Jews live, Jewish culture, for all practical purposes, is banned. The younger generation, for the most part, knows little to nothing of its Jewish heritage. In such circumstances (over a period of another generation or so), in both America and Russia, the identifiable Jewish community should, *logically speaking*, be reduced to a small number of diehards which would seemingly save *millions* of Jews from future oppression. In other regions throughout the world (excluding Israel), there is a similar assimilation process taking place. Orthodox (Oral Law) Jews, however, will probably not assimilate, but world Jewry is more than 85 percent non-Orthodox.

Furthermore, in Israel the picture is different than it may first appear. For instance, hundreds of thousands of Israeli Jews over the past thirty years have emigrated to the "lands of opportunity" (and the process seems to be picking up) and will most likely assimilate (given an extra generation or so) like their more settled Jewish kin.

In addition, the Jews remaining in Israel could, en masse, convert to Islam. This tactic was considered a viable option by the founder of modern Zionism himself, Theodore Herzl, who originally suggested that Jews, en masse, convert to Christianity. Theodore Herzl envisaged "a voluntary and honorable [mass Jewish] conversion" to Christianity. He even depicted, in his notes, the ceremony thereof: "in the broad light of day, at noon on a Sunday, a solemn and festive occasion accompanied by the pealing of bells... proudly and with a gesture of dignity...."[1] Only after realizing that the Jews (at that time) were unwilling to convert, did Herzl advocate mass return to the Jewish homeland.

It is this author's belief that had Herzl known that a Jewish state would bring more (not less) hostility towards Jews in its wake, he would have argued otherwise. For instance, if Herzl had known that a Jewish State would fail to desegregate the Jewish nation from the nations of the world, that it would be continuously surrounded by enemies attempting to liquidate it and its inhabitants, and that it would be refused normal diplomacy with the majority of the world's nations, he would have opted otherwise. Moreover, if he knew that the nations of the world would refuse to recognize the Jewish State's historical and present-day capital, that the assembly of nations (the United Nations) would officially label the movement he himself founded as *racism*, that after forty years the Jewish State would still need to justify its existence, that because of the existence of a Jewish State, Americans (both Jews and Gentiles alike) would be threatened by ever-growing world terrorism, that because of the Arab-Israeli conflict Western economies would be threatened and the specter of another World War less an illusion, and that despite Jewish and Israeli liberal efforts the Jewish State would remain a pariah among nations, then Theodore Herzl, the founding father of secular Zionism, would have argued differently!

Furthermore, to believe that the United States will always

182

come to the moral, economic, and military aid of Israel borders on the ridiculous. Realistically speaking, when the American economy starts flagging, when terrorism increases, when World War III becomes more a reality, and when Arab-Communist propaganda becomes more ingrained in American consciousness, American sympathy for the Jewish State could do an about-face.

Western "concern" was demonstrated by "enlightened" sympathizers less than fifty years ago, and there is no reason to believe that human nature has significantly changed. In short, less than fifty years ago Nazi atrocities were overlooked by the Western world, and the Jewish people were left once again to suffer the atrocities of an insane demagogue.[2] Is anyone today naive enough to believe it could not happen again?

More significant, however, is that the Israeli culture itself is more European-American than it is traditionally Jewish. In secular Israel (which is approximately 80 percent of the Jewish population) the native-born Israeli is much more tied in thought, dress, and behavior to the non-Jewish world than he is to the Jewish one. The secular Israeli soldier perceives himself more like the Western He-Man than the zealous Maccabee, the pious soldier of King David and Solomon, or a member of the righteous army of Joshua. The present-day secular Israeli was taught to be an "enlightened" Westerner, so why stop at the eleventh hour? Why promote an emotionally troublesome, dual identity? If traditional Judaism is not true (as secularists claim) then we must admit the deception and simply leave. We must refuse to suffer for the sake of some "man-made" romantic nationalism. We must have compassion for our children and their children, and dispel our racist attitudes in order that, at the very least, our progeny be spared untold pain and torment.

Accordingly, and without allowing sentimentality and emotionalism to interfere with intellectual consistency, organization sponsored campaigns, instead of targeting non-Jewish populations, must target Jewish populations to educate world Jewry about the dire need for *total* assimilation.

183

The Historical Paradox

Notwithstanding the above, an anomalous phenomenon (not discussed in chapter III) *which militates against the above strategy*, pertains to the *inconsistent* policy non-Jewish national or international powers have historically had towards Jews. *This inconsistency is not mentioned in most (if any) scholarly analyses of anti-Jewish hostility.* The inconsistency (or, more properly termed, paradox) is that although anti-Jewish powers, throughout history, have fervently attempted to assimilate the Jews into their respective empires and have, most often, been met by intransigence, the various periods in history (e.g., late medieval Spain, Russia during the late nineteenth and early twentieth centuries, and nineteenth- and twentieth-century Germany), when large Jewish populations were *visibly* in the process of relinquishing their Jewish identity and logically speaking, within a generation or so, there would have been few Jews left in those very lands, they were met by unprecedented persecution.

Moreover, the hostility toward the Jews during those times of mass assimilation was aimed primarily at the *assimilated Jew*, who only by a stretch of the imagination could be considered identifiably Jewish. Although in those periods of assimilation *all* Jews suffered (that is, both the assimilated and unassimilated ones), the *prime focus* of attack was the Jew who so fervently desired to be one with his non-Jewish compatriots, and for years prior was the primary target of assimilation.

The import of this phenomenon rests in its ability to counter the claim that Jewish suffering is a direct consequence of the Jews' historical stiff-necked separatism. Ironically, the very forces which so incessantly tried to assimilate Jews were now the chief antagonists obstructing the rapid assimilation process, and creating a division between Jew and non-Jew which even Jewish separatism, in its most extreme form, could not parallel.

This phenomenon is as historically unprecedented as Jewish longevity (discussed in chapter III). And like Jewish longevity, the claim could be made that it is coincidence, a quirk of fate, serendipity which happened to befall the Jewish people, or one could transcend secular social, psychological, and political theories which are based on commonalities and consistencies among individuals, groups, and political entities to the realm of *theology*, which has its own interpretations.

The one important general approach to anti-Jewish hostility that the distinguished psychologist, Gordon Allport, did *not* speak of in his classic *The Nature of Prejudice* is the *Theological Approach*. Three major religions (Christianity, Islam, and Judaism) all have well-defined but divergent views concerning the anti-Jewish phenomenon.

The Quran explains that because the Jews were unwilling to accept Allah's revelations, as communicated by his prophet Mohammad, they were cursed for all time to live an existence of "humiliation and wretchedness." The curse is not binding, however, once the Jew converts to Islam.

Christianity's interpretation of Jewish suffering was enunciated by St. John Chrysostom and St. Augustine in the fourth century. Both envisaged for the Jew an endless state of misery for his role in the crucifixion of Jesus. This "rejection and dispersion" by God would only be terminated by the Jew's acceptance of Jesus.

However, both Islam and Christian interpretations are inadequate for at least two reasons. *One*, the discrimination, persecution, and expulsion (from the Land of Israel) of Jews predates both Islam and Christianity by several hundred years. *Two*, from the inception of both Islam and Christianity up to the twentieth century, the vast majority of discrimination and persecution was meted out in the name of these two religions themselves (i.e., their predictions could hardly be called prophetic).

The Jewish Theory

Why were Jews so different from the other ancient nations who stayed together in both the national and religious sense while in the majority or in positions of power, but quickly disbanded if given the opportunity after being conquered and/or dispersed? Jews not only remained separate, but amidst the most brutal persecutions and multiple expulsions over an extraordinarily long period of time, they continued to maintain their separate identity and lifestyle (while oftentimes becoming an integral part of the larger non-Jewish culture).

A logical, though metaphysical, explanation which accounts for the Jews' continued existence (and paradoxical status vis-à-vis the dominant non-Jewish culture) is found in traditional Jewish literature, which to a great extent is the foundation of Christianity and Islam as well. These sources, recorded thousands of years ago, seem to explain Jewish longevity and the Jews' apparent inability to totally assimilate (whether voluntarily or involuntarily). For example:

1. In the Old Testament, God promised that the descendants of Abraham, Isaac, and Jacob would never be completely abandoned[3] even if they transgressed His Torah (Law).[4]

2. In the Jerusalem Talmud[5] it states that Jacob's offspring would always survive as a distinctive people.

3. In Leviticus: "I have set you apart from all other peoples."[6]

4. In Isaiah: "No weapon that is raised against you shall be successful."[7]

5. Despite the Jewish people's backslidings God promised that they would continue to exist as a nation, as is written in Isaiah: "The mountains may depart, and the hills may be removed, but My kindness will not depart from you, neither will My covenant of peace be removed."[8]

6. The non-Jewish prophet Bilam prophesized concerning the people of Israel: "They are a people who will dwell separately and among the nations of the world will not be counted."[9]

7. "And yet for all that, when they are in the land of their enemies, I will not cast them away, nor will I abhor them, to destroy them utterly, or to break My covenant with them."[10]

8. "For I am the Lord, I do not change; therefore you

186

children of Jacob are not consumed."[11]

9. "Thus says the Lord God of hosts, because you speak this word, behold, I will make my words in thy mouth fire, and this people [i.e., the Israelites] wood, and it shall devour them. Lo, I will bring a nation upon you from afar, O house of Israel, says the Lord: it is a mighty nation, it is an ancient nation, a nation whose language thou knowst not, neither dost thou understand what they say.... And they shall eat up thy harvest, and thy bread, what thy sons and thy daughters should eat: they shall eat up thy flocks and thy herds; they shall eat up thy vines and thy fig trees; they shall batter thy fortified cities, wherein thou dost trust, with the sword. *Nevertheless also in those [coming] days, says the Lord you will not be totally consumed.*"[12]

10. "A song of ascents, since my youth they have afflicted me. Let Israel now declare, since my youth they [the nations] have assailed me, but they never prevailed."[13]

11. The Midrash states that God vowed to the people of Israel that He would never exchange them for another people or nation, and that He would never permit them to dwell permanently in any land other than the Land of Israel.[14]

12. A further Midrash explains that during Jacob's prophetic dream,[15] God promised him that his seed would be like the dust of the earth, and as the earth survives all things so will Jacob's seed survive all the nations of the world. However, just as the earth is trodden upon by all, so will Jacob's seed be trodden upon.[16]

13. "When [the people of] Israel stood at Mount Sinai and received the Torah, God said to the Angel of Death: 'On all the nations of the world you have permission [to eventually destroy] but on this nation [Israel] you have no jurisdiction.'"[17]

14. "Hadrian, the emperor of Rome [circa 150 C.E.] asked the Jewish sage Rabbi Yehoshua: 'Is the sheep [i.e., Israel] stronger than the seventy wolves [i.e., the nations of the world] it stands among?' He replied: 'No, however great is the Shepherd Who rescues, guards, and destroys in behalf of the sheep.'"[18]

15. The Biblical verse "She [Israel] dwells among the nations, she finds no rest"[19] is explained thus:

> Rabbi Yudan the son of Rabbi Nechemya in the name of Rabbi Shimon son of Lackish said: "If she [Israel] found rest she would never return [to her indigenous culture and land], and similarly you find in the Book of Deuteronomy[20]; 'And among the nations you [Israel] will find no ease, neither shall the sole of thy foot have rest.'"[21]

16. The Midrash compares the nation of Israel to sand, and anti-Jewish powers to the ocean; "The first wave [of the ocean] says; 'now I'm going to flood the entire earth,' but when he reaches the sand he becomes impotent to go any further and dies out. Shouldn't the second [wave] have learned from the first? Likewise, Pharaoh [Egypt] arrogantly came [against Israel] and was destroyed by God.... Shouldn't the Amalekites have learned from the Egyptians [but they didn't].... And shouldn't the mighty Kings Sichon and Og have learned from the Amalekites [but they too came to fight Israel and were miraculously uprooted]?"[22]

17. "And that which comes into your [Israel's] mind will never come about, that you [Israel] say, 'We will be like the nations, like the families of the countries, to serve wood and stone.' As I live, says the Lord God, surely with a mighty hand, and with a stretched out arm, and with anger poured out, will I be King over you: and I will bring you out from the peoples and will gather you out of the countries in which you are scattered, with a mighty hand, and with a stretched out arm, and with anger poured out."[23]

18. "Thus said the Lord who established the sun for light by day, the laws of moon and stars for light by night. Who stirs up the sea into roaring waves, Whose name is Lord of Hosts: If these laws should ever be annulled by Me — declares the Lord — only then would the offspring of Israel cease to be a nation before Me for all time."[24]

Correspondingly, modern thinkers have likewise pondered

the metaphysics of Jewish survival. For example, Leo Tolstoy in his *What is the Jew?* wrote:

> What is the Jew? This is not as strange a question as it would first appear to be. Come let us contemplate what kind of unique creature is this whom all the rulers and all the nations of the world have disgraced and crushed and expelled and destroyed; persecuted, burned and drowned, and who despite their anger and their fury, continues to live and flourish. What is this Jew, whom they have never succeeded in enticing with all the enticements in the world, whose oppressors and persecutors only suggested that he deny (and disown) his religion and cast aside the faithfulness of his ancestors?!
>
> The Jew — is the symbol of eternity. He is the one whom they were never able to destroy, neither bloodbath nor afflictions, neither the fire nor the sword succeeded in annihilating him. He is the one who for so long has guarded the prophetic message and transmitted it to all mankind. A people such as this can never disappear.
>
> The Jew is eternal. He is the embodiment of eternity.[25]

In his book *The Ancient World*, Professor T.R. Glover similarly wrote:

> No ancient people has had a stranger history than the Jews.... The history of no ancient people should be so valuable, if we could only recover it and understand it.... Stranger still, the ancient religion of the Jews survives, when all the religions of every ancient race of the pre-Christian world have disappeared.... Again it is strange that the living religions of the world all build on religious ideas derived from the Jews.... This then is the problem offered by the Jews to the historian. The great matter is not, "What happened?" but "Why did it happen?" Why does this race continue? Why does Judaism live? How did it really begin?...Why did it come out so?[26]

Professor Nicholas Berdkilaev, of the Moscow Academy of Spiritual Culture, in his book *The Meaning of History* commented thus:

The Jews have played an all-important role in history. They are pre-eminently an historical people and their destiny reflects indestructibility...

Their destiny is too imbued with the 'metaphysical' to be...explained either in material or positive-historical terms.

I remember how the materialist interpretation of history, when I attempted in my youth to verify it by applying to it the destinies of peoples, broke down in the case of the Jews, where destiny seemed absolutely inexplicable from the materialistic standpoint. And, indeed, according to the materialistic and positivist criterion, this people ought long ago to have perished. Its survival is a mysterious and wonderful phenomenon demonstrating that the life of this people is governed by a special predetermination, transcending the process of adaptation expounded by the materialistic interpretation of history. The survival of the Jews, their resistance to destruction, their endurance under absolutely peculiar conditions and the fateful role played by them in history, all these point to the particular and mysterious foundations of their destiny.[27]

A contemporary example of the Jewish people's remarkable survival mechanism, was described in the secular Israeli newspaper *Maariv* (April 17, 1983):

Is this how things really happened? Just as they are told in the history books? And 650,000 Jews who escaped from the horrors of the Second World War and from the cruel struggle with the oppressive British — did they really build up this whole infantry on their own efforts? Six hundred fifty thousand who created a nation-state from emptiness and desolation?! And they stood in bitter warfare against the organized armies of five Arab countries? Five percent of the Jewish people, and not only did they strike a blow against every enemy that stood up against them, but absorbed hundreds of thousands of refugees from the remnants of European and Middle East Jewry. By all logic, and by all human reason, everything that happened in 1948 is in the category of the impossible. It was impossible with the limited arms that the

Jews possessed, with the rudimentary international support they managed to gather, with the limited resources that were available to them, to do all that they did. To bring a system of public services into operation from nothing. To establish a military industry from its beginning. To sustain supplies and minimal services, and to run a war that had no clear delineated front or rear lines, no organized lines of defense, no organized reserves of ammunition, and no expert commanders to lead its battalions![28]

The eighteenth-century Talmudic scholar, Rabbi Jonathan Eybeschutz, commented:

Will the atheist not be embarrassed when he reflects on Jewish history? We, an exiled people scattered sheep from antiquity, after all that we have brutally endured after thousands of years. There is no nation or people pursued as we. Many and powerful are those who aspired to totally destroy us but they never prevailed. How will the wise philosopher respond? Is this extraordinary phenomenon truly by chance?[30]

Dr. Isaac Breuer similarly expressed:

The "people of the Book" among the nations is the most fantastic miracle of all, and the history of this people is literally one of miracles. And one who sees this ancient people today, after thousands of years among the nations of the world, when he reads the Scripture [the Old Testament] and finds that they prophetically relate clearly and simply the ever-transpiring Jewish phenomenon, and does not fall on his face and exclaim "God, the Lord of Israel, He is God," then no other miracle will help him. For, in truth, this individual has no heart to understand, no eye to discern, and no ear to hear."[31]

In conclusion, the French author Jon DeBileda, during the latter part of the nineteenth century (i.e., before the Russian Revolution, Nazi Germany, and the modern Jewish State) described the situation thus:

In essence the Jewish people chuckle at all forms of anti-Semitism. Think all you want and you will not be able to find one form of brutality or strategy that has not been used in warfare against the Jewish people. I cannot be defeated says Judaism. All that you attempt to do to me today has been attempted 3,200 years prior in Egypt. Then tried the Babylonians and Persians.... Afterwards tried the Romans and then others and others....

There is no question that the Jews will outlive us all. This is an eternal people.... They cannot be defeated, understand this! Every war with them is a vain waste of time and manpower. Conversely, it is wise to sign a mutual covenant with them. How trustworthy and profitable they are as allies! [For instance] look at their patriotism, their commercial benefit, and their ambition and success in science, the arts, and politics! Be their friends and they will pay you back in friendship one-hundred fold! This is an exalted and chosen people![32]

Jewish Suffering

If Jews then are so intimately connected to God (as expressed in Biblical and Oral Law literature), then how and why have they been so trampled on throughout history? The traditional source for explaining Jewish suffering is again the Bible. In the Pentateuch, the concept of Jewish suffering plays a prominent role. Jewish suffering is predicted and elaborated on in the Biblical books of Leviticus and Deuteronomy, and throughout the Prophets and Holy Writings. Suffering is contingent on the Jewish people's collective actions. Benedictions are forthcoming for following the Torah (the Law), and maledictions for acting to the contrary. God's covenant with the Jewish people is understood as irreversible, obligating the Jewish nation to remain separate among the nations of the world through adherence to the Law, or conversely (that is, they will perforce remain separate) through discrimination and/or persecution.

It is important to emphasize at this point that the following explanation does not contradict the mechanisms, dynamics, and anomalies of anti-Jewish hostility described in earlier chapters. What it does mean, however, is that these processes are subject to a determinism different than the rational-materialistic approach most often espoused.

In the third book of the Pentateuch, Leviticus 26, it reads:

> If you follow My laws and are careful to keep My command-ments, I will provide you with rain at the right time, so that the land will bear its crops and the trees of the field will provide fruit. You will have your fill of food, and [you will] live securely in the land.
>
> I will grant peace in the land so that you will sleep without fear. I will rid the land of dangerous animals, and the sword will not pass through your land. You will chase away your enemies, and they will fall before your sword. Five of you will be able to chase away a hundred, and a hundred of you will defeat ten thousand.
>
> [But this is what will happen] if you do not listen to Me. If you come to denigrate My decrees, and grow tired of My laws,... I will then do the same to you. I will bring upon you feelings of anxiety, along with depression and excitement, destroying your outlook and making life hopeless.
>
> You will plant your crop in vain, because your enemies will eat it. I will direct My anger against you, so that you will be defeated by your foes, and your enemies will dominate you. You will flee even when no one is chasing you.
>
> I will make the land so desolate that [even] your enemies who live there will be astonished. I will scatter you among the nations, and keep the sword drawn against you. Your land will remain desolate, and your cities in ruin.
>
> The few of you who survive in your enemies' lands will [realize that] your survival is threatened as a result of your non-observance. [These few] will also [realize] that their survival has been threatened because of the non-observance of their fathers.
>
> But when the time finally comes that their stubborn spirit is humbled, I will forgive their sin.

Thus, even when they are in their enemies' land, I will not grow so disgusted with them nor so tired of them that I would destroy them and break My covenant with them.

Correspondingly, in Deuteronomy 28-30 it states:

If you obey God your Lord, carefully keeping all His commandments as I am prescribing them to you today, then God will make you highest of all the nations on earth. As long as you listen to God your Lord, all these blessings will come to bear on you.

If you do not obey God your Lord and do not carefully keep all His commandments and decrees as I am prescribing them for you today, then all these curses will come to bear on you.

God will send misfortune, confusion and frustration against you in all you undertake.

God will make you panic before your enemies. You will march out in one column, but flee from them in seven. You will become a terrifying example to all the world's kingdoms.

Your sons and daughters will be given to a foreign nation. You will see it happening with your own eyes, and will long for them all day long, but you will be powerless. A strange nation will consume the fruit of your land and all your toil. You will be constantly cheated and crushed.
You will go insane from what you will have to witness....

You will be an object of horror, a by-word and an abject lesson among all the nations where God will lead you.

You will have sons and daughters, but they will not remain yours, since they will be taken into captivity....
[These curses] will be a sign and proof to you and your children forever.
When you had plenty of everything, you would not serve God your Lord with happiness and a glad heart. You will therefore serve your enemies when God sends them against you, and it will be in hunger, thirst, nakedness and universal want. [Your enemy] will place an iron yoke on your neck so as to destroy you.

God will scatter you among the nations, from one end of the earth to the other. Among those nations you will feel insecure, and there will be no place for your foot to rest. There God will make you cowardly, destroying your outlook and making life hopeless.

There shall come a time when you shall experience all the words of blessing and curse that I have presented to you. There, among the nations where God will have banished you, you will reflect on the situation.

This mandate that I am prescribing to you today is not too mysterious or remote from you. It is not in heaven, so [that you should] say, "Who shall go up to heaven and bring it to us so that we can hear it and keep it?" It is not over the sea so [that you should] say, "Who will cross the sea and get it for us, so that we will be able to hear it and keep it?" It is something that is very close to you....

See! Today I have set before you [a free choice] between life and good [on one side], and death and evil [on the other].

I have commanded you today to love God your Lord, to walk in His paths, and to keep His commandments, decrees and laws. You will then survive and flourish....

The prophet Amos (3:1-2) similarly declared: "Hear this word that the Lord has spoken against you, O children of Israel... you only have I known of all the families of the earth, therefore I will punish you for all your iniquities."

The Jewish people are depicted as representing the word of God through His Torah. Their actions, therefore, are to be judged differently than others.[33] On this point, one of the leading Talmudists and Jewish mystics of the seventeenth century, the Maharal of Prague wrote:

It behooves you to ask, why have the chosen people suffered so greatly, while other nations seemingly sin much more yet receive relatively little punishment?... Therefore, you should know that the great unprecedented suffering that Israel has endured is because they have acted contrary to what was expected of them. Punishment is meted out in respect to the nation's responsibility [and Israel's responsibility is greater than others]. They [Israel], as opposed to other nations, must be exceedingly upright and they, unlike others, are held responsible for even slight deviations.[34]

Jewish Prophecy

"Remember the former things of old... declaring the end from the beginning, and from ancient times, the things that are not yet done" (Isaiah 46:10).

The Jewish experience is distinctly different from that of other nations. The historical process operating on others is less than evident when superimposed on Jews. However, under closer examination these events themselves conform to laws of their own.[35]

In several places the Bible warns that the Temple and the land will be destroyed, and mass exile from the Land of Israel will occur if the Jewish people (collectively) disregard their Law.[36] Prophecies which warn of the Temple's destruction and of exile appear primarily in two places, in Leviticus 26 and Deuteronomy 28 as described above. And twice the Jewish people were sent into exile, following the destruction of the First and Second Temple.[37]

1. Destruction of the First Temple and Exile

PROPHECY A: *"And I will bring a sword upon you, that shall avenge My covenant: and when you are gathered together within your cities, I will send a pestilence among you; and you shall be delivered into the hand of the enemy"* *(Leviticus 26:25).*

PROPHECY: Accordingly, in the year 444 B.C.E. the prophet Jeremiah predicted that the Temple would be destroyed by the King of Babylon, Nebuchadnezar, and that the people of Israel would be subsequently exiled and dispersed, while the land lie desolate for 70 years.[38]

196

HISTORY: Nineteen years later (425 B.C.E.) Nebuchadnezar began his two year siege of Jerusalem and conquered it.[39]

PROPHECY B: *The Unbearable Siege: Famine*
"I will cut off your food supply so that ten women will be able to bake bread in one oven, bringing back only [a small] amount of bread. You will eat, but you will not be satisfied" (Leviticus 25:26).

HISTORY: Concerning the destruction of the First Temple it states: "And on the ninth day of the fourth month the famine prevailed in the city, and there was no bread for the common people."[40]

PROPHECY C: *"And ye shall eat the flesh of your sons and the flesh of your daughters shall ye eat" (Leviticus 26:29).*

HISTORY: "Hands of compassionate women did boil their [dead] children: they were their food in the disaster of my poor people."[41]

PROPHECY D: *"And I will make your cities waste and bring your sanctuaries into desolation" (Leviticus 26:31).*

HISTORY: "On the seventh day of the fifth month, that was the nineteenth year of King Nebuchadnezar of Babylon, Nebuzaradan, the chief of the guards, an officer of the king of Babylon, came to Jerusalem. He burned the House of the Lord, the king's palace, and all the houses of Jerusalem; he burned down the house of every notable person. The entire Chaldean force that was with the chief of the guard tore down the walls of Jerusalem on every side."[42]

PROPHECY E: *"I will send...King Nebuchadnezar of Babylon... against this land and its inhabitants, and against all those nations round about. I will...make them a desolation, an*

object of hissing.... And those nations shall
serve the king of Babylon seventy years"
(Jeremiah 25:8-11).

HISTORY: "And those who had escaped from the
sword he carried away into exile to Babylon; where they were servants to him and
his sons until the Persian kingdom prevailed... to fulfill seventy
years."[43]

2. Destruction of the Second Temple and Exile

PROPHECY A: Jewish corpses not allowed burial.
"Your carcasses shall become food for all the
birds of the sky and all the beasts of the
earth, with none to frighten them" (Deuteronomy 28:26).

HISTORY: "Dead bodies were heaped up high along all
the main roads; and many who were anx-
ious to desert changed their minds and de-
cided instead to die within the walls, for hope of burial made
death in their own city appear the lesser evil. But the Zealots
[nationalists] had reached such a pitch of barbarity as to grant
interment to no one, whether killed within the city or on the
roads; as if they were pledged to destroy the laws of their own
country and those of nature as well, and to add pollution of the
Deity to their outrages against humanity, they left the dead to rot
in the sun."[44]

HISTORY: "Hadrian had a vineyard eighteen miles by
eighteen miles equal to the distance from
Tiberia to Tzippori. And he surrounded
the vineyard with a great wall two and a half meters high with
the bodies of Jews whom he had slaughtered at Betar. He
decreed as well that they would not be buried, but rather rot."[45]

PROPHECY B: Oppression and Extortion
"If you pay the bride price for a wife, another
man shall enjoy her. If you build a house, you

198

shall not live in it. If you plant a vineyard, you shall not harvest it. Your ox shall be slaughtered before your eyes, but you shall not eat of it; your ass shall be seized in front of you, and it shall not be returned to you; your flock shall be delivered to your enemies, with none to help you.

"A people you do not know shall eat up the produce of your soil and all your gains; you shall be abused and downtrodden continually until you are driven mad by what your eyes behold" (Deuteronomy 28:31).

HISTORY: "Gessius [the Roman high commissioner] paraded the wrongs he did to the [Jewish] nation openly *and indulged in every form of robbery and violence.* When pitiable things happened, he showed himself the most cruel of men; when disgraceful things, none was more shameless than he. No one did more to bring truth into disrepute; none thought out more subtle methods of crime. To make a profit out of individuals seemed to him too petty; *he plundered whole cities, ruined whole communities, and virtually announced to the entire country that everyone might become a bandit if he chose, as long as he himself received his share of the spoils.* The result of his avarice was desolation upon all the cities; many people deserted their ancestral homes and sought refuge in foreign provinces."[46]

HISTORY: "Many thousands fell dead during the numerous stages of the fighting. *Many cities were burnt and destroyed* both as a result of the fighting and of acts of revenge employed by the Roman legions to instill fear in the hearts of the people. *Agriculture was especially ravaged.* Large areas of mountains and valleys covered with fruit trees were destroyed. In many places, troops of Roman legions were dispatched to uproot entire tree plantations. *According to the testimony of Josephus, during the period of the siege of Jerusalem, all the trees surrounding the city were cut down and 'the Land was denuded and left bare.'"*[47]

The Final Resolution

PROPHECY C: *Abduction of children*
"Your sons and daughters shall be delivered to another people, while you look on; and your eyes shall strain for them constantly, but you shall be helpless" (Deuteronomy 28:32).

HISTORY: "Caesar picked out the tallest and most handsome of the lot and reserved them for the triumph. Of the rest, those that were over seventeen he put in chains and sent to hard labor in Egypt, while great numbers were presented by Titus to the provinces to perish in the theaters by sword or by wild beasts; those under seventeen were sold."[48]

PROPHECY D: *"The alien among you will rise higher and higher over you, while you will descend lower and lower.... He will become the master, while you the vassal" (Deuteronomy 28:43-44).*

HISTORY: Declaration of the Jewish deputies
"First, the plaintiffs were given permission to state their case and began by enumerating Herod's crimes. 'He was not a king whom they had to bear with,' [*For he was the son of Antipater the non-Jew Idumean*] they declared, 'but the most savage tyrant who ever lived. Many had been executed by him, and the survivors had suffered so much that they envied the dead. *Not only had he tortured individual subjects, but whole cities; he had crippled his own towns and embellished those of other people; he had shed the life blood of Judea to gratify foreigners. Depriving them of their old prosperity and their ancestral laws, he had reduced the people to poverty and utter lawlessness.'* The fact was that in the course of a few years the Jews had endured more calamities at Herod's hands than their ancestors had endured since they left Babylon to return to their country in the reign of Xerxes."[49]

200

PROPHECY E: *The strange Eagle from afar*
"God will bring upon you a nation from afar,
from the edge of the earth, swooping down as
an eagle. It will be a nation whose language
you do not understand, a sadistic nation, that
has no respect for the old and no mercy for
the young" (Deuteronomy 28:49-50).

HISTORY: "After Vespasian came the cavalry, the infantry, the cohort commanders and tri-
bunes, with an escort of picked troops.
Next the standards surrounding the eagle, which in the Roman
army precedes every legion, because it is the king and the most
fearless of all birds: they regard this as the symbol of their
empire and the portent of victory, whomever may be their
adversary."[50]

HISTORY: "The great eagle was one of the common
symbols of the Roman government, it
being found on the totem of every Roman
Legion. These 'eagles' were more than insignias. They served as
the representation of the deity of each legion, and as a result,
the eagle became the symbol of divine Rome and her army."[51]

HISTORY: "The rise of the Romans and their language
(Latin) upon the stage of history was, in
those days, a relatively new phenomenon.
Their language was unknown in the East until they appeared as
conquerors."[52]

PROPHECY F: *Famine*
"He who is most tender and fastidious
among you shall begrudge his brother and
the wife of his bosom and the children he has
spared to share with any of them the flesh of
the children that he eats, because he has
nothing else left as a result of the desperate
straits to which your enemy shall reduce you
in all your towns" (Deuteronomy 28:54-55).

HISTORY: "Pitiful was the fare and worthy of tears the spectacle, for while the strong had more than enough, the weak could only whimper. All human emotions yield to hunger, but of nothing is it so destructive as of shame; what at other times would claim respect is, in the time of famine, treated with contempt. *Thus it was that wives snatched food from their husbands, children from fathers, and — most pitiful of all — mothers out of the very mouths of their infants*; while their dearest ones were dying in their arms, they did not hesitate to deprive them of the life-giving morsels."[53]

PROPHECY G: *"And it shall come to pass, that as the Lord rejoiced over you to do good, and to multiply you; so the Lord will rejoice over you to destroy and annihilate you, and you will be torn from the land which you are about to occupy" (Deuteronomy 28:63).*

PROPHECY: "God will bring you back to Egypt in ships, along the way of which I spoke to you, that you should never see again. You will [try to] sell yourselves as slaves and maids, but no one will want to buy you" (Deuteronomy 28:68).

HISTORY: The fate of the captives "Because the soldiers were now growing weary of bloodshed, and survivors appeared constantly, Caesar gave orders to kill only those who offered armed resistance and to take alive all the rest. The troops slaughtered the aged and infirm; people in their prime who might be useful they herded into the Temple area and shut up in the Court of the women. He picked out the tallest and most handsome of the lot and reserved them for the triumph. *Of the rest, those that were over seventeen he put in chains and sent to hard labor in Egypt.*[54]

HISTORY: The Letter from Aristeas to Philocrates. *"And at that time approximately 100,000 Jews were taken from the land of the Jews to*

202

Egypt...the best and the most excellent were chosen, those at the height of their youthful prowess and fighting ability.... And the remaining masses of Jews, those who were too old or too young, as well as the women, were taken into servitude."[55]

HISTORY: "Now that Betar had been captured, everything came under Roman control while Jerusalem was reduced to a desolate mound. *Captives were sold into slavery in numbers too great to count*.... Each slave was sold for the price of a horse. *Those captives not sold were brought to the market place in Azza which*, because of the great multitude of slaves who were sold there, was called the market place of Hadrian. *Those who could not be disposed of there were herded into ships and taken to Egypt.* Many died in transit, whether by starvation or by shipwreck, while others were killed by cruel masters."[56]

PROPHECY H: *"When you betroth a woman, another man will sleep with her"* (Deuteronomy 23:30).

HISTORY: The Roman prefects would forcefully sleep first with any Jewish maiden betrothed on a particular day of the week.[57]

3. Long Range Occurrences

PROPHECY A: *"You will be an object of horror, a by-word and an abject lesson among all the nations where God will lead you"* (Deuteronomy 28:37).

HISTORY: The bowed Jew, up to the creation of the modern state of Israel, was for millennia a symbol of humiliation and persecution throughout Christendom and the Middle East. The famous Jewish commentator Rabbi Shlomo ben Yitzchak (1040-1105) explained the phrase "a byword" to mean that the nations of the world will speak of the Jewish people "again and again." This appears to be an accurate description even till the present.

For instance, in modern times, despite the fact that Jews represent significantly less than one-half of one percent of the world's population, how many headlines are devoted to issues on Jews, Judaism or Israel? And how many sessions at the United Nations concern Jews and/or Israel?[58]

HISTORY: "... But as I researched more deeply into the history of this people the feeling of dread and oppressiveness magnified within me at the sight of the willfully evil acts of violence that were perpetrated against them at every time in history and in almost every place in the world. The persecutions, the expulsions, the atrocities, the degradations, the countless murders that we find on these pages are part and parcel of the story of the Jewish people."[59]

HISTORY: "Of all the extreme fanaticism that plays havoc in man's nature, there is not one as traditional as anti-Semitism. The Jews cannot vindicate themselves in the eyes of these fanatics. If the Jews are rich, they are victims of theft. If they are poor, they are victims of ridicule. If they take sides in a war it is because they wish to gain advantage from the spilling of non-Jewish blood. If they espouse peace, it is because they are scared by their nature or traitors. If the Jew dwells in a foreign land he is persecuted and expelled. If he wishes to return to his own land, he is prevented from doing so."[60]

HISTORY: "The Jews have been objects of hatred in pagan, religious, and secular societies. Fascists have accused them of being Communists, and Communists have branded them capitalists. Jews who live in non-Jewish societies have been accused of having dual loyalties and Jews who live in the Jewish state have been condemned as 'racists.' Poor Jews are bullied, and rich Jews are resented. Jews have been branded as both rootless cosmopolitans and ethnic chauvinists. Jews who assimilate are often called a fifth column, while those who stay together often spark hatred for remaining different. Literally hundreds of millions of people have believed that Jews drink the blood of non-Jews, that they cause plagues and poison wells, that they plan to conquer the world, and that they murdered God himself."[61]

PROPHECY B: *Dispersion*
"God will scatter you among the nations, from one end of the earth to the other" *(Deuteronomy 28:64).*

PROPHECY: "God will then scatter you among the nations" (Deuteronomy 4:27).

PROPHECY: "And I will scatter thee among the nations, and disperse thee in the countries" (Ezekiel 22:15).

HISTORY: "The dispersion of the Jewish people over the face of the earth is a completely unique phenomenon in the history of the world. In the course of their long and pain-filled wanderings, and while preserving their national identity, willingly or not, this people has established residence in almost every inhabited land on earth."[62]

HISTORY: For 1,900 years from the destruction of the Second Temple (70 C.E.) to the establishment of the modern State of Israel (1948), the Jewish people have wandered literally around the world. This wandering was usually precipitated by intolerable spiritual and/or physical persecution. The scope of the Jews' nineteen hundred year exile is reflected in the lands from which they were, en masse, expelled. For example, in the third century (C.E.) they were expelled from Carthage (North Africa), in the fifth century from Alexandria (Egypt), in the sixth from provinces in France, and in the seventh from the Visigothic empire. In the ninth century they were expelled from Italy, in the eleventh from Mayence (Germany), in the twelfth from France, the thirteenth from England, the fourteenth from France, Switzerland, Hungary, Germany, and in the fifteenth from Austria, Spain, Lithuania, Portugal, and Germany. In the sixteenth and seventeenth centuries Jewish populations were expelled from Bohemia, Austria, Papal States, the

Netherlands, the Ukraine, Lithuania, and Oran (North Africa). In the eighteenth and nineteenth centuries they were expelled from Russia, Warsaw (Poland), and Galatz (Romania). In the twentieth century all Jews living in Nazi controlled lands were relocated, and from 1948 to 1952 hundreds of thousands of Jews managed to escape from the lands of Egypt, Lebanon, Syria, and Iraq.[63]

> PROPHECY C: *Fear and Insecurity*
> *"And upon those who are left alive of you I will send a faintness into their hearts in the lands of their enemies; and the sound of a shaken leaf shall chase them; and they shall flee, as fleeing from a sword, and they shall fall when none pursues. And they shall fall one upon another, as it were before a sword, when none pursues; and you shall have no power to stand before your enemies" (Leviticus 26:36-37).*

> PROPHECY: "Yet even among those nations you shall find no peace, nor shall your foot find a place to rest. The Lord will give you there an anguished heart and eyes that pine and a despondent spirit. The life you face shall be precarious; you shall be in terror, night and day, with no assurance of survival. In the morning you shall say, 'If only it were evening!' and in the evening you shall say, 'If only it were morning!' — because of what your heart shall dread and your eyes shall see" (Deuteronomy 28:65-67).

> HISTORY: For a detailed account of Jewish suffering in the Diaspora, see chapter V.

> HISTORY: The mark of fear was engraved upon the face of the wandering Jew throughout millennia of persecution. The Jewish people's suffering and bondage at the hands of ruthless and tyrannical despots imprinted a characteristic fear in their very being.[64]

> HISTORY: "The Torah [Bible] said: 'The Lord shall

give you a trembling heart, and failing of
eyes, and sorrow of mind. And you shall
fear day and night, and shall have no assurance of your life.'
There could be no clearer picture of the bitter fate and lack of
peace of mind of the Jew in the Diaspora.... Even when Jews
prospered, they lived in constant fear.

"The history of the Jewish nation in the Diaspora is a tale
of bloodshed. We left the Land of Israel at the point of a sword,
and that sword has never been sheathed."[65]

PROPHECY D: *Few in Number*
            "I will draw out a sword after you... and you
            shall perish among the nations, and the land
            of your enemies shall eat you up" (Leviticus
            26:33-38).

PROPHECY: "And you shall be left few in number
            among the nations whither the Lord shall
            lead you" (Deuteronomy 4:27).

HISTORY: Present day demographers claim that the
            Jewish people would number several hun-
            dred million (as opposed to approximately
thirteen million today) were it not for periodic physical persecution and annihilation.[66]

PROPHECY E: *Continued Existence*
            "And yet for all that, when they be in the land
            of their enemies, I will not cast them away...
            to destroy them utterly, and to break My
            Covenant with them" (Leviticus 26:44).

PROPHECY: See above in present chapter, where a de-
            tailing of Biblical and Oral Law prophe-
            cies concerning the Jew's continued exist-
ence are presented.

HISTORY: World Jewry 1988.

PROPHECY F: *The Land of Israel*
            Background Information — When the Land

of Israel was inhabited by Jews (i.e., from approximately 1200 B.C.E. to 423 B.C.E., and then again from 353 B.C.E. to 70 C.E., a combined total of 1,200 years) the land was considered "the beauty of all lands" (Ezekiel 20:6,15). Accordingly, in the book of Exodus (3:8) it states: "I have come down to rescue them from the Egyptians and to bring them out of that land [Egypt] to a good and spacious land, a land flowing with milk and honey."

The land was further described in the book of Deuteronomy (8:7-9):

> *For the Lord your God is bringing you into a good land, a land with streams and springs and fountains issuing from plain and hill; a land of wheat and barley, of vines, figs, and pomegranates, a land of olive trees and honey; a land where you may eat food without stint, where you will lack nothing; a land whose rocks are iron and from whose hills you can mine copper.*

Some twelve hundred years later, immediately preceding the second exile, the historian Josephus likewise described the beauty and bounty of the land thus:

> *For the whole area is excellent for crops or pasturage and rich in trees of every kind, so that by its fertility it invites even those least inclined to work on the land. In fact, every inch of it has been cultivated by the inhabitants and not a parcel goes to waste. It is thickly covered with towns, and thanks to the natural abundance of the soil, the many villages are so densely populated that the smallest of them has more than fifteen thousand inhabitants.[67]*

In light of the above scenario the following takes on greater significance.

PROPHECY: "And I will bring the land into desolation; and your enemies who dwell in it shall be astonished at it. I will scatter you among the nations... and your land shall be desolate, and your cities waste" (Leviticus 26:32-33).

The Resolution

PROPHECY: "And later generations will ask — the children who succeed you, and foreigners who come from distant lands and see the plagues and diseases that the Lord inflicted upon the land, all its soil devastated by sulfur and salt, beyond sowing and producing, no grass growing in it just like the upheaval of Sodom and Gomorrah, Admah and Zeboiim, which the Lord overthrew in His fierce anger — all nations will ask, 'Why did the Lord do thus to this land?'" (Deuteronomy 29:21-23).

PROPHECY: "I will make the land a desolate waste, and her proud glory shall cease; and the mountains of Israel shall be desolate, with none passing through" (Ezekiel 33:28-29).

PROPHECY: "For the mountains, I take up weeping and wailing. For the pastures in the wilderness, a dirge. They are laid waste; no man passes through.... I will turn Jerusalem into rubble, into dens for foxes. And I will make the towns of Judah a desolation without inhabitants" (Jeremiah 9:9-10).

HISTORY: The Land of Israel is located in the center of the Fertile Crescent, and forms the meeting ground for three continents. While inhabited by the Jews it was heavily populated and developed. However, once the Jewish people were exiled, it was left in ruins (by the Romans) and remained so for over eighteen hundred years. Following the Jewish exile many a people (e.g., Romans, Crusaders, Tartars, Mamelukes, Arabs, and Turks) conquered the land, and numerous wars were fought for its possession. However, all efforts to settle the land or cause its desolate wastes to blossom were in vain. It remained a barren wasteland until the Jewish people began returning, en masse, in the twentieth century.

HISTORY: In 1260, the Jewish Talmudist and mystic, Moses Nachmanides, while in the Land of

Israel, wrote to his son: "What shall I tell you about the land? There are so many forsaken places, and the desolation is great. It comes down to this: the more sacred the place the more it has suffered. Jerusalem is most desolate, Judea more so than Galilee."[68]

HISTORY: Mark Twain, visiting the Land of Israel in 1867, described it as:

"...[a] desolate country whose soil is rich enough, but is given over wholly to weeds — a silent mournful expanse.... A desolation is here that not even imagination can grace with the pomp of life and action.... We never saw a human being on the whole route.

"The Land of Israel dwells in sackcloth and ashes. The spell of a curse hovers over her which has blighted her fields and imprisoned her mighty potential with shackles. The Land of Israel is wasteland, devoid of delight. It is no longer to be considered a part of the world. It is reserved for poetry and legend, a land of dreams."[69]

HISTORY: In 1888, Professor Sir John William Dawson wrote:

"[Up until] today no people has succeeded in establishing national [control] in the Land of Israel.... No national unity or spirit of nationalism has acquired any hold there. The mixed multitude of itinerant tribes that managed to settle there did so only as temporary residents. It seems indeed that they too were awaiting the return of the permanent residents to the land."[70]

HISTORY: As late as the early twentieth century, the *Palestine Royal Commission* described the land thus:

"The road leading from Gaza to the north was only a summer track suitable for transport by camels and carts...no orange groves, orchards or vineyards were to be seen until one reached Yabna village....The western part, towards the sea, was

210

almost a desert.... The villages in this area were few and thinly populated. Many ruins of villages were scattered over the area, as owing to the prevalence of malaria, many villages were deserted by their inhabitants."[71]

HISTORY: Correspondingly, Nachmanides (thirteenth century), in his commentary on the book of Leviticus explained:

"...that which He stated here, 'and your enemies that shall dwell therein shall be desolate in it' constitutes a good tiding, proclaiming that during all our exiles, our land will not accept our enemies. This also is an assurance to us, for in the whole inhabited part of the world one cannot find such a good land which was always lived in and yet is as ruined as it is [today], for since the time that we left it, it has not accepted any nation or people, and they all try to settle it, but to no avail."[72]

Some seven hundred years later, despite repeated attempts to develop it, the land remained desolate. However, with the return of the Jewish people, the land once again has begun to bloom.

PROPHECY G: *"But you, O mountains of Israel, shall yield your produce and bear your fruit for My people Israel, for their return is near. For I will care for you: I will turn to you, and you shall be tilled and sown. I will settle a large population on you, the whole House of Israel; the towns shall be resettled, and the ruined sites rebuilt. I will multiply men and beasts upon you, and they shall increase and be fertile, and I will resettle you as you were formerly, and will make you more prosperous than you were at first. And you shall know that I am the Lord" (Ezekiel 36:8-11).*

PROPHECY: There is no surer sign for the subsequent Redemption, than when the Land of Israel becomes fertile again for the Jewish people (Talmud, Sanhedrin 98A).

The Final Resolution

PROPHECY: "As long as Israel does not dwell on its land, the land does not give her fruit as she is accustomed. When she will begin to re-flourish, however, and give of her fruit, this is a clear sign that the end — the time of Redemption is approaching, when all of Israel will subsequently return to the land" (Rabbi Shmuel Eliezer [The Maharsha], 1630).

HISTORY: Perhaps it may be inferred that the land, by giving of its fruits again, is preparing for the arrival of the entire Jewish nation. We ourselves are witness today to the fact that in a relatively short period of time Israel has undergone a remarkable transformation into a green and blossoming land, after thousands of years of desolation.[73]

PROPHECY H: *The Industrial Revolution*
Background Information — It is hard to imagine how three million Jews, in a country as small and geographically indefensible as Israel (particularly before 1967), could consistently prevail over more than one hundred million Arabs in adjacent and surrounding lands. Naturally speaking, this could only have occurred with today's technology. However, from a historical perspective, this technological boom, beginning (for all practical purposes) in the early nineteenth century, did not slowly and progressively evolve, but rather broke into history as a radical departure from the past.

Correspondingly, the Zohar, which is the primary classic of Jewish mysticism (the Kabbalah) attributed to the school of Rabbi Shimon bar Yochai (circa 120 C.E.), predicted that in the 600th year of the sixth millennium of the Hebrew calendar (corresponding to 1840 C.E.), unprecedented "scientific" break-throughs would occur. The Zohar reads:

"Every sixty years of the sixth millennium the gates of 'lower' wisdom will be 'strengthened' and 'rise up' gradually to become 'stronger.' Then (at the end of ten complete stages of sixty years each) at the end of 600 years into the sixth millennium [i.e., 1840], the gates of supernal knowledge will open 'above,' along with the

212

wellsprings of [secular] knowledge 'below.' This will begin the process whereby the world will prepare to enter the seventh millennium.

"This is symbolized by Israel who start preparing themselves, on the afternoon of the sixth day, for the Sabbath. In the same manner, the sixth millennium parallels Friday which is the sixth day of the week. Toward 'afternoon' of the sixth millennium everything is accelerated and all the preparations are readied for the Great Sabbath."[74]

HISTORY: Accordingly, at the turn of the nineteenth century, a revolution commenced in all areas of applied science.

Partial List of Scientific Discoveries[75]

1805	Dalton's Atomic Theory
1823	Ampere, electricity
1825	Laplace, formulas
1831	Joseph Henry, telegraph
1833	K. F. Gauss, electromagnetism
1834	Faraday, theory of electro-chemistry
1842	H. Joule, 2nd Law of Thermodynamics, Conservation of energy
1842	Doppler effect
1842	Radio
1845	Boolean algebra, basis for modern computer languages
1857	Louis Pasteur, breakthrough in discovery of microbes and immunization
1859	Bunsen and Kurchoff, spectroscopy
1864	Alfred Nobel, dynamite
1865	Mendel, laws of genetic inheritance
1869	Mendeleev, periodic table of elements
1873	Maxwell's formulas (electromagnetic)

HISTORY: "In one generation (from 1801 to 1840), more progress was made in all branches of science than in the thousands of years that passed since man first contemplated the stars and asked himself 'where is all this from?' "[76]

HISTORY: "The nineteenth century reached a greater degree of progress than all previous centuries put together in the understanding of nature and its laws. Important riddles of the universe were solved which were considered impossible to unravel at the beginning of the century. The veil was removed from science and from man's awareness of new frontiers whose existence was never suspected less than 100 years ago!"[77]

PROPHECY I: *Return to the Land*
"God will then bring back your remnants and have mercy on you. God your Lord will gather you from among the nations where He scattered you. Even if your diaspora is at the ends of the heavens, God your Lord will gather you up from there and He will take you back.

"God your Lord will then bring you to the land that your ancestors occupied, and you will occupy it" (Deuteronomy 30:3-5).

HISTORY: Despite the fact that over 70 percent of the Jewish people today reside outside the Land of Israel (and despite the relatively large present-day emigration rate), Jewish immigration, over the last 100 years, remains extraordinary. The Jewish people's striking return, since the establishment of Israel in 1948, is seen in the following statistics:

AFRICA		EUROPE	
140,365	Morocco	199,467	USSR
184,413	Algeria	168,533	Poland
14,703	Tunisia	260,188	Romania
35,778	Libya	39,887	Bulgaria
30,002	Egypt & Sudan	15,649	Germany
11,918	South Africa	23,459	Czechoslovakia
13,566	Rest of Africa	28,175	Hungary
		19,798	United Kingdom
		21,702	France
		37,009	Rest of Europe
430,745	TOTAL	813,867	TOTAL

214

AMERICA, OCEANIA		ASIA	
57,832	USA, Canada	60,136	Turkey
32,670	Argentina	129,497	Iraq
25,260	Rest of Latin America	46,411	Yemen
	and Oceania	69,755	Iran
		24,789	India, Pakistan
		26,644	Rest of Asia

PROPHECY J: *Return to Tradition*
"*There shall come a time when you shall experience all the words of blessing and curse that I have presented to you... You will then return to God your Lord, and will obey Him, doing everything that I am commanding you today. You and your children [will repent] with all your heart and with all your soul*" (Deuteronomy 30:1-2).

HISTORY: Though the number of non-observant (non-Orthodox) Jews today vastly exceeds the number of observant ones, the fact that traditional observance today is steadily increasing suggests that the above prophecy is materializing. (It should be understood that Judaism is not Christianity, and that for a non-observant Jew to become observant is an arduous task fraught with social unease, discipline, and serious study.) Simcha Meiri describes this phenomenon thus:

"Realistic" projections thirty or forty years ago envisioned the number of religious Jews as slowly but surely fading away. Observant Jews were to become a thing of the past within a generation or two. Not only has this prediction proven false, not only have religious institutions not emptied of their scholars, but, on the contrary, their numbers have increased. We are witnessing a great and gratifying spiritual rebirth which, although contrary to all human expectations, was specifically foretold in the Torah: 'And it shall come to pass, when all these things are come upon you... and you shall return unto the Lord your God and shall obey His voice.'[78]

"No one could have anticipated that the number of observant Jews would increase daily, and even today we still do not grasp the full significance and extent of this welcome turn of events, yet knowledge of it was plainly imparted to the prophet Amos:[79] 'Behold the days come, says the Lord God, that I will send a famine in the land, not a famine of bread, nor a thirst for water, but of hearing the words of the Lord.'"[80]

PROPHECY K: The Temple's Western Wall
In the Biblical book Song of Songs (2:9) it states: "Behold, he stands behind our wall." The Midrash explains: "Behind the Western Wall of the [Jerusalem] Temple [i.e., the wall in the verse is speaking of the Temple's Western Wall]. Why [the Midrash asks, is God figuratively standing there]? For God has sworn that it will never be destroyed."[81]

HISTORY: "During two thousand years of exile, Jerusalem was the scene of many battles and was razed and rebuilt no less than nine times. But although it was seized by nations who sought to erase any trace of its past glory, one thing remained intact. The Western Wall has miraculously stood to this very day. There were periods during which it was covered in dirt and rubbish, but it has never crumbled."[82]

PROPHECY L: The City Babylon
"And Yirmeyahu said to Seraya, When thou comest to Babylon and shalt see, and shalt read all these words; then shalt thou say, O Lord, thou hast spoken against this place, to cut it off, that none shall remain in it, neither man nor beast, but that it shall be desolate forever. And it shall be, when thou has made an end of reading this book, that thou shalt bind a stone to it, and cast it into the midst of Perat: and thou shalt say, Thus shall Babylon sink, and shall not rise" (Jeremiah 51:16-64).

The Resolution

PROPHECY: "And Babylon the glory of kingdoms, the beauty of the pride of the Kasdim, shall be as when God overthrew Sodom and Gommorah. It shall never be inhabited, neither shall it be dwelt in from generation to generation, neither shall the Arabs pitch tent there, neither shall the shepherds make their flock lie down there. But wild beasts of the desert shall lie there, and their houses shall be full of owls; and ostriches shall dwell there, and the scops owl shall hop about there. And jackals shall cry in their castles, and wild dogs in their pleasant palaces" (Isaiah 13:19-22).

PROPHECY: "And I will pay back to Babylon and to all the inhabitants of Kasdim all their evil that they have done in Zion [i.e., Jerusalem] in your sight, says the Lord...and I will stretch out my hand upon thee, and roll thee down from the rocks, and will make thee a burnt mountain...for thou shalt be desolate forever" (Jeremiah 51:24-26).

HISTORY: "The city of Babylon was the capital of the old Babylonian empire from about 2000 B.C.E. It was the metropolis of antiquity, the center of oriental civilization. Nebuchadnezar restored it in the middle of the sixth century (B.C.E.).

"After the reign of Cyrus, Babylon still continued to be an important city, remaining one of the capitals of the Persian empire. But gradually the city became more and more deserted. Alexander the Great intended to make it the center of his world empire, but his early death prevented this. And Babylon eventually passed from the scene. It was reduced to rubble and has remained in this condition until our time."[83]

HISTORY: "Why did the prophets endanger their credibility with a long range prophecy which would extend till the end of history? The demise of an empire and the destruction of a city are natural occurrences, but all the great cities of the ancient Near East were destroyed and rebuilt numerous times until the modern period. Damascus, Rabat Amon, Jericho, Jerusalem, Alexandria were all repeatedly rebuilt and are standing today on the ruins of their past. Why then was Babylon, the greatest and most glorious city of old, standing at the economic hub of empires that arose around her one after the other, transformed into an eternal desolation?"[84]

PROPHECY M: *Torah Continuity*
"When they are then beset by many evils and troubles, this song shall testify for them like a witness, since it will not be forgotten by their descendants" (Deuteronomy 31:21).

PROPHECY: "As for Me, this is My covenant with them, says the Lord... My words which I have put in your mouth, shall not depart out of your mouth, nor out of the mouth of your seed, nor out of the mouth of your seed's seed, says the Lord, from henceforce and forever" (Isaiah 59:21).

HISTORY: "We were... assured that the Torah would live forever in the nation.... For a nation that lived so long among other peoples, encountering alien cultures, this is nothing if not unnatural....

"The Torah faced many ordeals in its exile from the Land of Israel together with the nation. But whenever a center of Torah study was destroyed, others immediately took its place.... In every generation there were those who attempted to exterminate us or bring us, in various ways, to abandon our Torah.... The physical survival of the Jewish nation and its continued observance of the Torah are among the most astounding phenomena in human history. They are unparalleled in the annals of any other nation. Despite our contact with other cultures, the Torah was preserved unaltered in its original form. Even today, the daily routine and cultural life of observant [Orthodox] Jews the world over, whether shoemaker or famous scientist, is essentially the same as that of our forefathers some three thousand years ago."[85]

PROPHECY N: *The Messiah and Messianic Era*
Prophecies concerning the Messiah and the
pre-Messianic Era are discussed below.

Future Interests: The Messiah

The Talmud relates the following anecdote:

> When they [Rabbi Gamliel, Rabbi Eliezer Ben Azaria,
> Rabbi Joshua, and Rabbi Akiva] were going up to Jerusa-
> lem, and reached Mount Scopus they rent their clothing [as
> mourners witnessing the destroyed Temple]. When they
> reached the Temple Mount they saw a fox coming out of the
> area where the Holy of Holies once stood. They began to
> weep and Rabbi Akiva laughed! They said: "Why are you
> laughing?" He said: "Why are you weeping?" They said to
> him "A place of which it is written 'an alien who comes near
> shall die' and now foxes therein reside, and we should not
> cry?" He said to them "Just because that I laugh...for if the
> prophecy of Uriah [who described the Temple's destruction]
> had not materialized then I may fear that Zachariah's pro-
> phecy [who spoke of the Final Redemption] would also not
> transpire. Now that Uriah's prophecy has transpired, we
> may be assured that the prophecy of Zachariah will also
> be"...They said: "Akiva you have consoled us, Akiva you
> have consoled us!"[86]

Not all Jewish prophecies have been fulfilled. The last and
most important (for both Jew and non-Jew alike) prophecies
concerning the "End of Days" have yet to be realized: "And it
shall come to pass in the last days, that the mountain of the
Lord's house shall be established on the top of the mountains,
and shall be exalted above the hills; and all nations shall flow
unto it" (Isaiah 2:2).

According to traditional literature the Final Redemption
(for all humanity) is assured, but the process of getting there
(that is, via worldwide destruction or supernal benevolence) is
dependent on the Jewish people collectively. For example, the
Talmud states:

The son of Levi cites a contradiction, in the prophet Isaiah it is written "in its time" [i.e., the Final Redemption will come in its prescribed time], but it also is written there "I will hurry it up" [i.e., God will bring the Final Redemption before its appointed time]? [The Talmud then explains] If they [the Jews] *merit*, I [God] will hurry it up, if they *do not merit*, it will come in its prescribed time.[87]

The Maharsha (Rabbi Shmuel Eliezar) explains: "If the Jews merit by repentance and Torah observance, God will have compassion on them [and indirectly on the entire world], but if they do not return to Torah observance [i.e., do not merit] God will delay the Redemption until its prescribed time, and will only then redeem the Jewish people [amidst worldwide destruction and suffering]."
In the Zohar, it is likewise written:

We learn that all the time the people of Israel are in exile, if they merit God will have compassion and take them out of exile, and if they do not, God will delay them until the prescribed time. If the time comes and they are not fit to be redeemed, then God in the honor of His Own Name will not forget them completely.[88]

It must be emphasized, however, that the Jewish people are not directly responsible for the prophesized destruction (described below) before the "End of Days" (or better known as the pre-Messianic era) if it comes in its "prescribed time." Nonetheless, they are portrayed as having the potential of preventing it.
Talmudic and other traditional literature give signs of what life will be like "immediately" preceding the Messianic era (the term "immediate" is used loosely, and may represent a period of one or one hundred years depending on one's understanding of the following signs) if the redemption comes in its "prescribed time." For example:

1.   From several places in Jewish literature it becomes clear that if the Redemption comes in its "prescribed time" it

will not come all at once, but gradually, in a seemingly natural manner.[89]

2. "In the future the 'Sons of Ishmael' [the Arabs] will rule in the Holy Land while it is a wasteland for a prolonged period of time, and will hinder Israel from returning to its land."[90]

3. "There is no surer sign for the 'immediate' coming of the Messiah than when the Land of Israel becomes fertile again for the Jewish people."[91]

4. "If you see a period of time where constant and frightful sorrow confronts the Jewish people, anticipate the arrival of the son [i.e., descendant] of King David [who according to tradition will be the Messiah].[92]

5. "Immediately" preceding the coming of the Messiah all mankind will be frightened and dismayed by an excess of ongoing wars and tension between nations.[93]

6. "In the future, God will pay heed to the people of Israel's sorrow that will be caused by the Sons of Ishmael (the Arabs)."[94]

7. The Talmud[95] enumerates various happenings that will occur "immediately" before the Messianic era. They are:

A. The Jewish government will be run by non-observant Jews.
B. The wisdom of the Rabbis will be scorned.
C. Pious Jews will be ridiculed.
D. There will be great inflation.
E. This inflation will not be on account of lack of supply, and,
F. Truth will (seemingly) not exist. (The Talmud means by this that Jews will split up into several groups, each laying claim to the truth and making it difficult to discern true Judaism from the false.[96])

In addition, the wars predicted to occur immediately before the Messianic era (again, if the Redemption comes in its prescribed time) are reviewed briefly in the following:

1. "The son of [King] David [i.e., the Messiah] will not appear until the 'Roman' nation spreads out over the entire world."[97]

2. According to the prophet Daniel, ten kingdoms will spring forth from the fourth conquering empire (which according to the Midrash is Rome).[98] Thereafter another and final kingdom will arise from Rome but will be different from the first ten.[99]

3. It is this last kingdom from Rome who will spread out and conquer the entire world.[100]

4. Correspondingly, according to the prophet Ezekiel the final superpower to war with Israel (before the Messianic era) will come from the land of *Magog*.[101]

5. According to Josephus, who lived during the first century C.E., the land of Magog is *Scythia*.[102] And "according to the ancient Greeks, Scythia was a vast, undefined region lying north and east of the Black and Caspian Seas" [i.e., present day *Russia*].[103]

"Throughout classical literature *Scythia* meant all regions to the north and northeast of the Black Sea, and a Scythian any barbarian coming from those parts."[104]

6. The Jerusalem Talmud states that the land of Magog is *Gothia* (Goth).[105] And according to the *Encyclopaedia Brittanica*, the Goths (first century C.E.) inhabited the middle part of the basin of the Vistula River (i.e., central to eastern Poland), but under their sixth king (who was more contemporary in time with the redaction of the Talmud) migrated into *Scythia* (again, *present-day Russia*).

7. In the book *Yov'loth*, which is a history of the periods covered in the Books of Genesis and Exodus, written in approximately 110 B.C.E., the land of Magog is likewise identified as being to the north of the Black Sea. [The book *Yov'loth* is the earliest source for much of the material found in the Midrashic works of *Pirkey D'Rabbi Eliezer, Bereshit Rabatai, and Midrash Tadshe.*[106]]

8. After the destruction of the Western Roman empire by the Teutons, only Constantinople remained as the capital of

the (Eastern) Roman Empire (i.e., the Byzantine empire). And from the day the Russian king (Ivan III) betrothed the only niece (Sophia) of the *last Byzantine Roman emperor* (Constantine Palaeologus), Russian autocrats considered themselves the new emperors of the Roman empire. Russian aristocracy claimed that since the Greeks had been punished for their

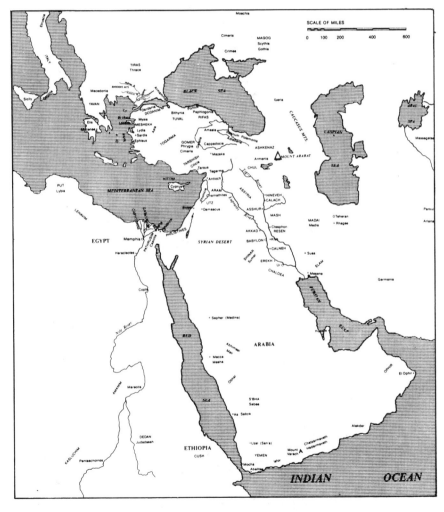

Nations of the Ancient World[107]

223

apostasy, their succession had to pass to the *third Rome* (Constantinople being the second) which was *Moscow*.[108] In addition, the Russian flag (before 1917) carried on it the double eagle sign of the Byzantine Roman empire.[109]

Before the Russian Revolution in 1917, the Imperial Standard of the Russian Czar was a double-headed eagle, black on a yellow field, an insignia adopted from the Byzantine Roman Empire of the fifteenth century.[110]

9.   According to the Zohar[111] the mechanics of the final war (again if the Redemption comes in its "prescribed time") will proceed in the following manner:

A. The Sons of Ishmael (the Arabs) will attempt to keep Israel from returning to its homeland.

B. The Sons of Ishmael will effect fierce wars, and Rome (Russia) will eventually wage war against them in order to take over their land and the Land of Israel.

C. Rome will succeed in taking over Muslim land but the Land of Israel will not be taken over.

D. *"One nation at the end of the world,"* together with other nations, will then challenge Rome, but these nations, after a period of three months, will be consumed.

E. After vanquishing all comers, Rome will attempt an all out attack against Israel. At that time, God will defend Israel, and Rome together with her allies will perish.

Other examples of what has or could transpire in the near future, as predicted in traditional Jewish literature, are:

1. In the Midrash, Rabbi Elazar taught that the pre-Messianic Era will usher in a generation with the power to consume itself.[112]
2. Neither parents nor the aged will be held in respect. The aged will be humiliated by the young and a man's household will be his enemies'. Arrogance will greatly increase and rebuke will be silenced. Religious students and studies will be held in disdain, and non-observant Jews will use the same studies to strengthen their own status.[113]
3. The Jewish people will return to the Land of Israel as a prelude to the Messianic Era.[114]
4. The pre-Messianic Era will begin with a measure of political independence for the Jewish people in their own land.[115]
5. This political independence will come with the permission of other nations.[116]
6. The Messiah will reveal himself in the Land of Israel.[117]
7. Rabbi Moses Ben Maimon (Maimonides, 1135-1204), wrote the following, concerning the awaited-for Messiah:

> If there comes a ruler from the House of David, who is immersed in the study of Torah like David his ancestor, following both the Written and Oral Law, who brings masses of Jews back to the ways of Torah, strengthening the Laws and fighting battles for the sake of Heaven, then it may be assumed that he is the Messiah. If he is further successful in rebuilding the Temple on its prior site and in bringing the dispersed Jews back to their Land, then his identity as the Messiah is a certainty.[118]

8. The generation before the Coming of the Messiah will be a lustful one without shame.[119]

9.   If the people of Israel desire to be like the other nations, the Redemption will come with "great anger."[120]

10.   The Jewish people will immigrate to the Land of Israel more out of non-Jewish hatred than of their own volition.[121]

11.   Before the Messiah comes, most people will have given up any hope or trust in a super-physical redemption.[122]

12.   During the period from the beginning of the pre-Messianic epoch to its finale, there will be great fighting and tumult in the world.[123]

13.   "Immediately" preceding the Redemption the Jews then called *Israel* will deny God's help, and will claim that their success is dependent wholly on their own efforts.[124]

14.   The conquering empire (which is posited above as Russia) will rule over the Jews nine months before the Messiah comes.[125]

15.   The Redemption will come when the Jewish people are unable to suffer any longer.[126]

16.   This last nation from Rome (Russia) will call all peoples of the world to be one people and to speak one language. It will also decree, that anyone who says the Jewish God is God will be executed.[127]

17.   Immediately preceding the Messiah, the Ishmaeli (Arab) "kingdom" will ally itself with the Roman nation.[128]

18.   Rabbi Saadia Gaon (882-942), received the tradition that the final two kings to sprout from the Roman empire, before the coming of the Messiah, will be the King of Russia (he explictly mentioned the name Russia) together with the King of Ishmael.[129]

19.   According to the Jewish proselyte and scholar Onkelos (circa 90 C.E.) and Jonathan ben Uzziel (circa 50 C.E.), the cryptic verse in Numbers (24:24) means that immediately preceding the Messiah, the Roman nation will send fleets of warships against various nations in the Middle East, and will wreak havoc.[130]

20.   The great Jewish scholar of the 18th century, the Vilna Gaon, told his students that when they see the *warships of*

Russia pass through the Bosporus straits they should put on their Sabbath clothes (i.e., their nicest clothing) for the Messiah is close at hand.[131]

21. According to various medieval Jewish commentators (e.g., Rashi, Eban Ezra, etc.) based on the Biblical verses in Daniel (11:40-42 and 12:1), when Rome begins to conquer the Middle East the peoples of the world will suffer as *never before in history*.[132]

22. Prior to the Messiah the Jewish people will establish for themselves a government in Jerusalem, and the Sons of Ishmael in conjunction with other nations will attack the Jewish state. The Jewish people will suffer greatly, but will prevail.[133]

23. Once Rome conquers Egypt, it will hear rumors that armies from the East and the North are coming against it. Rome will then go on the offensive .[134]

24. Once Rome begins to subjugate the Middle East, the Sons of Ishmael will seek help from "Western Rome."[135]

25. According to the prophet Daniel[136] (as opposed to the Zohar discussed above), and interpreted by Isenberg based solely on Talmudic and Midrashic sources, the *final war* will proceed as follows:

A. The king of Egypt will become highly arrogant and will cause great friction between himself and Rome.
B. The king of the North (i.e., Rome) will attack Egypt.
C. Certain Middle Eastern nations, including Egypt, will be consumed.
D. Other Middle Eastern nations will be left alone to do Rome's bidding. These nations will rule in Israel and other Mideast lands as Roman proxies.
E. After Rome has conquered various Mideast nations, rumors will circulate that other nations have come to attack it.
F. Rome will then divert its attention from the Middle East, to war with them.
G. After Rome has destroyed its adversaries, it will return to Jerusalem to establish its new capital there.

H. Once Rome rules in Jerusalem, *the suffering will be greater than ever before experienced.*

I. At that time, only the righteous will survive.

The Resolution

In conclusion, the upshot of the above is that the responsibility for ameliorating or, conversely, exacerbating anti-Jewish hostility devolves on the Jews themselves. If God did not give the Jewish people in particular special commandments to follow, then why be distinctively Jewish? (To suggest that God chose the Jewish people to be a model for mankind without instructing them on how to create that model is absurd and borders on racism.) Why in the name of some "man-made" ideology or historical identity should individuals allow themselves and their posterity to be hated, discriminated against, persecuted, and slain? Must Jews continue to make the same mistake as their forefathers, who for reasons of "ignorance," "obstinacy," or "arrogance" preferred poverty, torture, and murder to fraternity and opportunity?! In short, if the only reason for staying together is to maintain the *most hated* "man-made" ideology and lifestyle known to history, then Jews must immediately disband.

However, if God did indeed give the Torah with its multiple commandments to the Jewish people, then by abandoning their responsibilities (regardless of whether they remain Jews in name or not) they are again creating their own misfortune and indirectly the misfortune of others.

Just as thousands of years ago the prophet Elijah exclaimed: "How long will you waver between two opinions? If the Lord be God, follow Him; but if [you believe in] Baal, follow him,"[137] so today must Jewish leaders demand no less from the Jewish people. There is no third alternative. All else is rationalization and self-deception. World Jewry cannot continue to straddle over both sides of this important issue (and remain undisturbed), but must categorically decide for their own sake, the sake of their children, and possibly for all mankind!

XI / The Present-Day Jewish Phenomenon

*Your destroyers and those that
lay you waste will come from you.*
(Isaiah 49:17)

The importance of this chapter depends on how seriously the reader has taken the previous ten. If the Torah is indeed authentic, then it is imperative to examine the present level of Torah observance and to understand the reasons for it. It is not enough to simply describe in general what the Jewish people are or are not observing; the sources of non-observance must be clarified as well. Without clarification, any attempt to rectify matters will fail.

The major problem for individuals seeking *true* Judaism today is that various groups all claim to be authentic forms of Judaism, and have their own criteria for deciding what makes a "good" Jew. The three main groups in America are Reform, Conservative, and Orthodox (Oral Law) Judaism.

The Reform movement originated in Germany in the early nineteenth century, and was transported to America during the large German-Jewish immigration which began in the 1840s. By the second half of the nineteenth century it appeared that the future of Jews in America would be found in the Reform movement.[1]

229

The Conservative movement is more of an American pheno-menon, originating as a reaction to Reform Judaism which it deemed "too Reform,"[2] and achieved primacy in America (in terms of number of constituents) after World War II.

While espousing different philosophies, both movements deny the binding (Divine) authority of the Oral Law, and proclaimed at their inception the *unadaptability* of Orthodox (Oral Law) Judaism, which they viewed as an anachronism. They portrayed themselves as legitimate forms of Judaism, whose destiny it was to succeed the "antiquated" Orthodox tradition and lead contemporary Jewry in "enlightened" Western society.

According to the Reform and Conservative leaders, they were not trying to sever the Jewish people's relationship to traditional Judaism, but rather attempting to save Judaism, which allegedly could not adapt without an overhaul in behavior and perspective. Although this was their claim, the following arguments suggest that these leaders were more interested in breaking with traditional Judaism than they were in providing American Jewry with a true spiritual experience.

1. Their claim to succeed traditional Judaism was based on the alleged inability of traditional Judaism to adjust and adapt to the American way of life. However, historically, in contrast to their claim, the *only* Jewish movement to ever adapt (i.e., adaptation as a viable *Jewish entity* among the majority non-Jewish population) to *all* types of cultures and societies, throughout history, was the same "unadaptable" form of Judaism known today as Orthodoxy! Therefore, either the Reform and Conservative leaders were unaware of Jewish history, or their claim was specious, used only to rationalize their break with tradition.

2. The second argument which questions the true intent of Reform and Conservative leaders concerns their attempt to adapt the tenets of traditional Judaism to the new American lifestyle. Even if we charge Reform and Conservative leaders with a lack of perspective concerning Jewish history, the question still needed to be asked is: How much of an effort was

made, and how many generations of Jews in America had passed, before these leaders concluded that traditional Judaism was outdated? The answer to both questions is nil (i.e., it was never given a chance). Evidence to support this claim is based on the number of Jews residing in America during the turn of the century. In 1880 and 1900 the percentage of Jews in America was approximately 5 and 15 percent, respectively, of what it was in 1972. The source of this growth rate was the mass immigration of Jews from Eastern Europe during the turn of the century and thereafter.[3]

The mores and language of America were foreign to these immigrants, whose primary thought was to provide their families with food and shelter. Their lifestyle was and remained primarily Eastern European. It was their children, the *first generation* of Jews born in America, that had the first opportunity to create an optimal synthesis of traditional Judaism and American culture.* However, this opportunity was never capitalized on, for first generation American-born Jews, who started raising families of their own immediately preceding and following World War II, followed (whether knowingly or unknowingly) the Reform and Conservative leaders' claim concerning the "inevitable" need for change. In effect, this was the *first generation* able to test traditional Judaism's resilience, but instead it accepted its mentors' ahistorical and non-empirical claims, concerning the "dated" Judaism of its forebears.

3.   Reform and Conservative Judaism are not too dissimilar from other Jewish sects in the past (e.g., Sadducees, Bitosim, and Karaites) who also attempted to abolish the binding authority of the Oral Law. Both Reform and Conservative Judaism deny the Divinity of the Oral Law, and in regards to the Written Law (the Pentateuch) there exists a variation of

---

* The number of Jews who arrived from Germany in the 1840s was insignificant in comparison with the number of Eastern European Jews who arrived at the turn of the century. Moreover, the German Jews brought with them the traditions of Reform.

opinion within the groups themselves. Denying the Divine nature of the Oral Law (and to a lesser extent the Written Law) should not be taken lightly, for it implies: (1) that the redactors of the Talmud flagrantly lied when they declared that the Oral Law was given by God[4], and that some or most of the places throughout the Pentateuch where it states "And God spoke to Moses" (and other introductions with the same expressed meaning) are fabrications (to suggest these statements are open to interpretation, like other more obscure passages in the Talmud or Bible is to deny the possibility for objective communication among people), and (2) that the millions of Jewish men, women, and children who were savagely raped, pillaged, tortured, and murdered *only* because they believed the detailed law was God-given and therefore refused to deviate from its precepts were cruelly misled and mistaken.

4. The Bible without interpretation is little more than an amorphous body of terse phraseology, which can be portrayed as representing the most sublime of values, but conversely manipulated to justify the most serious of crimes. Moreover, it is literally *impossible* for any group of people to conduct themselves individually or collectively on the basis of the Bible alone. If we were honest with ourselves, we would be forced to admit that if there *never* was an accompanying body of legislation, *then the Bible itself is a lie*. For a righteous God (and in Judaism there is no such thing as unrighteousness when pertaining to God) could never hold a people responsible for something impossible to clearly understand and apply.

For example: the commandment we call *tefillin* is spoken of no less than four times in the Bible, but like other commandments is totally incomprehensible without an *accompanying body of legislation*. More specifically, the Biblical verses are:
   A. "And thou shalt bind them for a sign upon thine hand, and they shall be as frontlets between thine eyes."[5]
   B. "...and bind them for a sign upon your hand, and they shall be as frontlets between your eyes."[6]
   C. "And it shall be for a sign unto thee upon thine hand, and for a memorial between thine eyes."[7]

D.   "And it shall be for a sign upon thine hand, and for frontlets between thine eyes."[8]

Who could explain, from the above verses, what a *sign* and *frontlet* are made of? What should they look like? Where on the hand should they be placed, and if "between the eyes" is to be taken literally, then why have Jews, throughout history, done otherwise? And must everyone put on tefillin, and at all times? These are only a small sample of the many questions needed to be addressed if the commandment is to be practically applied. It is illogical to assume that a God-given law was delivered so ambiguously as to depend on the arbitrary whim of each succeeding generation. In short, there are only two possibilities: either the Bible is a fraud, or there was indeed accompanying legislation.

A further example is the commandment of *tzitzit*. In the Bible it states:

> And the Lord spoke to Moses, saying, speak to the children of Israel, and bid them that they make fringes on the corners of their garments throughout their generations, and that they put upon the fringe of each corner a thread of blue: and it shall be to you as a fringe.[9]

Who could explain what a "fringe" looks like? What kind of material is it made from? Must it be attached to every form of clothing such as one's undershirt and winter hat? Must everyone wear "fringes" and at all times? Are we foolish enough to attach woolen threads to linen clothing, and thereby (according to another Biblical passage) transgress an explicit prohibition of wearing wool and linen together, which is what Jews used to be permitted to do with their *tzitzit* when they had threads of that special blue?[10]

Even the most seemingly explicit Biblical command, the commandment of *circumcision*, without added legislation is *inexplicable*. For example, in the book of Genesis it reads:

> ...every male among you shall be circumcised. You shall circumcise the flesh of your *orlah*... Thus shall My covenant

be marked in your flesh as an everlasting pact. And if any male who is uncircumcised fails to circumcise the flesh of his *orlah*, that person shall be cut off from his kin; he has broken My covenant.[11]

In most Bibles the above word *orlah* is translated as "foreskin," which implies the male genitals. However, based strictly on the Written text, this is an arbitrary and forced translation. The reason is that the word *orlah* when mentioned in other places in the Bible refers specifically to the *mouth*, the *ear*, and the *heart*.[12] In fact, nowhere in the Written text (Bible) does the word *orlah* refer specifically to the genitals. Contextually, it would be more logical to decree that circumcision be done on the heart, for in Deuteronomy it states: "Circumcise therefore the *orlah* [foreskin] of your heart."[13] In other words, if decisions were based exclusively on the Written text, we today would be performing heart surgery on all male infants eight days of age and older.[14]

However, if we do *arbitrarily* declare that *orlah* means the foreskin of the genitals, other *unanswerable* questions still need to be addressed. For instance, how is the operation performed? What happens when the eighth day falls on the Sabbath, during which operations, in general, are prohibited? And what does it mean when it says that one who refrains from performing this commandment will be "cut off"?[15]

A further example pertains to slaughtering an animal for food purposes, of which it says in the Book of Deuteronomy: "...you need only slaughter your cattle and small animals that God will have given you *in the manner that I have prescribed.*"[16] However, nowhere in the Bible did God prescribe how the animal is to be slaughtered.[17]

It further states in Deuteronomy[18] that a betrothed woman who transgresses is not to receive the same punishment as one married. However, the Bible does not explain the distinction between the act of betrothal and that of marriage.[19]

The Bible, by itself, is even contradictory. For example in Leviticus it states: "Seven days you shall eat unleavened bread,"[20] but in Deuteronomy it states: "Six days you shall eat unleavened bread."[21] In truth, these nebulous and contradictory statements are easily reconciled *via the Oral Law*, but in and of themselves are unintelligible.

In effect, what has been shown regarding the commandments of *tefillin, tzitzit, circumcision, ritual slaughter, marriage, engagement,* and the *prohibition of eating unleavened bread (on Passover)* is similarly seen in regards to all other commandments, mentioned ever so briefly in the Written Law. To accept or partially accept the Divinity of the Written Torah without accepting the authority of an accompanying legislation is to make a mockery of the Bible and of Judaism.

The nineteenth century Jewish scholar, Rabbi Samson Raphael Hirsch compared the relationship between the Written and the Oral Law with the relationship between notes taken at a lecture and the lecture itself. The notes are clear to one who heard the lecture, but incomprehensible to one who did not. In other words, the Written Law is consistent and logical to one guided by the Oral Law, but objectively incomprehensible to one who is not.

Moses Maimonides, in his *Introduction to Mishna Torah,* explains the historical transmission of the Oral Law. He writes:

> All the precepts which Moses received on Sinai, were given together with their interpretation [the Oral Law]....
>
> Although the Oral Law was not committed to writing, Moses taught the whole of it, to his *court* [the equivalent of our present-day yeshiva or university].... So too, Joshua, throughout his life, taught the Oral Law. Many elders received the Oral Law from Joshua. Eli received it from the elders and from Phineas. Samuel, from Eli and his court. David, from Samuel and his court. Ahijah, the Shilonite... received the Oral Law from David and his court. Elijah received it from Ahijah and his court. Elisha, from Elijah and his court. Yehoyada the priest, from Elisha and his court. Zechariah, from Yehoyada and his court. Hosea, from Zechariah and his court. Amos, from Hosea and his court. Isaiah, from Amos and his court. Micah, from Isaiah

and his court. Joel, from Micha and his court. Nahum, from Joel and his court. Habakkuk, from Nahum and his court. Zephaniah, from Habakkuk and his court. Jeremiah, from Zephaniah and his court. Baruch the son of Neriah, from Jeremiah and his court. Ezra and his court received it from Baruch and his court. The members of Ezra's court were called "The Men of the Great Assembly." They were Haggai, Zechariah, Malachi, Daniel, Chananiah, Mishael, Azariah, Nehemiah, Mordecai, Zerubabel and many other sages, numbering altogether one hundred and twenty elders. The last of them was Simon the Just, who is included among the hundred and twenty. He received the Oral Law from all of them.... Antigonos of Socho and his court received the Oral Law from Simon the Just and his court. Jose the son of Yoezer of Zeredah, and Joseph the son of Yochanan of Jerusalem and their court, from Antigonos and his court. Joshua the son of Perahiah, and Nitai the Arbelite and their court, from Jose the son of Joezer and Joseph the son of Johanan and their court. Judah the son of Tabbai, and Simeon the son of Shetah and their court received from Joshua the son of Perahiah and Nitai the Abelite and their court. Shemaiah and Abtalion, proselytes of righteousness, and their court received from Judah and Simon and their court. Hillel and Shammai and their court received from Shemaiah and Abtalion and their court. Rabban Yochanan the son of Zaccai, and Rabban Simeon the son of Hillel received from Hillel and his court. Rabban Yochanan had five [outstanding] disciples who were the most distinguished among the scholars who received the Oral Law from him. They were Rabbi Eliezer the Great, Rabbi Joshua, Rabbi Jose the Priest, Rabbi Simeon the son of Nathaniel, and Rabbi Elazar the son of Arach. Rabbi Akiba the son of Joseph received the Oral Law from Rabbi Eliezer the Great. Joseph, his father, was a proselyte of righteousness. Rabbi Ishmael and Rabbi Meir, the son of a proselyte of righteousness, received the Oral Law from Rabbi Akiba. Rabbi Meir and his colleagues also received it from Rabbi Ishmael. The colleagues of Rabbi Meir were Rabbi Judah, Rabbi Jose, Rabbi Simeon, Rabbi Nehemiah, Rabbi Eleazar the son of

Shammua, Rabbi Yochanan, the sandal-maker, Simon the son of Azzai and Rabbi Hananiah the son of Teradion. Rabbi Akiba's colleagues received the Oral Law from Rabbi Eliezer the Great. The colleagues of Rabbi Akiba were Rabbi Tarfon, the teacher of Rabbi Jose the Galilean, Rabbi Simeon the son of Eleazar, and Rabbi Yochanan the son of Nuri. Rabban Gamaliel the Elder received the Oral Law from Rabban Simeon, his father, a son of Hillel the Elder. Rabban Simon his son, received it from him. Rabban Gamaliel his son, received it from him. Rabban Simeon his son, received it from him. Rabbi Judah the son of Rabban Simeon, called Our Teacher the Saint, received the Oral Law from his father and from Rabbi Eleazar the son of Shammua, and from Rabbi Simeon, his father's colleagues. Our Teacher, the Saint, compiled the Mishna. From the time of Moses [circa 1250 B.C.E.] to that of Our Teacher the Saint [circa 200 C.E.], no work had been composed from which the Oral Law was *publicly* taught. In each generation, the head of the existing court, or the Prophet at that time wrote down for his private use a memorandum of the traditions which he had heard from his teachers, and which he taught orally in public. So too, each student wrote down, according to his ability, the expositions of the Torah as he heard them....

All the Sages heretofore mentioned were the greatest scholars of the successive generations; some of them were presidents of colleges, some exilarchs, and some were members of the great Sanhedrin; besides them were thousands and myriads of disciples and fellow-students. Ravina and Rav Ashi were the last of the Talmudic sages. It was Rav Ashi who compiled the Babylonian Talmud [circa 500 C.E.] in the land of Shinar (Babylonia), about a century after Rabbi Yochanan had compiled the Jerusalem Talmud. These two Talmuds contain an exposition of the Mishna and an elucidation of its abstruse points.[22]

However, while the Jewish people were dispersed throughout the known world, even the complete Talmud required further clarification. Therefore, the most erudite and accepted of the Jewish scholars in each generation had the task of explaining the Oral Law (Talmud), to the Jewish people. In 1180 C.E., Maimonides, in his *Mishna Torah*, wrote:

> At this time there have been many afflictions and our imme-
> diate troubles have overshadowed everything else and the
> wisdom of our Sages has been lost and the knowledge of our
> scholars has become obscure.... Because of that, I embol-
> dened myself, I, Moses ben Maimon the Sephardi, and I took
> strength from God and I studied all of these books and I
> decided to compile... from them concerning what is forbid-
> den and what is permitted so that there will be one complete
> Oral Law, comprehensible to everyone without need for
> questioning or dissection.[23]

Notwithstanding Maimonides' efforts, the Talmud remained the mainstay of Jewish study.

Other medieval Torah giants (e.g., the Rif, the Rosh, Rabbi Yaakov ben Asher, etc.) also produced works which made the Oral Law significantly more accessible. In 1565, Rabbi Joseph Karo produced the *Shulchan Aruch*, which was an Oral Law compendium based on Talmudic and post-Talmudic sources. Today, in the latter part of the twentieth century, Orthodox (Oral Law) Jews still live by the *Shulchan Aruch*, which is an unbroken chain of tradition from Moses to the Jewish people of today (some 3,250 years later!).

Accordingly, it is interesting to note the conversation between "the Rabbi" and the King of the Khazars, "Al Kha-zari," in the literary classic *The Kuzari* by Rabbi Yehuda HaLevi (1074-1141). In the following conversation the Rabbi argues against a particular Jewish sect, the Karaites, who accepted the Divinity of the Written Law, but (like the Reform and Conservative) denied Oral Law authority:

> *The Rabbi:* The acknowledgment of tradition is therefore
> incumbent upon us as well as upon the Karaites, as upon
> anyone who admits that the Torah [the Pentateuch], in its
> present shape and as it is read, is the Torah of Moses.
> *Al Khazari:* This is exactly what the Karaites say. But as they
> have the written Torah, they consider the tradition [Oral
> Law] superfluous.

The Present-Day Jewish Phenomenon

The Rabbi: Far from it. If the consonantic text of the Mosaic Book requires so many traditional classes of vowel signs, accents, divisions of sentences and masoretic signs for the correct pronunciation of words, how much more for the comprehension of the same? The meaning of a word is more comprehensive than its pronunciation! When God revealed the verse: "*This month shall be unto you the beginning of months*" (Exod. 12:2), how was there no doubt whether He meant the calendar of the Copts — or rather the Egyptians — among whom they lived, or that of the Chaldeans who were Abraham's people in Ur-Kasdim; or solar or lunar months, or lunar years which are made to agree with solar years as is done in embolismic years. I wish the Karaites would give me a satisfactory answer to questions of this kind. I would not hesitate to adopt their view, as it pleases me to be enlightened. I further wish to be instructed on the question as to *what makes an animal lawful for food; whether "slaughtering" means cutting its throat or any other mode of killing?...* I should desire an explanation of the forbidden fat, seeing that it lies in the stomach and entrails close to the lawful fat, as well as of the rules of *cleansing the meat*. Let them draw me the line between the fat which is lawful and that which is not, inasmuch as there is no difference visible. Let them explain to me where the *tail of the sheep*, which they declare unlawful, ends. One of them may possibly forbid the end of the tail alone, another the whole hind part! I desire an explanation of the *lawful and unlawful birds*, excepting the common ones, such as the pigeon and turtle dove. How do they know that the hen, goose, duck, and partridge are not unclean birds? I further desire an explanation of the words: "*Let no man go out of his place* [*on the seventh day*]" (Exod. 16:29). Does this refer to the house or precincts, estate — where he can have many houses — territory, district, or country? For the word "place" can refer to all of these. I should, further, like to know *where the prohibition of work on the Sabbath is detailed*. Why pens and writing material are not admissible in the correction of a Scroll [on the Sabbath day], but lifting a heavy book, or a table, or eatables, entertaining guests and all cares of hospitality should be permitted, although the guests would be resting and the host be kept employed? This applies even more to women and servants, as it is written: "That thy manservant and thy maidservant rest as well as thou" (Deut. 5:14)!... Then, again, I wish to see a Karaite give *judgment between two parties* according to the chapters in Exodus 21 and Deuteronomy 21. For that which appears plain in the Written Torah is yet obscure, and much more so are the obscure passages, because the Oral supplement was relied upon. I should wish to hear the deductions he draws from the case of the daughters of Zelophehad to questions of *inheritance* in general. I want to know *the details of circumcision, fringes and the tabernacle*; why it is incumbent on him to say *prayers*; whence he derives his belief in *reward and punishment* in the *world after death*; how to deal with laws which interfere with each other, *as circumcision or the paschal lamb with the Sabbath, which must yield to which*, and many other matters which cannot be enumerated in general, much less in detail.[24]

The Study

After describing the seeming hypocrisy of Reform and Conservative Judaism, it is interesting to note these movements empirically. This was done by taking a random sample of over eight hundred Jewish adults for the city of Chicago (as part of the author's 1985 doctoral dissertation),[25] and questioning them on issues of prime importance to *all* of mainstream Jewry. Groups representing Orthodox, Conservative, Reform, and Nonaffiliated Jews were compared with respect to their positions on three issues. They were: *Jewish identity, Jewish education*, and the *State of Israel*.

The study's objective was to investigate the groups' accomplishments or failures, over the last generation, in relation to their claims made only a generation or two earlier.

Participants

A random sample of 811 Jewish adults from Chicago proper participated in the study, which began in February of 1985. Three-fourths of the respondents were selected randomly from the phone book on the basis of "distinctively Jewish names." This procedure is commonly used when conducting surveys on Jewish populations, and no significant differences have been found between Jews with common Jewish names and those without.

To ensure a solid representation of Orthodox Jewry, who comprise less than 10 percent of Chicago's Jewish population, the remaining participants were drawn randomly from mailing lists of all major Orthodox Jewish organizations and schools in Chicago.

Procedure

Data were collected at the Bernard Horwich Jewish Community Center of Chicago, where two rooms and ten telephones were obtained for a period of one month. The telephones were the property of the Jewish Federation of Metropolitan Chicago, and twenty university students were trained to conduct the interviews.

All participants were asked the same attitudinal, behavioral, demographic, and general-knowledge questions dealing with religious affiliation, education, observance, and Israel.

Observance Results

At the outset, participants were asked which type of synagogue they belong to, and also questions concerning their religious activities and beliefs. The following table represents the complete *Religious Observance Scale* according to group affiliation.

Note: In the following tables, NA = Nonaffiliated, R = Reform, C = Conservative, and O = Orthodox. Participants affiliated with other Jewish religious movements were not included in light of their relatively small numbers. N = number of participants.

JEWISH OBSERVANCE SCALE

	(N=79)	(N=114)	(N=231)	(N=322)
	R	C	O	NA

1. Do you *refrain* from eating bread and bread products on Passover?

Yes	56%	75%	99%	37%
No	44%	25%	1%	63%

2. Do you *refrain* from driving on Saturday?

Yes	1%	9%	91%	8%
No	99%	91%	9%	92%

3. Do you keep Kosher?

Yes	5%	31%	96%	10%
No	95%	69%	4%	90%

4. Do you believe in God?

Yes	92%	91%	100%	81%
No	8%	9%	0%	19%

5. Do you fast on Yom Kippur?

Yes	69%	80%	99%	48%
No	31%	20%	1%	52%

6. Do you eat pork?

Yes	61%	40%	1%	67%
No	39%	61%	99%	33%

7. Do you fast on Tisha B'Av?

Yes	1%	8%	87%	5%
No	99%	92%	13%	95%

8. Do you believe in a "world to come" after one dies in this world?

Yes	16%	39%	92%	34%
No	84%	61%	8%	66%

(Observance Scale Continued)

	(N=79) R	(N=114) C	(N=231) O	(N=322) NA

9. Do you believe that the Bible was given to the Jews by God?

	R	C	O	NA
Yes	38%	70%	97%	46%
No	62%	30%	3%	54%

10. Do you attend synagogue services weekly?

	R	C	O	NA
Yes	21%	22%	73%	4%
No	79%	78%	27%	96%

11. [For Men Only] Do you put on Tefillin daily?

	(N=38)	(N=68)	(N=96)	(N=174)
Yes	3%	6%	90%	6%
No	97%	94%	10%	94%

12. [For Women Only] Do you light Sabbath candles?

	(N=42)	(N=47)	(N=135)	(N=148)
Yes	48%	60%	99%	18%
No	52%	40%	1%	82%

Jewish Identity

The American Reform and Conservative rationale for breaking with traditional Judaism was its "unadaptable" and "anachronistic" nature. Therefore, according to their claims, Orthodox Judaism in 1985 should be a dying breed, and Reform and Conservatism movements should be American Jewry's propelling forces today. This issue was therefore investigated.

It was also important to learn what type of religious background the Nonaffiliated Jews (i.e., nonaffiliated with any synagogue) come from today. Nonaffiliated Jews, in general, were seen as representing a substantive loss of Jewish identity for the following four reasons:

1. *Intermarriage:* Results showed that 42 percent of all married Nonaffiliated Jews between the ages of twenty-one

and forty were currently married to Gentiles (i.e., spouses that had not converted to any branch of Judaism). This rate of intermarriage was *ten times* greater than for those individuals presently affiliated with Reform, Conservative, and Orthodox Judaism. Correspondingly, Jews having Gentile spouses scored lowest, as a group, on all major Jewish issues.

2. *Jewish Organization Affiliation:* Reform, Conservative, and Orthodox Jews were 2.5 times more likely to be members of some Jewish organization (other than synagogue membership) than were Nonaffiliated Jews.

3. *Marital Status:* Nonaffiliated Jews (between the ages of thirty-five and fifty-five) were six times more likely to never have been married than their Reform, Conservative, and Orthodox counterparts.

4. *Divorce Rate:* The divorce rate among the Nonaffiliated (between the ages of thirty-five and fifty-five) was more than three times that of Reform, Conservative, and Orthodox adherents.

Results

The first objective was to investigate Reform and Conservative claims concerning the unadaptability of Orthodoxy. According to their claims, the younger generation of Jews today should have significantly abandoned the Orthodoxy of their parents. In addition, Reform and Conservative constituencies should, at the very least, be maintaining their numbers.

All participants were asked their religious affiliation and the religious affiliation of their parents. Participants with children and/or grandchildren over the age of twenty were asked the type of synagogue their children and/or grandchildren are presently affiliated with.

In order to determine the rate of increase over the last generation, a comparison was made between the religious affiliation of present-day young adults (between the ages of twenty-one and forty) and their parents. The following table

244

represents the differences in religious affiliation over the last generation.

Parents' Religious Affiliation	Children's Religious Affiliation				
	(N=408) NA	(N=67) R	(N=120) C	(N=293) O	Total
(N=126) NA	81%	3%	3%	10% =	97%
(N=167) R	65%	22%	8%	3% =	98%
(N=296) C	49%	7%	31%	12% =	99%
(N=303) O	16%	2%	2%	76% =	96%

This table can be understood by the following example of parents who are or were (if deceased) affiliated with Reform Judaism: 167 parents (who had children between the ages of twenty-one and forty) were affiliated with the Reform movement. Of their children (between the ages of twenty-one and forty) *65 percent* today are Nonaffiliated, *22 percent* are still affiliated with the Reform movement, *8 percent* affiliated with the Conservative movement, and *3 percent* affiliated with Orthodoxy (in addition, *2 percent* are affiliated with other movements *unspecified* in the table).

Specifically, *65 percent* of the young adults whose parents are or were Reform are today Nonaffiliated, *49 percent* whose parents are or were Conservative are today Nonaffiliated, and *16 percent* from Orthodox households are presently Nonaffiliated. Accordingly, the growth rate of the four groups, over the last generation, has been:

Nonaffiliated	=	+224%
Reform	=	- 60%
Conservative	=	- 59%
Orthodox	=	- 3%

The maintenance of any group is not completely dependent on its inter-generational drop-out or accretion rate. It is, in addition, dependent on the birthrate of its members. Therefore the birthrate of participants was compared. When birthrate was taken into account (in conjunction with inter-generational group movement), the change over *one generation* was:

Nonaffiliated	=	+203%
Reform	=	- 63%
Conservative	=	- 58%
Orthodox	=	+ 9%

Once birthrate was taken into account, the *Nonaffiliated* group *increased +203 percent* over the last generation, the Reform and Conservative groups *decreased 63 percent and 58 percent* respectively, and the Orthodox group has *increased by 9 percent.*

The Land of Israel

The *official platforms* of both Reform and Conservative Judaism today emphasize their positive relationship to the Land of Israel. For example, as early as 1937 the Reform movement's *Guiding Principles of Reform Judaism* declared the Jewish people's responsibility to build and recreate the Jewish homeland. Furthermore, in 1975, on the hundredth anniversary of the founding of the Hebrew Union College (the Reform movement's institution for training rabbis) their statement of principles, the *Centenary Perspective*, was issued. In it they proclaimed their relationship to the Land and State of Israel. It reads:

> We are privileged to live in an extraordinary time, one in which a third Jewish Commonwealth has been established in our people's ancient homeland. We are bound to that land and to the newly reborn State of Israel by innumerable religious and ethnic ties. We have been enriched by its culture and ennobled by its indomitable spirit. We see it providing unique opportunities for Jewish self-expression. We have both a stake and a responsibility in building the State of

246

Israel, assuring its security and defining its Jewish character. We encourage aliya [immigration] for those who wish to find maximum personal fulfillment in the cause of Zion.[26]

The *Conservative* movement also emphasizes its positive relationship to the Land of Israel. For example, one of its founding fathers, Solomon Schechter, was active in the Zionist Organization of America and was a delegate at several Zionist congresses and conventions. According to Conservative sources

> Dr. Schechter...made the JTS [The Jewish Theological Seminary, the institution which trains Conservative rabbis] an institution for the graduation not only of rabbis, but also of Zionists. Without exception, its rabbis... have carried the message of Zionism to all parts of America.[27]

Another of its main proponents, Rabbi Louis Ginzberg, proclaimed: "Jewish nationalism without religion would be a tree without fruit, Jewish religion without Jewish nationalism would be a tree without roots."[28] As early as 1927, (Conservative) Rabbi Israel Goldstein reported that the Zionist Organization of America looks on the Conservative rabbinate "as the rabbinical bulwark of American Zionism."[29] In 1928 the Conservative Rabbinical Assembly, at its annual convention, called for support of colonists in Palestine and aid to the Zionist movement. And in 1978, Rabbi Robert Gordis, one of today's leading Conservative proponents, wrote:

> In particular, no other aspect of Jewish experience is even remotely comparable to the impact of the State of Israel in rekindling the "spark of the Jew" in the hearts of our youth the world over. In a world that has seemed to vow death and destruction for the Jewish people, Israel has given us a new gift of life.[30]

Furthermore, the affinity to the modern State of Israel should theoretically be more intense among Reform and Conservative adherents (than among the Orthodox) since Israel's official policy, like their own, is not bound by Oral Law tradition.

Results

The criteria for measuring participants' relationship to Israel was based on two behavioral indices, and less importantly, on participants' attitudes toward the Jewish State and their level of knowledge of the Middle East.

The first index was based on the question: *If things in the U.S. remain as they are, do you have any real intention of ever settling in Israel?*

Responses, grouped according to synagogue affiliation, were:

Intention to Ever Settle in Israel	Synagogue Affiliation			
	(N=318) NA	(N=79) R	(N=113) C	(N=221) O
Yes	8%	1%	7%	51%
No	92%	99%	93%	49%

According to the above, the percentages of Nonaffiliated, Reform, and Conservative participants who have the intention of ever settling in Israel are *8 percent*, *1 percent*, and *7 percent* respectively. In contrast, the percentage of Orthodox Jews who intend to someday settle in Israel is 51 *percent*.

The second index was based on the question: *How many times have you visited Israel?*

According to six individual comparisons, the Orthodox group has visited Israel significantly more than the other three. In addition, there were no significant differences among the other groups, when compared with each other.

The *Israel Attitude Scale* and the *Middle East Knowledge Scale* were deemed secondary in importance when evaluating the relationship between American Jews and the Land of Israel, in light of their overly general nature. Overly general, because a positive Jewish identity (regardless of affiliation) should itself predispose the individual to inquire about and support Jewish interests in the Middle East.

According to the six individual comparisons, *Orthodox* adherents had significantly more positive attitudes towards Israel than the others. The *Conservative* group, however, produced significantly more positive attitudes than the *Nonaffiliated* group.

The last comparison was based on participants' level of knowledge concerning recent Middle Eastern history. Again, the Orthodox group had significantly greater knowledge of happenings in the Middle East than did the others, and no differences were found when comparing the other groups with one another.

Based on the findings, one question which needs to be addressed is: Why is there such a discrepancy between Orthodox adherents and the adherents of the Reform and Conservative? Have Reform and Conservative leaders *just failed* to stir up their constituencies in relation to the Jewish homeland? Are the Orthodox leaders such powerful and charismatic personalities vis-a-vis their Reform and Conservative counterparts? Are Orthodox Jews so inherently different from the Reform and Conservative?

A second question is: How is it possible that no differences (barring one) were registered among Reform, Conservative, and the Nonaffiliated? Are the Reform and Conservative constituencies so obtuse and insensitive as to totally "turn off" their leaders' exhortations regarding their ancestral homeland? Or perhaps they sense something else, something deeper than their leaders' towering oratory.

Jewish Education

Jewish education is another area in which the policy of all three movements ostensibly converge. Officially, all deem Jewish education a highly important and integral aspect of Judaism. For example, Rabbi David Einhorn (1809-1879), who made his *Reform* imprint both in Germany (Birkenfeld) and later in America (Baltimore), stated the following:

> The religious training of our children should be thoroughly Jewish and instructed with the spirit of the Sinaitic teaching. This is a task of supreme importance, a task to which we should bend every effort. Here no obstacle should block our path.... We will point out to our children the world-redeeming power, the ever-widening significance of the Sinaitic teaching which is everenduring; the changeable character of its outward forms, the glorious triumphs it has achieved.... When synagogue, school, home, and our life in general are imbued with such a spirit, we can rest assured that we shall have given our heritage an abiding place in the hearts of our offsprings....[31]

Accordingly, in the *Guiding Principles of Reform Judaism*, the emphasis on Jewish education was expressed thusly: "The perpetuation of Judaism as a living force depends upon religious knowledge and upon the education of each new generation in our rich cultural and spiritual heritage."[32]

The *Conservative* approach to Jewish education is as seemingly positive as the Reform. For example, a staunch exponent of Conservative Judaism, Rabbi Dr. Israel J. Kazis, declared:

> ...we must strive to produce, as did our ancestors, dedicated custodians of our heritage who will with equal conviction and devotion cherish it, enhance it, and transmit it with love and loyalty to their children and children's children. The development of such devoted Jews requires above all an intensive pursuit of Jewish learning for only in the rich soil of knowledge can the seeds of appreciation and love of our heritage flourish.... The dictum Talmud Torah K'neged Kulam, the study of Torah takes precedence over all other

precepts, must guide and inform the philosophy and policy of Jewish community life in America.... Only knowledgeable Jews are in a position to develop the intellectual appreciations and spiritual affinities which are prerequisites for the cultivation of an authentic and meaningful Judaism.[33]

The emphasis on Jewish education was further expressed by Rabbi Robert Gordis (1978), in Principle 4 of his *Seven Principles of Conservative Judaism*. He writes:

Jewish knowledge is the privilege and duty of every Jew, not merely of the rabbi and the scholar. A Hebrewless Judaism that has surrendered to ignorance and has ceased to create new cultural and spiritual values is a contradiction in terms, and must perish of spiritual anemia. The regular study of Torah on whatever level is incumbent on every Jew, a supreme commandment second to none.[34]

Results

The index for measuring participants' level of *fundamental* Jewish knowledge was a set of ten *elementary* questions on Jewish history, Jewish holidays, the Bible, the Talmud, the Prophets, Prayer, and the Hebrew language. The following data represent the complete *Religious Knowledge Scale*, according to synagogue affiliation.

JEWISH RELIGIOUS KNOWLEDGE SCALE

	(N=80) R	(N=112) C	(N=231) O	(N=323) NA
1. Could you tell me the name of the Jewish New Year?				
Correct	80%	80%	96%	76%
Incorrect	20%	20%	4%	24%
2. On what date was the 1st and 2nd Temple in Jerusalem (the Beit Hamikdosh) destroyed?				
Correct	16%	21%	78%	10%
Incorrect	84%	79%	22%	90%

251

JEWISH RELIGIOUS KNOWLEDGE SCALE

	(N=80) R	(N=112) C	(N=231) O	(N=323) NA

3. On which Jewish holiday do some Jews wave around a palm branch (a lulav)?

Correct	55%	61%	95%	36%
Incorrect	45%	39%	5%	64%

4. What were the names of the three Jewish Patriarchs?

Correct	47%	45%	89%	33%
Incorrect	53%	55%	11%	67%

5. Could you give me an example of what is meant in the Bible by "an eye for an eye"?

Correct	3%	8%	59%	7%
Incorrect	98%	92%	41%	93%

6. Who brought the Jewish people into the Land of Canaan after they had left Egypt?

Correct	14%	17%	66%	13%
Incorrect	86%	83%	34%	87%

7. What is the Oral Law?

Correct	17%	21%	69%	14%
Incorrect	84%	80%	31%	86%

8. What is the name of the morning service?

Correct	11%	28%	88%	10%
Incorrect	89%	72%	12%	90%

9. Could you tell me who the chief commentator of the Talmud is whose commentary is found on the same page as the Talmud itself?

Correct	11%	26%	74%	12%
Incorrect	89%	74%	26%	88%

10. Could you spell for me the word Shabbat in Hebrew?

Correct	22%	29%	83%	19%
Incorrect	79%	71%	17%	81%

The Present-Day Jewish Phenomenon

Summary of Results

	Non-affiliated (N=323)	Reform (N=80)	Conservative (N=112)	Orthodox (N=231)
0-2 Correct	72%	58%	48%	7%
3-5 Correct	16%	30%	31%	10%
6-8 Correct	7%	11%	16%	25%
9-10 Correct	5%	1%	5%	58%

In summary, the percentage of Nonaffiliated, Reform, and Conservative participants who obtained scores of 25 percent correct or lower were 72 percent, 58 percent, and 48 percent respectively. In contrast, only 7 percent of Orthodox participants scored 25 percent or lower.

Similarly, the percentages of Nonaffiliated, Reform, and Conservative participants who obtained scores of 90 percent correct or higher were 5 percent, 1 percent, and 5 percent respectively. In contrast, 58 percent of the Orthodox participants scored 90 percent or higher.*

In effect, these results do not reflect a lack of knowledge, but rather an *abysmal ignorance*, most probably unparalleled in Jewish history. Is it conceivable that 70 to 80 percent of the American adult population would be unable to spell the word *CAT*? And yet, the so-called backbone of American Judaism (i.e., Reform and Conservative) is unable to spell its Hebrew equivalent. What of their holy proclamations? Where are the intelligent baby boomers who grew up as Reform and Conservative Jews? How is it possible they know *nothing* of Judaism? How is the older generation of Reform and Conservative Jews, as well, devoid of Jewish knowledge? Where are the Reform and Conservative rabbis, and what (in the name of Heaven) are they teaching?

---

* Despite the vast difference in *elementary Jewish knowledge* between the Orthodox group and others, no significant difference was registered when participants' *secular educational level* was compared. In short, the average secular educational level of all four groups was a drop above the B.A. level.

The Final Resolution

Significance of Findings

Stated briefly, the importance of the above analyses and findings are:

1. *To Refute Arab Propaganda.* One of the many propaganda themes circulated by Arab and Communist propagandists alike, is that Zionism or the resettlement of the Jewish people in the Middle East has nothing to do with Judaism, but is an outgrowth of secular European imperialism. Notwithstanding its falsity based on activities of modern Zionism since 1880, in conjunction with historical Judaism, the present study adds another dimension. It does this by demonstrating that the concept of Zionism (i.e., the living and being in Zion, a name used by the Prophets some twenty-seven hundred years ago in reference to the Land of Israel and/or Jerusalem) in Chicago, ˹t least, is an almost absolute Orthodox concept and phenomenon, far removed from secular European imperialism.

2. *Ethics.* For over three thousand years, literally tens of millions of Jews have been mercilessly pillaged, tortured, and slaughtered because they would not renounce their Jewish nationalism (i.e., relationship to the Land of Israel) or Torah, and yet according to the present findings (and extrapolating to the entire United States) millions of Jews have significantly relinquished both their nationalism and Torah within one (at maximum two) generations in the name of Judaism itself! The above analyses indicate that American Jews were led into abandoning their rich cultural and spiritual heritage without understanding what they were indeed abandoning. In effect, Jews (like others) deserve the right — for their own sake, the sake of their ancestors, and their progeny — to *consciously* and intelligently choose to abandon their traditions, without being tacitly pressured into doing so (i.e., by remaining ignorant of Judaism and believing in the legitimacy of Reform and Conservative Judaism, the Jewish masses are perforce prevented from making any intelligent decision regarding their abandonment of tradition).

3. *For Jewish Youth.* An unusually large number of young

American Jews (i.e., many times over their proportion in the general American population) have been recruited, over the last twenty years, into the religious cults of the Moonies, Hare Krishna, Jews for Jesus, drug cults of all types, or imported-to-America eastern religions, in their search for spirituality (whether the cult or religion is intellectually palatable is immaterial). These youth are not products of Orthodoxy, but primarily are from families affiliated, at some time, with Reform or Conservative Judaism.[35] As long as Reform and Conservative Judaism are portrayed as legitimate forms of Judaism these youth will probably never return. Their sincere (albeit at times disoriented) response is: "We know all about Judaism [i.e., Reform and Conservative] for we grew up in it, and found it devoid of meaning, and therefore are looking elsewhere." If Reform and Conservativism are not exposed for what they are, other youth will inevitably follow and become equally ensnared in these and other religious cults.

4. *To Attenuate Jewish Suffering.* According to the above (overall) analysis, the factor most responsible for anti-Jewish hostility is the "threatening" nature of Jewish separatism. This separatism can be a blessing or a curse. In essence, Jewish distinctiveness may claim its origins in one of two ways. Either God wants the Jewish people to be distinct and perforce they will remain distinct, or else this separatism is a man-made artifact, historically and cruelly perpetuated by Jewish leaders throughout history.

If the latter is true, then all Jewish people holding on "presumptuously" to their Jewish identity (in any form) are generating their own suffering and the suffering of future generations. However, if the former is true, then when the Jewish people (collectively) are acting in accordance with tradition they will be blessed, and cursed when they are not.

Reform and Conservative constituents do little of what is required according to Jewish law. Following therefrom, they are perforce the primary agents of their own suffering. In other words, whichever position one adopts, Reform and Conservative Jews, at the very least, are responsible for their own suffering. If Judaism is of human origin, then by obstinately retaining their Jewish identity (instead of *totally* assimilating) they are unwittingly inflicting hardship and suffering on themselves and their progeny. Inversely, if the Torah is true, they continue to sow the seeds of affliction (by their non-observance), but in this not only for themselves and their descendants, but for the entire Jewish people and non-Jewish world as well.

In conclusion, if traditional Judaism is not some ingenius propaganda ploy, but rather God's purpose for the Jewish people (and indirectly for all mankind), then only through a return to tradition can true unity and peace be achieved.

References

Chapter I

1. Exodus (23:7).
2. Psalms (119:104).
3. Ibid. (119:163).
4. Tractate *Avot* (1:18). Jerusalem: Ortsel, 1960.
5. Tractates *Shabbos* (55A), *Yoma* (69B), and *Sanhedrin* (67A).
6. Josephus. Antiquities (XI, 3.3-9). In L. Ginzberg (Ed.) *The Legends of the Jews*. Philadelphia: Jewish Publication Society of America, 1968.
7. Hirsch, S.R. "How Does Our Time Relate to Truth and Peace?" In *Collected Writings of Rabbi Samson Raphael Hirsch*. New York: Feldheim, 1984, pp. 321-25.

Chapter II

1. Planck, M. *Where Is Science Going?* Woodbridge: Ox Bow Press, 1981, pp. 168-69.
2. Charniovsky, A. *Between Science and Religion*. Tel Aviv: Joshua Chachik Publishing, 1965.
3. Numbers (2:32).
4. E.g., Exodus (16:3) and Numbers (14:22).
5. E.g., Exodus (6:6) and Deuteronomy (5:6).
6. Miller, A. *Behold a People*. New York: Balshon, 1968.
7. Feldman, E. "Changing Patterns in Biblical Criticism." In A. Carmel and C. Domb (Eds.), *Challenge: Torah Views on Science and Its Problems*. Jerusalem: Feldheim, 1978.
8. Ganor, N.R., "Who Were the Phoenicians?" In A. Sutton and Arachim Staff (Eds.), *Pathways to the Torah*. Jerusalem: Arachim, 1985.
9. Kaufman, Y. *The Religion of Israel: From Its Beginnings to the Babylonian Exile*. Chicago: University of Chicago Press, 1960.
10. E.g., Keller, W. *The Bible as History*. New York: Wm. Morrow, 1956; Negev, A. *Archaeological Encyclopedia of the Holy Land*. New York: Putnam, 1972.
11. In Keller, pp. 117-18.

12. Albright, W.F. *Archaeology and the Religion of Israel.* New York: Anchor Books, 1969, p. 96.
13. Albright, W. F. *The Biblical Period.* New York: Harper & Row, 1963, pp. 1-3.
14. In Sutton et al., p. G1.
15. Velikovsky, I. *Ages in Chaos.* New York: Doubleday, 1952.
16. Ibid.
17. Ibid.
18. Ibid.
19. Ibid.
20. Ibid.
21. *Encyclopaedia Judaica.* Jerusalem: Keter, 1973.
22. Radday, Y.T., Shore, H., Pollatschek, M.A., & Wickman, D. *Genesis, Wellhausen and the Computer.* In Sutton et al.
23. Ibid.
24. Krosney & Schmueloff. *The National Jewish Ledger.* April, 1986.
25. Ibid.
26. Abelson, C. M. Bias and the Bible. In Carmell et al.
27. Ibid.
28. Ibid.
29. Keller. End of Introduction.
30. Grayzel, S. *A History of the Jews.* New York: Mentor, 1968.
31. See Carmell et al.
32. Newton, I. *Opticks.* New York: Dover, 1952, pp. 369-70.
33. Einstein, A. *Comment Je Vois Le Monde.* New York: Philosophical Library, 1949, pp. 12-13.
34. Popper, K.R. *Conjectures and Refutations.* London: Routledge & K. Paul, 1969, p. 36.
35. In Sutton et al., p. 13.
36. In W. J. Broad. "Creationists Limit Scope of Evolution Case." *Science*, 1981, *211*, 1332.
37. Sutton et al.
38. Ibid.
39. Hooton, E.A. *Up from the Ape.* New York: Macmillan Co., 1946.
40. Sutton et al.
41. Ibid.
42. Dewar, D. & Shelton, H.A. *Is Evolution Proved?* London: Hollis & Carter, 1947.
43. Lewin, R. "Evolutionary Theory Under Fire." *Science*, November 21, 1980, *210*, 883.
44. Kerkut, G. A. *Implications of Evolution.* New York: Pergamon Press, 1960.
45. Sutton et al.

258

References

46. Moore J.N. & Slusher, H.A. *Biology; A Search for Order in Complexity.* Grand Rapids: Zondervan, 1976.
47. Ibid.
48. Sutton et al.
49. Ibid.
50. Ibid.
51. Ibid.
52. Ibid.
53. Ibid.
54. Ibid.
55. Brinkman, R.T. "Dissociation of Water Vapor and Evolution of Oxygen in the Terrestrial Atmosphere." *Journal of Geophysical Research*, 1969, *74*, 5355-68.
56. Sutton et al.
57. Ibid.
58. Hill, D.E. "Thermodynamics and Kinetics of Spontaneous Generation." *Nature*, 1960, *186*, 693-94.
59. Ibid.
60. Abelson, P.H. "Chemical Events on the Primitive Earth." *Proceedings of the National Academy of Sciences*, 1966, *55*, 1365-72.
61. Ponnamperuma, C., Shimoyama, A., Yamada, M., Hobo, T., & Pal, R. "Possible Surface Reactions on Mars: Implications for Viking Biology Results." *Science*, 1977, *197*, 455-57.
62. Dickerson, R.E. "Chemical Evolution and the Origin of Life." *Scientific American*, 1978, 239, 70-87.
63. Sutton et al.
64. Ibid.
65. Ibid.
66. Hoyle, F. & Wickramasinghe, N.C. *Evolution from Space: A Theory of Cosmic Creation.* New York: Simon & Schuster, 1982.
67. Sutton et al.
68. Green, D.F. & Goldberger, R.F. *Molecular Insights into the Living Process.* New York: Academic Press, 1967.
69. Lipson, H.S. "A Physicist Looks at Evolution." Physics Bulletin, 1980, 31, 138.
70. Sutton et al., p. I7.
71. Ibid., p. I8.
72. Ibid.
73. Macbeth, N. *Darwin Retried; An Appeal to Reason.* Boston: Gambit, 1971.
74. Sutton et al., p. I8.
75. Ibid.
76. Ibid., p. I13.

77. Ibid., p. I4.
78. Macbeth, p. 126.
79. Sutton, p. I12.
80. Ibid.
81. Charniovsky, A. *Between Science and Religion.* Tel Aviv: Joshua Chachik Pub., 1965.
82. Bergman, S.H., "Can Transgression Have an Agent?" *Yad Vashem Studies,* 1963, 5, 7-15.
83. Sutton et al., I16.
84. E.g., Keller; Negev.
85. Deuteronomy (5:2-3).
86. Ibid. (4:32-35).
87. Exodus (14:10-11).
88. Ibid. (16:2).
89. Ibid. (17:4).
90. Numbers (17:6).
91. Biberfeld, P. *Universal Jewish History; Vol. I.* New York: Feldheim, 1962.
92. Exodus (4:10-14).
93. Sutton et al., p. E8.
94. Ibid.
95. Deuteronomy (16:3).
96. Ibid. (4:9-10).
97. Ibid. (5:15, 16:12, 24:18).
98. Ibid. (9:7).
99. Ibid. (25:17-19).
100. Ibid. (6:20-21).
101. Ibid. (8:18-19).
102. Ibid. (24:9).
103. Ibid. (8:2).
104. Malamot, A. *A History of the Jewish People.* Cambridge, Mass.: Harvard University Press, 1976, p. 33.
105. HaLevi, J. *The Kuzari.* New York: Schocken Books, 1964.
106. Cohen, S. "Divine Origin of the Torah." In D. Kiel (Ed.), *Return to the Source.* New York: Feldheim, 1984.
107. Leviticus (11:2-8).
108. Sutton et al., p. F13.
109. Menkin. Kerem Petahya. Ibid.
110. Tractate *Chullin* (60B). Jerusalem: Ortsel, 1960.
111. Deuteronomy (31:10-12).
112. Exodus (34:23-24).
113. Leviticus (25:1-5, 18-22).
114. Sutton et al.

References

115. Numbers (5:11-30).
116. Job (28:21).
117. Ibid. (11:9).
118. Tractate *Avot* (9:26). Jerusalem: Ortsel, 1960.
119. Sutton et al.
120. Krosney et al.
121. Ibid.
122. Deuteronomy (31:16-19).
123. I.B.M. Machshavot. In Sutton et al. p. C41.
124. E.g., ibid. (28:63-64).
125. Genesis (1:1-5).
126. Leviticus (1:15).
127. Numbers (34:9-12).
128. E.g., Leviticus (26:3-43).
129. Exodus (34:35; 35:1-5).
130. Leviticus (23:29-30).
131. Genesis (3:21-24).
132. Ibid. (49:25).
133. Deuteronomy (32:3-7).
134. Genesis (28:2-7).
135. Ibid. (50:24-25).
136. Meiri, S. "Burden of Proof." In Kiel (Ed.), *Return to the Source*. New York: Feldheim, 1984, p. 104.

Chapter III

1. Flannery, E.H. *The Anguish of the Jews*. New York: Macmillan Co., 1965, p. xi.
2. E.g., Flannery. Grosser, P.E., and Halperin, E.C. *The Causes and Effects of Anti-Semitism*. New York: Philosophical Library, 1978. Ruether, R.R. *Faith and Fratricide: The Theological Roots of Anti-Semitism*. New York: Seabury Press, 1979.
3. Prager, D., and Telushkin, J. *Why the Jews? The Reason for Anti-Semitism*. New York: Simon & Schuster, 1983.
4. See Tapsell, R.F. *Monarchs, Rulers, Dynasties, and Kingdoms of the World*. New York: Facts on File Inc., 1983.
5. Twain, M. "Concerning the Jews." *Harpers Magazine,* September, 1899.
6. *Encyclopedia Judaica: 1973-1982 Decemial Book*. Jerusalem: Keter, 1982.
7. Ibid., 1972.
8. Lipset, S.M. and Ladd, E.C. "Jewish Academics in the United States:

Their Achievements, Culture, and Politics." In M. Fine and M. Himmelfarb (Eds.), *American Jewish Yearbook 1971.* Philadelphia: Jewish Publication Society of America, 1971.

9. Tractate *Gittin* (60B). Jerusalem: Ortsel, 1960.
10. Exodus 31:14.
11. Deuteronomy, 112:12.
12. Ibid., 24:1-4.
13. Tractate *Shabbos* (31A).
14. Tractate *Sukkah* (28A).
15. *Sefer Ha'Ikarim.* Jerusalem, 1960.
16. Schimmel, H.C. *The Oral Law: A Study of the Rabbinic Contribution of Torah She-Be-Al-Peh.* Jerusalem: Feldheim, 1971.

Chapter IV

1. Deuteronomy (4:35).
2. Ibid. (4:39).
3. Matthew (19:17). *Self Pronouncing* edition. Cleveland: World Publishing Co., 1941.
4. Numbers (23:19).
5. Gevirtz, E. *L'hovin Ul'haskil: A Guide to Torah Hashkofoh, Questions and Answers on Judaism.* New York: Feldheim, 1980.
6. Isaiah (2:4).
7. Ibid. (11:9).
8. Micha (5:2).
9. Amos (9:11).
10. Isaiah (42:4).
11. Mark (9:1). *Self Pronouncing* edition. Cleveland: World Publishing Co., 1941.
12. Ibid. (13:30).
13. Gevirtz.
14. Deuteronomy (13:1-6).
15. Matthew (12:8).
16. Gevirtz.
17. Ibid.
18. Isaiah (7:14).
19. Leviticus (21:3).
20. Micha (5:1).
21. Gevirtz.
22. Isaiah (23).
23. Gevirtz.
24. Levine, S. *You Take Jesus, I'll Take God: How to Refute Christian*

References

Missionaries. Los Angeles: Hameroh Press, 1980.

25. Ibid.
26. Ibid.
27. Isaiah (64:5-8).
28. Ecclesiastes (7:20).
29. Leviticus (17:11).
30. Hebrews (9:22). *Self Pronouncing* edition. Cleveland: World Publishing Co., 1941.
31. Deuteronomy (24:16).
32. See Ezekiel (33:11,19), and Jeremiah (36:3).
33. Levine.
34. Jeremiah (23:5,7).
35. Levine.
36. Ibid.
37. Psalms (118:22).
38. Samuel I (16:12).
39. Levine.
40. Ibid.
41. Ibid.
42. Ibid.
43. Matthew (5:17).
44. Ibid. (12:1-5).
45. Acts (15:1). *Self Pronouncing* edition. Cleveland: World Publishing Co., 1941.
46. Levine.
47. Malachi (4:L4).
48. Levine.
49. Kaplan, A. *The Real Messiah: A Jewish Response to Missionaries*. New York: N.C.S.Y., 1985.
50. John (14:6). *Self Pronouncing* edition. Cleveland: World Publishing Co., 1941.
51. Exodus (20:2).
52. Kaplan.
53. Ibid.
54. Deuteronomy (18:18).
55. John (1:45).
56 Acts (3:22; 7:37).
57. Kaplan.
58. Deuteronomy (34:10).
59. Exodus (19:9).
60. Kaplan.
61. Psalms (22:17).
62. Kaplan.

Chapter V

1. *Encyclopaedia Judaica.* Jerusalem: Keter, 1973.
2. *Midrash Bereshit Rabbah.* Jerusalem: Vaharmon, 1965.
3. Ibid.
4. Genesis (12:1).
5. *Midrash Seder Eliyahu Rabbah* (5.27). In L. Ginzberg (Ed.), *The Legends of the Jews.* Philadelphia: Jewish Publication of America, 1968.
6. *Yashar Noah* (236-66). In L. Ginzberg (Ed.), *The Legends of the Jews.* Philadelphia: Jewish Publication of America, 1968.
7. *Midrash Bereshit Rabbah.*
8. *Midrash Beit HaMidrash.* Jerusalem: Wahrman-Boos, 1967.
9. *Perkei D'Rebbe Eleazar.* Jerusalem: M. Liman, 1969.
10. *Midrash Beit HaMidrash.*
11. Genesis (21:12).
12. Ibid., 37:28.
13. Ibid., 41:43-44.
14. Ibid., 47:14-26.
15. Ibid., 47.
16. Exodus (1:7).
17. Miller, A. *Behold a People.* New York: Balshon, 1968.
18. See Ezekiel (20:5-7).
19. *Midrash Tanchuma.* Warsaw: Y.G. Monk, 1879.
20. Josephus. Antiquities.
21. Midrash Hagodol. Jerusalem: Mossad HaRav Kook, 1956.
22. *Midrash Mekilta (Pischa).* In *Mekilta De Rebbe Ishmael.* Philadelphia: Jewish Publication Society of America, 1976.
23. *Midrash Shemot Rabbah.* In *Midrash Rabbah.* Jerusalem: Levin-Epstein, 1965.
24. *Midrash Hagodol* (II, 43). In L. Ginzberg (Ed.), *The Legends of the Jews.* Philadelphia: Jewish Publication of America, 1968.
25. Exodus (1:10).
26. Ibid.
27. Tractate *Sotah* (11A). Jerusalem: Ortsel, 1960.
28. *Midrash Shemot Rabbah.*
29. Genesis (41:35).
30. Exodus (1:12).
31. Genesis (17:8).
32. Exodus (1:13).
33. Ibid. (1:16).
34. Ibid. (1:22).
35. Genesis (41:43-44).

References

36. Ibid. (47:25).
37. Ibid. (50:3).
38. Ibid. (47:6).
39. Scherman, N. and Zlotowitz, M. *History of the Jewish People: The Second Temple Era.* New York: Mesorah Publications, 1982.
40. Esther (3:8-9).
41. Tractate *Megillah* (11A). Jerusalem: Ortsel, 1960.
42. Esther (3:12-13).
43. *Midrash Abba Gurion.* In A. Jellinek (Ed.), *Beit HaMidrash.* Jerusalem: Wahrman-Boos, 1967.
44. Esther (2:22).
45. Ibid. (2:17).
46. Tractate *Megillah* (12B).
47. *Midrash Esther Rabbah.* In *Midrash Rabbah.* Bnai Brak: Tiferet Zion, 1963.
48. *Midrash Abba Gurion.*
49. *Midrash Pesikta Rabosi.* Vilna, 1880.
50. *Targum Yerushalmi.* In L. Ginzberg (Ed.) *The Legends of the Jews.* Philadelphia: Jewish Publication Society of America, 1968.
51. *Midrash Panim Aherim.* Ibid.
52. Esther (3:5, 5:13).
53. Perkei D'Rebbe Eleazar.
54. *Midrash Abba Gurion.*
55. Ibid.
56. Talmud Tractate *Megillah* (12B).
57. *Midrash Panim Acherim.* In L. Ginzberg (Ed.), *The Legends of the Jews.* Philadelphia: Jewish Publication Society of America, 1968.
58. *Midrash Esther.* In L. Ginzberg (Ed.), *The Legends of the Jews.* Philadelphia: Jewish Publication Society of America, 1968.
59. Esther (10:3).
60. E.g., See Biblical books of Genesis (17:8), Exodus (6:8), Jeremiah (7:7), and Ezekiel (28:25).
61. *Encyclopaedia Judaica.*
62. Scherman & Zlotowitz.
63. Mason, S. F. *A History of the Sciences.* New York: Collier Books, 1968.
64. Scherman & Zlotowitz.
65. Grayzel, S. *A History of the Jews.* New York: Mentor, 1968.
66. Miller, A. *Torah Nation.* New York: Balshon, 1971.
67. Scherman & Zlotowitz.
68. *Encyclopaedia Judaica.*
69. Scherman & Zlotowitz.
70. Ibid.
71. Ibid.

72. Ibid.
73. *Encyclopaedia Judaica.*
74. Ibid.
75. Josephus. The Jewish Wars.
76. Scherman & Zlotowitz.
77. Perlmutter, N., and Perlmutter, R.A. *The Real Anti-Semitism in America.* New York: Arbor House, 1982, p. 54.
78. *Encyclopaedia Judaica.*
79. Ibid.
80. Talmud Tractate *Taanith* 26B. Jerusalem: Ortsel, 1960.
81. Grosser, P.E., and Halperin, E.G. *The Causes and Effects of Anti-Semitism.* New York: Philosophical Library, 1978.
82. Lamprecht, S.P. *Our Philosophical Traditions.* New York: Appleton-Century-Crofts, 1955.
83. New Testament Matthew (5:17-18). *Self-Pronouncing* edition. Cleveland: World Publishing Co., 1941.
84. Ibid. (15:24).
85. See: (A) Ruether, R.R. *Faith and Fratricide: The Theological Roots of Anti-Semitism.* New York: Seabury Press, 1979. (B) Gager, J.G. *The Origins of Anti-Semitism: Attitudes towards Judaism in Pagan and Christian Antiquity.* New York: Oxford University Press, 1983.
86. Gager.
87. Flannery, E.H. *The Anguish of the Jews.* New York: Macmillan Co., 1965.
88. Ibid.
89. Ibid.
90. Talmud Tractate *Sanhedrin.* Jerusalem: Ortsel, 1960.
91. Kaplan, A. *Handbook of Jewish Thought.* New York: Maznaim, 1979.
92. Grosser & Halperin.
93. Ibid.
94. Ibid.
95. Prager, D., and Telushkin, J. *Why the Jew? The Reason for Anti-Semitism.* New York: Simon & Schuster, 1983.
96. Grosser et al.
97. Prager et al.
98. Flannery.
99. Prager et al.
100. Quran (Sura 46:11). In *The Koran Interpreted.* New York: Macmillan Co., 1970.
101. Baidawi. Cited in A. I. Katch, *Judaism and the Koran.* New York: A.S. Barnes & Co., 1962.
102. Katch, A.I. *Judaism and the Koran.* New York: A. S. Barnes & Co., 1962.
103. Ibid., Intro. p. 10.

References

104. Prager et al.
105. Ibid.
106. Grosser et al.
107. Ibid.
108. Peters, J. *From Time Immemorial: The Origins of the Arab-Jewish Conflict over Palestine.* New York: Harper & Row, 1984.
109. Ibid.
110. Prager et al.
111. Davis, L.J. *Myths and Facts 1985: A Concise Record of the Arab-Israeli Conflict.* Washington, D.C.: Near East Report, 1984, p. 133.
112. Prager et al.
113. Flannery.
114. Ibid.
115. Grosser et al.
116. Ibid.
117. Ibid.
118. Flannery.
119. Grosser et al.
120. Ibid.
121. Ibid.
122. Prager et al.
123. Ibid.
124. Bottomore, T.D. *Karl Marx: Early Writings.* New York: McGraw-Hill, 1964.
125. Great Soviet Encyclopaedia (1952). Cited in Prager et al.
126. Prager et al.
127. Fisch, D.A. *Jews for Nothing: On Cults, Intermarriage, and Assimilation.* New York: Feldheim, 1984.
128. Grayzel.
129. Prager et al.
130. Anti-Defamation League of B'nai B'rith. *Hate Groups in America: A Record of Bigotry and Violence.* New York: Anti-Defamation League of B'nai B'rith, 1982.
131. Goldberg, M.H. *Just Because They're Jewish.* New York: Scarborough House, 1981.
132. Dawidowicz, L.S. *The War Against the Jews, 1933-1945.* New York: Bantam Books, 1975, p. 3.
133. Prager et al.
134. Goldberg, p. 207.
135. Ibid.
136. Dawidowicz.
137. Ibid., p. 28.
138. See (A) Morse, A.D. *While Six Million Died: A Chronical of American Apathy.* New York: Random House, 1968. (B) Wyman, D.S. *The*

The Final Resolution

Abandonment of the Jews. New York: Pantheon Books, 1984.
139. Scherman et al., p. xiv.

Chapter VI

1. Sherif, M. *In Common Predicament.* Boston: Houghton Mifflin Co., 1966.
2. Ibid., p. 85.
3. Ibid.
4. Fromm, E. *Escape from Freedom.* New York: Farrar & Rinehart, 1941, pp. 44-45.
5. Maslow, A.H. "The Authoritarian Character Structure." *The Journal of Social Psychology.* 1943, *18,* p. 46.
6. Adorno, T.W. "Types and Syndromes." In Adorno, T.W., Frenkel-Brunswik, E., Levinson, D.J., and Sanford, R.N. (Eds.) *The Authoritarian Personality.* New York: Harper & Row, 1950.
7. Wasserman, E.B. *Kovatz Ma'amarim.* Jerusalem. Gitler & Associates, 1963.
8. Jaakobi, S. "Land of Israel." In D. Kiel (Ed.), *Return to the Source.* New York: Feldheim, 1984, pp. 47-48.
9. Psalms (132:13).
10. Deuteronomy (11:12).
11. Psalms (137:5-6).
12. Talmud Tractate *Ketuboth* (110B). Jerusalem: Ortsel, 1960.
13. Leviticus (25:38).
14. *Ketuboth* (111A).
15. Deuteronomy (12:29).
16. *Sifri (Parshat Re'eh).*
17. Psalms (52:15).
18. *Sifri (Parshat Re'eh).*
19. Tractate *Shabbos* (88A). Jerusalem: Ortsel, 1960.
20. Halevi, Y. (12th century C.E.). *The Kuzari.* New York: Schocken Books, 1964.
21. *Zohar (Acharey Mot).* Jerusalem: Ortsel, 1960.
22. Talmud Tractate *Yoma* (39A). Jerusalem: Ortsel, 1960.
23. Maimonides (12th century C.E.). In A. Kaplan, *Handbook of Jewish Thought.* New York: Maznaim, 1979.
24. Tractate *Avodah Zarah* (5B). Jerusalem: Ortsel, 1960.
25. Numbers (15:39).
26. Halevi.
27. Kaplan.
28. Tractate *Berachoth* (35B). Jerusalem: Ortsel, 1960.

References

29. *Bereshit Rabbah* (11.8). Jerusalem: Vaharmon, 1965.
30. Talmud Tractate *Sanhedrin* (100A). Jerusalem: Ortsel, 1960.
31. *Tanchuma Hakadoom V'Hayashan* (3.6). In *Midrash Tanchuma*. New York: Sefer, 1946.
32. Tractate *Temurah* (16A). Jerusalem: Ortsel, 1960.
33. *Shemot Rabbah* (47.1-4). In *Midrash Rabbah*. Jerusalem: Levin-Epstein, 1965.
34. *Bamidbar Rabbah* (22.2). In *Midrash Rabbah*. Jerusalem: Levin-Epstein, 1965.
35. *Midrash Abba Gurion*. In A. Jellinek (Ed.), *Beit HaMidrash*. Jerusalem: Wahrman-Boos, 1967.
36. Jeremiah (2:3).
37. Tractate *Taanith* (2:6). Jerusalem: Torah Mitzion, 1968.
38. Isaiah (43:10).
39. Ibid. (51:16).
40. Ibid. (42:6).
41. Psalms (68:35).
42. Kaplan.
43. Exodus (19:5-6).
44. Deuteronomy (26:17-19).
45. *Shemot Rabbah*.
46. *Zohar (Parshat Ha'azinu)*.
47. Deuteronomy (33:9).
48. Psalms (135:4).
49. Leviticus (20:24).
50. Ibid. (20:26).
51. Deuteronomy (7:6-8).
52. Gevirtz, E. *L'hovin Ul'haskil: A Guide to Torah Hashkofoh, Questions and Answers on Judaism*. New York: Feldheim, 1980.
53. Ibid.

Chapter VII

1. Dunham, D.C. *Kremlin Target: USA; Conquest by Propaganda*. New York: I. Washburn, 1961, pp. xiii-xiv.
2. Shultz, R.H. and Godson, R. *Dezinformatsia: Active Measures in Soviet Strategy*. Washington, D.C.: Pergamon-Brassey, 1984.
3. Miller, A. *Behold a People*. New York: Balshon, 1968.
4. *Midrash Tanchuma*. Warsaw: Y.G. Monk, 1879.
5. *Midrash Yashar Shemot*. In *Sefer HaYashar HaShalem*. Jerusalem: Etz Chaim, 1968.
6. Exodus (1:9-10).
7. *Targum Yerushalmi*. In L. Ginzberg (Ed.), *The Legends of the Jews*

(vol. 4). Philadelphia: The Jewish Publication Society of America, 1968.

8. *Midrash Abba Gurion.* In A. Jellinek (Ed.), *Beit HaMidrash.* Jerusalem: Wahrman-Boos, 1967.

9. *Midrash Esther.* In Ginzberg, pp. 410-12.

10. Reinach, T. Cited in E.H. Flannery, *The Anguish of the Jews.* New York: Macmillan Co., 1965, p. 8.

11. Ibid.

12. Flannery.

13. Reinach.

14. Flannery.

15. Trachtenberg, J. *The Devil and the Jew: The Medieval Conception of the Jew and its Relation to Modern Anti-Semitism.* Philadelphia: Jewish Publication Society of America, 1983.

16. Josephus. Against Apion (II).

17. Ruether, R.R. *Faith and Fratricide: The Theological Roots of Anti-Semitism.* New York: Seabury Press, 1979.

18. Flannery, p. 19.

19. Ibid., pp. 20-21.

20. Prager, D. & Teluskin, J. *Why the Jews? The Reason for Anti-Semitism.* New York: Simon & Schuster, 1983, p. 86.

21. Grosser, P.E. & Halperin, E.G. *The Causes and Effects of Anti-Semitism.* New York: Philosophical Library, 1978.

22. Flannery.

23. Ibid.

24. Ibid., p. 20.

25. Ibid., p. 21.

26. Ibid.

27. Goldberg, M.H. *Just Because They're Jewish.* New York: Scarborough House, 1981.

28. Ibid.

29. Ibid.

30. Flannery, p. 48.

31. Goldberg, p. 57.

32. Flannery, p. 152.

33. Ibid.

34. Prager et al., p. 107.

35. In Grosser et al., p. 376.

36. Quran (3:60). *The Koran Interpreted.* New York: Macmillan Co., 1970.

37. Ibid. (5:15).

38. Quran. In Grosser at al., p. 376.

39. Ibid.

40. Ibid.

41. Quran (9:30).

42. Ibid. (5:55).
43. Ibid. (2:95).
44. Ibid. (2:5-10).
45. Ibid. (5:65).
46. Ibid. (2:90-95).
47. Ibid. (5:10).
48. Ibid. (5:45).
49. Ibid. (3:105).
50. Ibid. (59:1).
51. Ibid. II (98:5).
52. Cited in L. J. Davis, *Myths and Facts 1985; A Concise Record of the Arab-Israeli Conflict.* Washington, D.C.: Near East Research, Inc., 1984, p. 198.
53. Ibid.
54. Ibid.
55. Ibid., p. 199.
56. Ibid., pp. 200-1.
57. Ibid., p. 202.
58. Ibid.
59. Kondracke, M. *Chicago Sun-Times*, January 25, 1985.
60. Prager et al.
61. Fisch, D. A. *Jews For Nothing: On Cults, Intermarriage, and Assimilation.* New York: Feldheim, 1984, pp. 173-74.
62. The International Center for the Study of Anti-Semitism. *Anti-Semitism.* Jerusalem: Hebrew University.
63. Ibid.
64. Ibid.
65. Ibid.
66. Grosser et al.
67. Flannery.
68. Ibid.
69. Ibid.
70. Grosser et al.
71. Davidowicz, L.S. *The War Against the Jews, 1933-1945.* New York: Bantam Books, 1975, p. 21.
72. Ibid., p. 24.
73. Ibid., p. 26.
74. Ibid.
75. Ibid., p. 211.
76. Ibid., p. 220.
77. Ibid., p. 223.
78. Goldberg.
79. Ibid.
80. Ibid., pp. 205-6.

271

Chapter VIII

1. See: (A) Givet, J. *The Anti-Zionist Complex*. Englewood Cliffs, N.J.: SBS Publishing, 1982. (B) Seidman, H. *United Nations: Perfidy and Perversion*. New York: M.P. Press, 1982.
2. Seidman, p. 5.
3. Givet, pp. xii-xiii.
4. Seidman, p. vii.
5. See: (A) Abu-Lughod, I.A. (Ed.), *The Transformation of Palestine*. Evanston, Ill.: Northwestern University Press, 1971. (B) Said, E.W. *The Question of Palestine*. New York: Times Books, 1979.
6. See: (A) Davis, L. J. & Decter, M. *Myths and Facts, 1982: A Concise Record of the Arab-Israeli Conflict*. Washington, D.C.: Near East Research, Inc., 1982. (B) Peters, J. *From Time Immemorial: The Origins of the Arab-Jewish Conflict over Palestine*. New York: Harper & Row, 1984.
7. Davis et al.
8. E.g., (A) Interview with King Hussein. *Time Magazine*, July 26, 1982, p. 23. (B) Johnson, M. *Time Magazine*, August 9, 1982, p. 24. (C) Muller, H. *Time Magazine*, October 18, 1982, p. 34.
9. Muller.
10. Peters.
11. Ibid.
12. Ibid.
13. Kessler, J.S. & Schwaber, J. *The AIPAC College Guide: Exposing the Anti-Israel Campaign on Campus*. Washington, D.C.: American Israel Public Affairs Committee, 1984.
14. Muravchik, J. *Misreporting Lebanon*. Washington, D.C.: Heritage Foundation, 1983.
15. Gerol, I., "TV Exaggerates Lebanese Damage." *The Citizen*, October 30, 1982, B2.
16. C.O.M.A. *Media Onslaught on Israel*. Santa Monica, Calif.: Committee on Media Accountability, 1983.
17. Davis et al.
18. Merari, A. *PLO: Core of World Terror*. Jerusalem: Carta, 1983.
19. Mandel R., "Israel in 1982: The War in Lebanon." In M. Himmelfarb & D. Singer (Eds.), *American Jewish Yearbook, 1984*. New York: American Jewish Committee, 1983.
20. Palestinian National Covenant (1968). In Davis.
21. "Britain Israel Public Affairs Committee." *The PLO Exposed*. London: Britain Israel Public Affairs Committee, 1982.
22. Tal, E. *Now the Story Can Be Told*. Tel Aviv: Achduth Press, 1982.
23. Kessler et al.
24. Ibid.

References

25. E.g., (A) Forster, A. & Epstein, B.R. *The New Anti-Semitism*. New York: McGraw-Hill, 1974. (B) Pilzer, J. *Anti-Semitism and Jewish Nationalism*. Virginia Beach, Va.: Donning Co., 1981.
26. Quinley, H.E. & Glock, C.Y. *Anti-Semitism in America*. New Brunswick, N.J.: Transaction Inc., 1983.
27. Peters.
28. Palestine Royal Commission Report. In Davis.
29. Cirino, R. *Power to Persuade*. New York: Bantam Books, 1974.
30. Epstein, E.J. *News From Nowhere*. New York: Vintage Books, 1974.
31. Davis et al.
32. Chafetz, Z. *Double Vision: How the Press Distorts America's View of the Middle East*. New York: Wm. Morrow & Co., 1985, p. 17.
33. Ibid., p. 19.
34. Ibid., p. 51.
35. Ibid., pp. 51-52.
36. Ibid., p. 78.
37. Ibid., p. 93.
38. Perlmutter, N. & Perlmutter, R.A. *The Real Anti-Semitism in America*. New York: Arbor House, 1982.
39. Newfield, J. *The Village Voice*. New York, 1981.
40. Chafetz.
41. Sartre, J.P. *Anti-Semite and Jew*. New York: Schocken Books, 1976, pp. 94-95.
42. Ibid., pp. 95-96.
43. Ibid., pp. 102-3.
44. Ibid., p. 109.

Chapter IX

1. Hoge, D.R. and Carrol, J.W., "Christian Beliefs, Non-Religious Factors and Anti-Semitism." *Social Forces*, 1975, *4*, 581-94.
2. E.g., (A) Ettinger, S., "The Origins of Modern Anti-Semitism." *Dispersion and Unity*, 1969, *9*, 17-37. (B) Parsons, T., "Postscript to the Sociology of Modern Anti-Semitism." *Contemporary Jewry*, 1980, *1*, 31-38.
3. Bettleheim, B. and Janowitz, M. *Social Change and Prejudice: Dynamics of Prejudice*. New York: Free Press of Glencoe, 1964.
4. Meyers, D.A. *Social Psychology*. New York: McGraw Hill, 1983.
5. See: (A) Rosennan, S., "Psychoanalytic Reflections on Anti-Semitism." *Journal of Psychology and Judaism*, 1977, *2*, 3-23. (B) Tumin, M. "Anti-Semitism and Status Anxiety: A Hypothesis." *Jewish Social Studies*, 1971, *4*, 307-16.
6. Bettleheim et al.

7. Berkowitz, L., "Whatever Happened to the Frustration-Aggression Hypothesis?" *American Behavioral Scientist*, 1978, *21*, 691-708.
8. E.g., (A) Green, R.G. "Effects of Frustration, Attack, and Prior Training in Aggressiveness Upon Aggressive Behavior." *Journal of Personality and Social Psychology*, 1968, *9*, 316-21. (B) Berkowitz, L., Cochran, S.T. and Embree, M.C. "Physical Pain and the Goal of Aversively Stimulated Aggression." *Journal of Personality and Social Psychology*, 1981, *40*, 687-700.
9. Berkowitz, p. 703.
10. Grosser, P.E. and Halperin, E.G. *The Causes and Effects of Anti-Semitism*. New York: Philosophical Library, 1978.
11. E.g., (A) Adorno, T.W., Frenkel-Brunswik, D., Levinson, D.J. and Sanford, R.N. *The Authoritarian Personality*. New York: Harper & Row, 1950. (B) Bettleheim et al. (C) Saenger, G. *The Social Psychology of Prejudice*. New York: Harper & Row, 1969.
12. Allswang, B. *Anti-Judaism, Anti-Semitism, Anti-Zionism: A Theoretical and Empirical Analysis of the Anti-Jewish Phenomenon throughout Its History to the Present*. Doctoral dissertation submitted to the Social-Psychology Department of Loyola University of Chicago, 1985.
13. Netanyahu, B. How Central is the Palestinian Problem? *The Wall Street Journal*, April 5, 1983.
14. Quinley, H.E. and Glock, C.Y. *Anti-Semitism in America*. New Brunswick, N.J.: Transaction Inc., 1983.
15. Selznick, G.J. and Steinberg, S. *The Tenacity of Prejudice: Anti-Semitism in Contemporary America*. New York: Harper & Row, 1969.
16. Perlmutter, N. and Perlmutter, R.A. *The Real Anti-Semitism in America*. New York: Arbor House, 1982, p. 186.
17. Davis, L.J. *Myths and Facts 1985: A Concise Record of the Arab-Israeli Conflict*. Washington, D.C.: Near East Research, Inc., 1984, pp. 139-40.
18. In J.S. Kessler and J. Schwaber, *The AIPAC College Guide: Exposing the Anti-Israel Campaign on Campus*. Washington, D.C.: AIPAC, 1984, p. 24.
19. Ibid., pp. 24-25.
20. Ibid.
21. Drayer, M. and Klanner, M. "Fighting Anti-Israel Propaganda." *Near East Report*, 1983, *27*, 130.
22. In Kessler et al., p. 4.
23. Ibid.

Chapter X

1. Sachar, H.M. *A History of Israel: From the Rise of Zionism to Our Time*. New York: Alfred A. Knopf, 1981, p. 38.

References

2. *Am Sigula*. Jerusalem: D'var Yerushalyim, 1981; Gilbert, M. *Auschwitz and the Allies*. New York: Holt, Rinehart, & Winston, 1981; Morse, A.D. *While Six Million Died*. New York: Random House, 1968; Wyman, D.S. *The Abandonment of the Jews*. New York: Pantheon Books, 1984.
3. Exodus (32:13).
4. Leviticus (26:44).
5. Tractate *Taanith* (2:6). Jerusalem: Torah Mitzion, 1968.
6. Leviticus (20:26).
7. Isaiah (54:17).
8. Ibid. (54:10).
9. Numbers (23:9).
10. Leviticus (26:44).
11. Malachi (3:6).
12. Jeremiah (5:8-14).
13. Psalms (129:1-2).
14. *Seder Eliahu Rabbah* (18:141-47). Jerusalem: Vaharmon, 1960.
15. Genesis (28:12-14).
16. *Bereshit Rabbah* (69:4-5). Jerusalem: Vaharmon, 1965.
17. *Midrash Shemot Rabbah* (32). In *Midrash Rabbah*. Jerusalem: Levin-Epstein, 1965.
18. *Midrash Esther Rabbah* (10:11). In *Midrash Rabbah*. B'nai Brak: Tiferet Zion, 1963.
19. Lamentations (1:3).
20. Deuteronomy (28:65).
21. *Eicha Rabbah* (10.) In *Midrash Rabbah*. B'nai Brak: Tiferet Zion, 1963.
22. *Yalkut Shimoni* (*Parshat Balak*). Jerusalem.
23. Ezekiel (20:32-34).
24. Jeremiah (31:35-36).
25. In A. Sutton and Arachim Staff (Eds.), *Pathways to the Torah*. Jerusalem: Arachim, 1985, p. A9.
26. Glover, T.R. *The Ancient World: A Beginning*. Westport, Conn.: Greenwood Press, 1979, pp. 184-87.
27. Berdkilaev, N. *The Meaning of History*. Cleveland: Meridian Books, 1962, pp. 86-87.
28. In Sutton et al., p. A7.
29. Ibid.
30. Eybeschutz, J. In *Am Sigula*, p. 109.
31. Bruer, I. *Moreah*. Jerusalem: Mosad HaRav Kook, 1982, pp. 98-99.
32. In *Am Sigula*, pp. 120-21.
33. Ibid.
34. Maharal. *Netzach Yisroel* (80:12). Warsaw: Freedberg, 1886.
35. Sutton et al.
36. Leviticus (26:14-32); Deuteronomy (11:16-17).
37. Sutton et al.

38. Jeremiah (25:8-11).
39. See Kings II (25).
40. Ibid. (25:3).
41. Lamentations (4:10).
42. Kings II (25:8).
43. Chronicles II (36:20-21).
44. Josephus. The Jewish World (4-6:3).
45. Jerusalem Talmud, Tractate *Ta'anith* (84-85). Jerusalem: Torah Mitzion, 1968.
46. Josephus (2-14:2).
47. "History of the Nation Israel in Ancient Days." In Sutton et al., B38.
48. Josephus (6-9:2).
49. Ibid. (2-6:2).
50. Ibid. (3-6:2).
51. Sutton et al., p. B36.
52. Ibid.
53. Josephus (5-10:3).
54. Ibid. (6-9:2).
55. In Sutton et al., p. B38.
56. Munter the Historian. In Sutton et al., p. B38.
57. Tractate *Ketuboth* (3B). Jerusalem: Ortsel, 1960.
58. Meiri, S. "Burden of Proof." I.D. Kiel (Ed.), *Return to the Source.* New York: Feldheim, 1984.
59. Gilbert, M. *Atlas of Jewish History.* New York: Dorset Press, 1985, in Preface.
60. Lloyd George (1923). In Sutton et al., p. B43.
61. Prager, D. & Telushkin, J. *Why the Jews? The Reason for Anti-Semitism.* New York: Simon & Schuster, 1983, p. 17.
62. Leschzinsky. "The Jewish Dispersion." In Sutton et al., p. B47.
63. Grosser, P.E. and Halperin. E.G. *The Causes and Effects of Anti-Semitism.* New York: Philosophical Library, 1978.
64. Sutton et al.
65. Meiri, pp. 107-8.
66. Ibid.
67. Josephus (3-3:2).
68. Nachmanides, M. "Epistle to his Son Nachmon." In *Kitvai Ramban Volume I.* Jerusalem: Mossad HaRav Kook, 1964, pp. 367-68.
69. Twain, M. *The Innocents Abroad.* In Sutton et al., p. B67.
70. Cited in Sutton et al., p. B67.
71. In Davis, L.J. *Myths and Facts 1985: A Concise Record of the Arab-Israeli Conflict.* Washington, D.C.: Near East Researach, Inc., 1984, p. 10.
72. Nachmanides, M. In *Mikraot Gedolot Vayikra* (26:32). New York: Pardes, 1951.

References

73. Sutton et al.

74. *Zohar* (Parashat Vayera). Jerusalem: Mossad HaRav Kook, 1964.

75. Sutton et al., p. B84.

76. Van Loon, H. W. *The Story of Mankind.* New York: Liveright, 1984, p. 321.

77. Charniovsky, A. *Between Science and Religion.* Tel Aviv: Joshua Chachik Publishing, 1965.

78. Deuteronomy (30:1-2).

79. Amos (8:11).

80. Meiri, pp. 112-13.

81. *Shir HaShirim Rabbah.* In *Midrash Rabbah.* Jerusalem: Levin-Epstein, 1965.

82. Meiri, p. 111.

83. Biberfeld, P. *Universal Jewish History, Volume I.* New York: Spero Foundation, 1948, p. 22.

84. Sutton et al., p. B91.

85. Meiri, pp. 109-10.

86. Tractate *Makot* (24B). Jerusalem: Ortsel, 1960.

87. Tractate *Sanhedrin* (98A). Jerusalem: Ortsel, 1960.

88. *Zohar (Acharey Mot,* 66).

89. E.g., (A) Jerusalem Talmud Tractate *Yoma* (3:2). (B) *Midrash Tehillim* (18). In *Midrash Shochar Tov Al Tehillim.* Jerusalem: Midrash, 1968. (C) *Zohar* (1:170A). In A. Kaplan, *The Real Messiah?* New York: NCSY, 1985.

90. *Zohar (Vaera,* p. 32).

91. Tractate *Sanhedrin* (98A).

92. Ibid.

93. E.g., (A) *Bereshit Rabbah* (42). In *Midrash Rabbah.* (B) *Yalkut Shemoni* (on Isaiah 60).

94. *Pirkey D'Rabbi Eliezer* (32). Jerusalem: M. Kilman, 1969.

95. Tractate *Sotah* (49B). Jerusalem: Ortsel, 1960.

96. Tractate *Sanhedrin* (97A).

97. Tractate *Yoma* (10A).

98. *Midrash Daniel.* Jerusalem: Mekeetze Nerdameem, 1968.

99. Daniel (7:23-24).

100. Isenberg, R. *Chavlai Meshiach Bizmanainu.* Tel Aviv: Chidekel, 1970.

101. Ezekiel (38).

102. Josephus. *Antiquities.*

103. *Brittanica World Language.* London: Encyclopaedia Brittanica, 1954.

104. *Encyclopaedia Brittanica.* London: 1954.

105. Tractate *Megillah* (1:19). Jerusalem: Torah Mitzion, 1985.

106. Kaplan, A. *The Living Torah.* New York: Maznaim, 1985.

107. Ibid., p. 42.

108. *Encyclopaedia Brittanica.*
109. Campbell, G. & Evans, I.O. *The Book of Flags.* London: Oxford University Press, 1969.
110. Ibid.
111. *Zohar (Vaera,* 32). Jerusalem: Mossad HaRav Kook, 1964.
112. *Pesikta Rabosi* (end of no. 1). Vilna: 1880.
113. Tractate *Sanhedrin* (97A).
114. Cited in Kaplan.
115. Tractate *Sanhedrin* (98).
116. Nachmonides (1194-1270).
117. Cited in Kaplan.
118. Ibid., (11:4).
119. Tractate *Sanhedrin* (97A). See Rashi.
120. Ibid., (105A). See Rashi.
121. See Mitsudath Daveed on Ezekiel (20:33-34). In *Mikraot Gedolot.* New York: Friedman, 1971.
122. Tractate *Sanhedrin* (97).
123. Nachmonides (1194-1270). *Kitvai Ramban Volume II* (516). Jerusalem: Mossad HaRav Kook, 1964.
124. See Rabbi Joseph Kara on Isaiah 48:1-5. Cited in Kaplan.
125. Tractate *Sanhedrin* (98B). See Rashi.
126. Chaim, C. *Shem Olam* (Chapter 12). Warsaw: 1897; Cited in Isenberg.
127. *Pesikta Zutrata.* Cited in Isenberg.
128. *Midrash Daniel.* Cited in Isenberg.
129. Isenberg.
130. In *Mikraot Gedolot Numbers.* New York: Friedman, 1971.
131. Isenberg.
132. In *Mikroat Gedolot Daniel.* New York: Friedman, 1971.
133. *Zohar Bereshit.* Cited in Isenberg.
134. See Isenberg. Based on Daniel (11:43-44).
135. *Pesikta Rabosi* (37:2). See Isenberg.
136. Daniel (11:40-42; 12:1).
137. Kings I (18:22).

Chapter XI

1. Sklare, M. (Ed.). *American Jews/A Reader.* New York: Behrman House, 1983.
2. Liebman, C.S. "The Religion of American Jews." In Sklare.
3. Gartner, L.P. "Immigration and the Formation of American Jewry," 1840-1925. In Sklare.
4. E.g., (A) Talmud Tractate *Shabbos* (31A). Jerusalem: Ortsel, 1960. (B) Tractate *Berachoth* (5A). Ibid. (C) Tractate *Gittin* (60B).

References

5. Deuteronomy (6:8).
6. Ibid. (11:18).
7. Exodus (13:9).
8. Ibid. (13:16).
9. Numbers (15:37-39).
10. Sutton, A. and Arachim Staff. *Pathways to the Torah*. Jerusalem: Arachim, 1985.
11. Genesis (17:10-14).
12. E.g., (A) Exodus (6). (B) Jeremiah (6, 9).
13. Deuteronomy (10:16).
14. Sutton et al.
15. Ibid.
16. Deuteronomy (12:21).
17. Schimmel, H.C. *The Oral Law*. Jerusalem: Feldheim, 1971.
18. Deuteronomy (22).
19. Sutton et al.
20. Leviticus (23:6).
21. Deuteronomy (12;21).
22. Maimonides, M. *Mishna Torah*. Jerusalem: Mosad HaRav Kook, pp. 5-11.
23. Ibid., pp. 14-15.
24. HaLevy, J. *The Kuzari* (3:33-35). New York: Schocken Books, 1964.
25. Allswang, B. *Anti-Judaism, Anti-Semitism, Anti-Zionism: A Theoretical and Empirical Analysis of the Anti-Jewish Phenomenon throughout Its History to the Present*. A doctoral dissertation submitted to the Social Psychology Department of Loyola University of Chicago, 1985.
26. Rosenthal, G.S. *The Many Faces of Judaism*. New York: Behrman House, 1978, pp. 69-70.
27. Raphael, M.L. *Profiles in American Judaism*. San Francisco: Harper & Row, 1984.
28. Ibid.
29. Ibid.
30. Gordis, R. *Understanding Conservative Judaism*. New York: Rabbinical Assembly, 1978, p. 100.
31. Plaut, W.G. *The Rise of Reform Judaism*. New York: World Union for Progressive Judaism, 1963.
32. Plaut, W.G. *The Growth of Reform Judaism*. New York: World Union for Progressive Judaism, 1965.
33. Kazis, I.J. "Meeting the Challenge to Jewish Survival." In M. Berger, J.A. Geffen, M.D. Hoffman (Eds.), *Roads to Jewish Survival*. New Yorck: Bloch, 1967, p. 167.
34. Gordis, p. 217.
35. Fisch, D.A. *Jews for Nothing*. New York: Feldheim, 1984.

Bibliography

Aban, Ezra. In *Mikraot Gedolot; Daniel.* New York: Friedman, 1971.

Abelson, C.M. "Bias and the Bible." In A. Carmell & C. Domb (Eds.). *Challenge: Torah Views on Science and Its Problems.* Jerusalem: Feldheim Publishers, 1978.

Abelson, P.H. "Chemical Events on the Primitive Earth." *Proceedings of the National Academy of Science,* 1966, *55,* 1365-1372.

Abu-Lughod, I.A. (Ed.). *The Transformation of Palestine: Essays on the Origin and Development of the Arab-Israeli Conflict.* Evanston, Ill.: Northwestern University Press, 1971.

Adorno, T.W. "Types and Syndromes." In T.W. Adorno, E. Frenkel-Brunswik, D.J. Levinson, and R.N. Sanford (Eds.). *The Authoritarian Personality.* New York: Harper & Row, 1950.

Adorno, T.W., Frenkel-Brunswik, E., Levinson, D.J., and Sanford, R.N. *The Authoritarian Personality.* New York: Harper & Row, 1950.

Aharoni, Y. "Canaanite Israel During the Period of Israeli Occupation." In A. Sutton & Arachim Staff (Eds.), *Pathways to the Torah.* Jerusalem: Arachim, 1985.

Albright, W.F. *The Biblical Period.* New York: Harper & Row, 1963.

Albright, W.F. *Archaeology and the Religion of Israel.* New York: Anchor Books, 1969.

Allport, G. *The Nature of Prejudice.* New York: Addison-Wesley, 1954.

Allswang, B. *Anti-Judaism, Anti-Semitism, Anti-Zionism: A Theoretical and Empirical Analysis of the Anti-Jewish Phenomenon throughout Its History to the Present.* Doctoral dissertation submitted to the Social-Psychology Department of Loyola University of Chicago, 1985.

Am Sigula. Jerusalem: D'var Yerushalyim, 1981.

Anti-Defamation League of B'nai B'rith. *Hate Groups in America: A Record of Bigotry and Violence*. New York: Anti-Defamation League of B'nai B'rith, 1982.

Baidawi. Cited in A.I. Katch, *Judaism and the Koran*. New York: Perpetua, 1962.

Berdkilaev, N. *The Meaning of History*. Cleveland: Meridian Books, 1962.

Bergman, S.H. "Can Transgression Have an Agent? On the Moral-Judical Problem of the Eichmann Trial." *Yad Vashem Studies, 5,* 1963, 7-15.

Berkowitz, L. "Whatever Happened to the Frustration-Aggression Hypothesis?" *American Behavioral Scientist*, 1978, *21*, 691-708.

Berkowitz, L., Cochran, S.T., and Embree, M.C. "Physical Pain and the Goal of Aversively Stimulated Aggression." *Journal of Personality and Social Psychology,* 1981, *40*, 687-700.

Bettelheim, B., and Janowitz, M. *Social Change and Prejudice: Dynamics of Prejudice*. New York: Free Press of Glencoe, 1964.

Biberfeld, P. *Universal Jewish History*, vol. 1. New York: Feldheim, 1962.

Bottomore, T.B. *Kark Marx: Early Writings*. New York: McGraw-Hill, 1964.

Brinkman, R.T. "Dissociation of Water Vapor and Evolution of Oxygen in the Terrestrial Atmosphere." *Journal of Geophysical Research, 74*, 1969, 5355-5368.

Britain Israel Public Affairs Committee. *The PLO Exposed*. London: Britain Israel Public Affairs Committee, 1982.

Britannica World Language. Edition of Funk and Wagnell's New Practical Standard Dictionary. London: Encyclopaedia Britannica, 1954.

Bruer, I. *Moriah*. Jerusalem: Mossad HaRav Kook, 1982.

Campbell, A., & Evans, I.O. *The Book of Flags*. London: Oxford University Press, 1969.

Cawley, J. "Canada Accuses German of Writing Off Holocaust." *Chicago Tribune*, February 3, 1985, p. 5.

Chafetz, Z. *Double Vision: How the Press Distorts America's View of the Middle East*. New York: William Morrow & Co., 1985.

Charniovsky, A. *Between Science and Religion*. Tel Aviv: Joshua Chachik Publishing, 1965.

Bibliography

Chavel, C.B. *The Law of the Eternal Is Perfect.* New York: Shilo, 1983.

Chicago Tribune. "Percy Held Talks with Palestinians." December 31, 1981.

Cirino,R. *Power to Persuade.* New York: Bantam Books, 1974.

Cohen, I. "Myths and Facts on the Middle East Mishegoss." *Jewish Chicago.* New Year, 1984, pp. 18-22.

Cohen, S. "Divine Origin of the Torah." In D. Kiel (Ed.). *Return to the Source.* New York: Feldheim Publishers, 1984.

Cohen, S.M. *Attitudes of American Jews Towards Israel and Israelis: The 1983 National Survey of American Jews and Jewish Communal Leaders.* New York: American Jewish Committee, 1983.

C.O.M.A. *Media Onslaught on Israel.* Santa Monica, Calif.: Committee on Media Accountability, 1983.

Davidowicz, L.S. *The War Against the Jews, 1933-1945.* New York: Bantam Books, 1975.

Davis, L.J. *Myths and Facts 1985: A Concise Record of the Arab-Israeli Conflict.* Washington, D.C.: Near East Research, Inc., 1984.

Davis, L.J., and Decter, M. *Myths and Facts 1982: A Concise Record of the Arab-Israeli Conflict.* Washington, D.C.: Near East Research, Inc. 1982.

DeBileda, J. In *Am Sigula.* Jerusalem: D'var Yerushalyim, 1981.

Dewar, D., & Shelton, H.S. *Is Evolution Proved? A Debate Between Douglas Dewar and H. S. Shelton.* London: Holis & Carter, 1947.

Dickerson, R.E. "Chemical Evolution and the Origin of Life." *Scientific American, 239,* 1978, 70-87.

Drayer, M., & Kanner, M. "Fighting Anti-Israel Propaganda." *Near East Report,* 1983, *27,* 130.

Dunham, D.C. *Kremlin Target: U.S.A.; Conquest by Propaganda.* New York: I. Washburn, 1961.

Einstein, A. *Comment je Voi le Monde.* New York: Philosophical Library, 1949.

Eliezer, S. *Maharsha: Talmud Tractate Baba Kama.* Vilna edition. Jerusalem: Ortsel, 1960.

Eliezer, S. *Maharsha: Talmud Tractate Succah.* Vilna edition. Jerusalem: Ortsel, 1960.

Emden, J. *Sulam Beit Al.* In *Sidut Beit Yaacob.* New York: Mefitzay Torah, 1950.

Encyclopaedia Britannica. London, 1954.

Encyclopaedia Judaica. Jerusalem: Keter Publishing House, 1973.

Encyclopaedia Judaica: 1973-82 Decennial Book. Jerusalem: Keter, 1982.

Epstein, E.J. *News from Nowhere.* New York: Vintage Books, 1974.

Etkin, W. "The Religious Meaning of Contemporary Science." In A. Carmell and C. Domb (Eds.). *Challenge: Torah Views on Science and Its Problems.* Jerusalem: Feldheim Publishers, 1978.

Ettinger, S. "The Origins of Modern Anti-Semitism." *Dispersion and Unity,* 1969, *9,* 17-37.

Eybeschutz, J. In *Am Sigula.* Jerusalem: D'var Yerushalyim, 1981.

Fisch, D.A. *Jews for Nothing: On Cults, Intermarriage, and Assimilation.* New York: Feldheim Publishers, 1984.

Flannery, E. H. *The Anguish of the Jews.* New York: Macmillan Co., 1965.

Forster, A., and Epstein, B. R. *The New Anti-Semitism.* New York: McGraw-Hill, 1974.

Fromm, E. *Escape from Freedom.* New York: Farrar & Rinehart, 1941.

Gager, J. G. *The Origins of Anti-Semitism: Attitudes towards Judaism in Pagan and Christian Antiquity.* New York: Oxford University Press, 1983.

Gartner, L. P. "Immigration and the Formation of American Jewry, 1840-1925." In M. Sklare (Ed.), *American Jews: A Reader.* New York: Behrman House, 1983.

Geen, R. G. "Effects of Frustration, Attack, and Prior Training in Aggressiveness upon Aggressive Behavior." *Journal of Personality and Social Psychology,* 1968, *9,* 316-21.

Gerol, Ilya. "TV Exaggerates Lebanese Damage." Ottowa, Canada: *The Citizen,* October 30, 1982.

Gevirtz, E. *L'haveen U' L'Haskeel: A Guide to Torah Hashkofoh, Questions and Answers on Judaism.* New York: Feldheim Publishers, 1980.

Gilbert, M. *Atlas of Jewish History.* New York: Dorset Press, 1985.

Gilbert, M. *Auschwitz and the Allies.* New York: Holt, Rinehart, & Winston, 1981.

Ginzberg, L. *The Legends of the Jews.* Philadelphia: The Jewish Publication Society, 1968.

Givet, J. *The Anti-Zionist Complex.* Englewood, N.J.: SBS Publishing, 1982.

Glover, T.R. *The Ancient World: A Beginning.* Westport, Conn.: Greenwood Press, 1979.

Goldberg, M.H. *Just Because They're Jewish.* New York: Scarborough House, 1981.

Bibliography

Goot, A.K., and Rosen, S.J. *The Campaign to Discredit Israel.* Washington, D.C.: American Israel Public Affairs Committee, 1983.

Gordis, R. *Understanding Conservative Judaism.* New York: Rabbinical Assembly, 1978.

Grayzel, S. *A History of the Jews.* Philadelphia: Jewish Publication Society of America, 1968.

Great Soviet Encyclopaedia (1952). Cited in D. Prager and J. Telushkin. *Why the Jews? The Reason for Anti-Semitism.* New York: Simon & Schuster, 1983.

Green, D.F., & Goldberger, R.F. *Molecular Insights into the Living Process.* New York: Academic Press, 1967.

Grosser, P.E., and Halperin, E.G. *The Causes and Effects of Anti-Semitism.* New York: Philosophical Library, 1978.

HaLevy, J. *The Kuzari.* New York: Schocken Books, 1964.

Harris, L., and Associates. Cited in H.E. Quinley and C.Y. Glock, *Anti-Semitism in America.* New Brunswick, N.J.: Transaction Inc., 1983.

Hirsch, S.M. "How Does Our Time Relate to Truth and Peace?" in *Collected Writings of Rabbi Samson Raphael Hirsch.* New York: Feldheim Publishers, 1984.

Hoge, D.R., and Carroll, J.W. "Christian Beliefs, Non-Religious Factors, and Anti-Semitism." *Social Forces*, 1975, *4*, 581-94.

Hooton, E.A. *Up from the Ape.* New York: Macmillan Co., 1946.

Hoyle, F., & Wickramasinghe, N.C. *Evolution from Space: Theory of Cosmic Creation.* New York: Simon & Schuster, 1982.

Hull, D.E. "Thermodynamics and Kinetics of Spontaneous Generation." *Nature, 186*, 1960, 693-94.

Hussein. "Interview with King Hussein." *Time*, July 26, 1982, p. 23.

The International Center for the Study of Antisemitism. *ANTI-SEMITISM.* Jerusalem: Hebrew University.

Isaacs, J. *Our People: History of the Jews.* New York: Shulsinger Bros., 1975.

Isenberg, R. *Chavlai Meshiach Bizmanainu.* Tel-Aviv: Chidekel, 1970.

Jaakobi, S. "Land of Israel." In D. Kiel (Ed.), *Return to the Source.* New York: Feldheim Publishers, 1984.

Jakobovits, I. Foreword. In H.C. Schimmel, *The Oral Law: A Study of the Rabbinic Contribution to Torah SheBe-Al-Peh.* Jerusalem: Feldheim Publishers, 1971.

Johnson, M. *Time Magazine*, August 9, 1982, p. 24.

Josephus. *Against Apion. The Life and Works of Josephus.* Philadelphia: John C. Winston Co., 1936.

Josephus. *Antiquities. The Life and Works of Josephus.* Philadelphia: John C. Winston Co., 1936.

Josephus, F. *Complete Works of Flavius Josephus.* Grand Rapids, Mich.: Kregel, 1970.

Josephus. *The Jewish Wars. The Life and Works of Josephus.* Philadelphia: John C. Winston Co., 1936.

Kaganoff, B.C. *A Dictionary of Jewish Names and Their History.* New York: Schocken Books, 1977.

Kaplan, A. *Handbook of Jewish Thought.* New York: Maznaim, 1979.

Kaplan, A. *The Living Torah.* New York: Maznaim, 1985.

Kaplan, A. *The Real Messiah: A Jewish Response to Missionaries.* New York: N.C.S.Y., 1985.

Kapustin, M. "Biblical Criticism: A Traditionalist View." In A. Carmell and C. Domb (Eds.), *Challenge: Torah Views on Science and Its Problems.* Jerusalem: Feldheim Publishers, 1978.

Katsh, A.I. *Judaism and the Koran.* New York: Perpetua, 1962.

Katzir, A. "In the Midst of the Scientific Revolution." In A. Sutton & Arachim Staff (Eds.), *Pathways to the Torah.* Jerusalem: Arachim, 1985.

Kaufman, Y. *The Religion of Israel: From Its Beginnings to the Babylonian Exile.* Chicago: University of Chicago Press, 1960.

Kazis, I.J. "Meeting the Challenge to Jewish Survival." In M. Berger, J.S. Geffen, M.D. Hoffman (Eds.), *Roads to Jewish Survival.* New York: Bloch, 1967.

Keniston, K. *Youth and Dissent: The Rise of a New Opposition.* New York: Harcourt Brace Jovanovich, 1971.

Keller, W. *The Bible as History: A Confirmation of the Book of Books.* New York: Wm. Morrow, 1956.

Kerkut, G.A. *Implications of Evolution.* New York: Pergamon Press, 1960.

Kessler, J.S., and Schwaber, J. *The AIPAC College Guide: Exposing the Anti-Israel Campaign on Campus.* Washington, D.C.: American Israel Public Affairs Committee, 1984.

Kondracke, M. *Chicago Suntimes.* January 25, 1985.

Krsoney & Schmueloff. *The National Jewish Ledger.* April, 1986.

Lamprecht, S.P. *Our Philosophical Traditions: A Brief History of*

Philosophy in Western Civilization. New York: Appleton-Century-Crofts, 1955.

Levi, L. *Torah and Science: Their Interplay in the World Scheme.* Jerusalem: Feldheim Publishers, 1983.

Levine, S. *You Take Jesus, I'll Take God: How to Refute Christian Missionaries.* Los Angeles: Hamoroh Press, 1980.

Lewin, R. "Evolutionary Theory Under Fire." *Science, 210,* 1980, 883-87.

Liebman, C.S. "The Religion of American Jews." In M. Sklare (Ed.), *American Jews/A Reader.* New York: Behrman House, 1983.

Lindsey, H. *The Late Great Planet Earth.* Grand Rapids, Mich.: Zondervan, 1977.

Lindsey, H. *The 1980's: Countdown to Armageddon.* New York: Bantam Books, 1981.

Lipset, S.M., & Ladd, E.C. "Jewish Academics in the United States: Their Achievements, Culture and Politics." In M. Fine and M. Himmelfarb (Eds.), *American Jewish Yearbook 1971.* Philadelphia: Jewish Publication Society of America, 1971.

Lipson, H.S. "A Physicist Looks at Evolution." *Physics Bulletin, 31,* 1980, 138.

Ma'ariv Newspaper. April 17, 1983.

Macbeth, N. *Darwin Retried: An Appeal to Reason.* Boston: Cambit, 1971.

McKay, J.P., Hill, B.D., & Buckler, J. *A History of World Societies.* Boston: Houghton Mifflin, 1984.

Machshavot I.B.M. "Sociobiology–Nature Within Man." In A. Sutton & Arachim Staff (Eds.), *Pathways to the Torah.* Jerusalem: Arachim, 1985.

McLellan, D. *Karl Marx: His Life and Thought.* New York: Harper & Row, 1973.

Maharal. *Netzach Yisroel.* Warsaw: Freedberg, 1886.

Maimonides, M. *Mishna Torah: Hilchot Melachim.* Jerusalem: Mosad HaRav Kook, 1972.

Maimonides, M. *Mishna Torah, Hilchot Tshuvah.* Jerusalem: Mosad HaRav Kook, 1972.

Maimonides, M. *Mishna Torah, Introduction.* Jerusalem: Mosad HaRav Kook, 1972.

Maimonides, M. *Mishna Torah: Sefer Mada.* Jerusalem: Mosad HaRav Kook, 1972.

Maimonides, M. *Shemoneh Perakim.* In *Talmud Tractate Avoda Zara.* Vilna edition. Jerusalem: Ortsel, 1960.

Malamot, A. *A History of the Jewish People.* Cambridge, Mass.: Harvard University Press, 1976.

Mandel, R. "Israel in 1982: The War in Lebanon." In M. Himmelfarb and D. Singer (Eds.), *American Jewish Yearbook, 1984.* New York: American Jewish Committee, 1983.

Maslow, A.H. "The Authoritarian Character Structure." *The Journal of Social Psychology*, 1943, *18*, 401-411.

Mason, S.F. *A History of the Sciences.* New York: Collier Books, 1968.

Meiri, S. "Burden of Proof." In D. Kiel (Ed.), *Return to the Source.* New York: Feldheim Publishers, 1984.

Merari, A. *PLO: Core of World Terror.* Jerusalem: Carta, 1983.

Meyers, D.A. *Social Psychology.* New York: McGraw-Hill, 1983.

Midrash Agadat Ester. Israel: 1964.

Midrash Abba Gurion. In A. Jellinek (Ed.), *Bet ha-Midrasch.* Jerusalem: Wahrmann-Boos, 1967.

Midrash Bamidbar Rabbah. In *Midrash Rabbah.* Jerusalem: Levin-Epstein, 1965.

Midrash Beit Hamidrash. Jerusalem: Wahrman-Boos, 1967.

Midrash Bereshit Rabbah. Jerusalem: Vaharmon, 1965.

Midrash Daniel. Jerusalem: Mekeetze Nerdemeein, 1968.

Midrash Eicha Rabbah. In *Midrash Rabbah.* Bnai Brak: Tiferet Zion, 1963.

Midrash Esther. In L. Ginzberg (Ed.), *The Legends of the Jews.* Philadelphia: Jewish Publication Society of America, 1968.

Midrash Esther Rabbah. In *Midrash Rabbah.* Bnai Brak: Tiferet Zion, 1963.

Midrash Hagadol (Shemot). Jerusalem: Mosad HaRav Kook, 1956.

Midrash Mekilta; Pischa. In *Mekilta De-Rebbe Ishmael.* Philadelphia: Jewish Publication Society of America, 1976.

Midrash Panim Aherim. In L. Ginzberg (Ed.), *The Legends of the Jews.* Philadelphia: Jewish Publication Society of America, 1968.

Midrash Pesikta Rabosai. Vilna: n.p., 1880.

Midrash Pesikta Zutrata, Parshat Balak. In A. Kaplan, *The Real Messiah.* New York: National Conference of Synagogue Youth, 1985.

Bibliography

Midrash Pirke D'Rabbi Eleazer. Jerusalem: M. Kliman, 1969.

Midrash Tehillim. In *Midrash Shockar Tov al Tehillim.* Jerusalem: Midrash, 1968.

Midrash Rabbah. Jerusalem: Levin-Epstein, 1965.

Midrash Seder Eliyahu Rabbah. Jerusalem: Vaharmon, 1960.

Midrash Shemot Rabbah. In *Midrash Rabbah.* Jerusalem: Levin-Epstein, 1965.

Midrash Shir Ha-Shirim. Jerusalem: Ktav Yad Vasefer, 1971.

Midrash Tanchuma. Warsaw: Y.G. Monk, 1879.

Midrash Tanchuma Hakadoom V' Ha-Yashan. In *Midrash Tanchuma.* New York: Sefer, 1946.

Midrash Vayikra Rabbah. In *Midrash Rabbah.* Bnai Brak: Tiferet Zion, 1963.

Midrash Yalkut Shemoni. Jerusalem.

Midrash Yashar Noah. In *Sefer HaYashar HaShalem.* Jerusalem: Etz Chaim, 1968.

Midrash Yashar Shemot. Sefer HaYashar HaShalem. Jerusalem: Etz Chaim, 1968.

Miller, A. *Behold a People.* New York: Balshon, 1968.

Miller, A. *Torah Nation.* New York: Balshon, 1971.

Moore, J.N., & Slusher, H.S. *Biology: A Search for Order in Complexity.* Grand Rapids, Mich.: Zondervan, 1976.

Moorhead, P.S. & Kaplan, M.M. (Eds.). *Mathematical Challenges to the Neo-Darwinian Interpretation of Evolution.* Philadelphia: Wistar Institute Press, 1967.

Morse, A.D. *While Six Million Died: A Chronicle of American Apathy.* New York: Random House, 1968.

Muller, H. *Time Magazine.* October 18, 1982, p. 34.

Muravchik, J. *Misreporting Lebanon.* Washington, D.C.: Heritage Foundation, 1983.

Nachmonides, M. Perush on Vayikra. In *Mikraot Gedolot Vayikra.* New York: Pardes, 1951.

Nachmonides, M. *Igeret* to His Son Nachman. In *Kitvai Ramban Volume I.* Jerusalem: Mosad HaRav Kook, 1964.

Nachmonides, M. *Kitvai Ramban Volume II.* Jerusalem: Mossad HaRav Kook, 1964.

Nachmonides, M. "Prayer at the Ruins of Jerusalem." In C.B. Chavel (Ed.), *Ramban: Writings and Discourses Volume II.* New York: Shilo, 1978.

Negev, A. *Archaeological Encyclopedia of the Holy Land*. New York: Putnam, 1972.

Netanyahu, B. "How Central Is the Palestinian Problem?" *The Wall Street Journal*, April 5, 1983.

Newfield, J. *The Village Voice*. New York, 1981.

New Testament, *Matthew*. Self-pronouncing edition. Cleveland, Ohio: World Publishing Co., 1941.

New Testament. *Hebrews*. Self-pronouncing edition. Cleveland, O.: World Publishing Co., 1941.

Newton, I. *Opticks*. New York: Dover, 1952.

Nimrod, D. *Peace Now: Blueprint for National Suicide*. Quebec: Dawn, 1984.

Old Testament, *Amos; Daniel; Deuteronomy; Ester; Exodus; Ezekiel; Genesis; Isaiah; Jeremiah; Kings I; Leviticus; Malachi; Numbers; Psalms*. The Jerusalem Bible edition. Jerusalem: Koren Publishers, 1980.

Onkelos. In *Mikraot Gedolot: Numbers*. New York: Friedman, 1971.

Or L'Ameen. Jerusalem: D'var Yerushalyim, 1983.

Palestinian National Covenant (1968). In L. Davis, *Myths and Facts 1985: A Concise Record of the Arab-Israeli Conflict*. Washington, D.C.: Near East Report, 1984.

Parsons, T. "Postscript to the Sociology of Modern Anti-Semitism." *Contemporary Jewry*, 1980, *1*, 31-38.

Perlmutter, N., and Perlmutter, R.A. *The Real Anti-Semitism in America*. New York: Arbor House, 1982.

Peters, J. *From Time Immemorial: The Origins of the Arab-Jewish Conflict over Palestine*. New York: Harper & Row, 1984.

Pilzer, J. *Anti-Semitism and Jewish Nationalism*. Virginia Beach, Va.: Donning Co., 1981.

Planck, M. *Where Is Science Going?* Woodbridge, Conn.: Ox Bow Press, 1981.

Plaut, W.G. *The Rise of Reform Judaism*. New York: World Union for Progressive Judaism, 1963.

Plaut, W.G. *The Growth of Reform Judaism*. New York: World Union for Progressive Judaism, 1965.

Poincarbe, H. *The Foundations of Science*. Washington, D.C.: University Press of America, 1982.

Ponnamperuma, C., Shimoyana, A., Yamada, M., Hobo, T., & Pal, R. "Possible Surface Reactions on Mars: Implications for Viking

Biology Results." *Science, 197,* 1977, 455-57.

Popper, K.R. *Conjectures and Refutations: The Growth of Scientific Knowledge.* London: Routledge & K. Paul, 1969.

Prager, D., and Telushkin, J. *Why the Jews? The Reason for Anti-Semitism.* New York: Simon & Schuster, 1983.

Prigogine, I., Nicolis, G., & Babloyantz, A. "Thermodynamics of Evolution." *Physics Today, 25,* 1972, 23-28.

Quinley, H.E., and Glock, C.Y. *Anti-Semitism in America.* New Brunswick: Transaction Inc., 1983.

Quran. In *The Koran Interpreted.* New York: Macmillan Co., 1970.

Radday, Y.T., Shore, H., Pollatschek, M.A., & Wickman, D. "Genesis, Wellhausen and the Computer." In A. Sutton (Ed.), *Pathways to the Torah.* Jerusalem: Arachim, 1985.

Raphael, M.L. *Profiles in American Judaism.* San Francisco: Harper & Row, 1984.

Rifkin, J. *Algeny.* New York: Viking Press, 1983.

Rosenman, S. "Psychoanalytic Reflections on Anti-Semitism." *Journal of Psychology and Judaism,* 1977, *2,* 3-23.

Rosenthal, G.S. *The Many Faces of Judaism: Orthodox, Conservative, Reconstructionist, and Reform.* New York: Behrman House, 1978.

Ruether, R.R. *Faith and Fratricide: The Theological Roots of Anti-Semitism.* New York: Seabury Press, 1979.

Sachar, H.M. *A History of Israel: From the Rise of Zionism to Our Time.* New York: Alfred A. Knopf, 1981.

Saenger, G. *The Social Psychology of Prejudice.* New York: Harper & Row, 1969.

Said, E.W. *The Question of Palestine.* New York: Times Books, 1979.

Sancton, T.A. *Time Magazine.* June 28, 1982, p. 17.

Sanford, R.N., Adorno, T.W., Frenkel-Brunswik, E., and Levinson, D.J. "The Measurement of Implicit Anti-Democratic Trends." In T.W. Adorno, E. Frenkel-Brunswik, D.J. Levinson, and R.N. Sanford (Eds.), *The Authoritarian Personality.* New York: Harper & Row, 1950.

Sartre, J.P. *Anti-Semite and Jew.* New York: Schocken Books, 1976.

Scherman, N. Foreword. In M. Prager, *Sparks of Glory.* New York: Mesorah Publications, 1985.

Scherman, N., and Zlotowitz, M. *History of the Jewish People: The Second Temple Era.* New York: Mesorah Publications, 1982.

Schimmel, H.C. *The Oral Law: A Study of the Rabbinic Contribution to Torah She-Be-Al-Peh*. Jerusalem: Feldheim Publishers, 1971.

Schurer, E. *The History of the Jewish People in the Age of Jesus Christ*. Edinburgh: T & T Clark Ltd., 1973.

Schwartzman, S.D. *Reform Judaism Then and Now*. New York: Union of American Hebrew Congregations, 1971.

Sefer Ha'Ikarim. Jerusalem, 1960.

Seidman, H. *United Nations: Perfidy and Perversion*. New York: M. P. Press, 1982.

Selznick, G.J., and Steinberg, S. *The Tenacity of Prejudice: Anti-Semitism in Contemporary America*. New York: Harper & Row, 1969.

Sherif, M. *In Common Predicament*. Boston: Houghton Mifflin Co., 1966.

Shultz, R.H., and Godson, R. *Dezinformatsia: Active Measures in Soviet Strategy*. Washington, D.C.: Pergamon-Brassey, 1984.

Sierksma, K.L. *Flags of the World 1669-1670*. Holland: S. Emmering, 1966.

Simon, E.H. "On Gene Creation." In A. Carmel and C. Domb (Eds.), *Challenge: Torah Views on Science and Its Problems*. Jerusalem: Feldheim Publishers, 1978.

Sklare, M. *The Conservative Movement/Achievements and Problems*. In M. Sklare (Ed.), *American Jews/A Reader*. New York: Behrman House, 1983.

Smith, W.E. *Time Magazine*. July 26, 1982, p. 25.

Sutton, A., & Arachim Staff. *Pathways to the Torah*. Jerusalem: Arachim, 1985.

Tal, E. *Now the Story Can Be Told*. Tel-Aviv: Achduth Press, 1982.

Talmud. Tractate *Avoda Zara*; Tractate *Avot*; Tractate *Baba Batra;* Tractate *Berakoth*; Tractate *Chullin*; Tractate *Gittin*; Tractate *Hagiga*; Tractate *Ketuboth*; Tractate *Megilla*; Tractate *Nedarim*; Tractate *Pesachim*; Tractate *Sanhedrin*; Tractate *Shabbos*; Tractate *Sota*; Tractate *Succah*; Tractate *Ta'anith*; Tractate *Yoma*. Vilna edition. Jerusalem: Ortsel, 1960.

Talmud. Tractate *Ooktzeen*. Jerusalem: Hotzaot Hatalmud.

Talmud Jerusalem. Tractate *Megilla*; Tractate *Yevamot*; Tractate *Yoma*. Jerusalem: Torah Mitzion, 1968.

Talmud Jerusalem. Tractate *Taanith*. New York: M. P. Press, 1976.

Tapsell, R.F. *Monarchs, Rulers, Dynasties, and Kingdoms of the World*. New York: Facts on File Inc., 1983.

Targum Yerushalmi. In L. Ginzberg (Ed.), *The Legends of the Jews*.

Philadelphia: Jewish Publication Society of America, 1968.

Time Magazine, February 5, 1979, p. 51.

Trachtenberg, J. *The Devil and the Jew: The Medieval Conception of the Jew and its Relation to Modern Anti-Semitism*. Philadelphia: Jewish Publication Society of America, 1983.

Tumin, M. "Anti-Semitism and Status Anxiety: A Hypothesis." *Jewish Social Studies*, 1971, *4*, 307-16.

Turner, R.K. In W.J. Broad, "Creationists Limit Scope of Evolution Case." *Science, 211*, 1981, 1331-32.

Twain, M. "Concerning the Jews." *Harpers Magazine*, September, 1899.

Twain, M. *The Innocents Abroad; or the New Pilgrims Progress*. New York: Harper & Row, 1911.

Uzziel, J.B. In *Mikroat Gedolot; Numbers*. New York: Friedman, 1971.

Van Loon, H.W. *The Story of Mankind*. New York: Liveright, 1984.

Velikovsky, I. *Ages in Chaos*. New York: Doubleday, 1952.

Wald, G. "The Origin of Life." *Scientific American, 191*(2), 1954, 45-53.

Wasserman, E.B. *Kovatz Ma'amareem*. Jerusalem: Gitler & Associates, 1963.

Wyman, D.S. *The Abandonment of the Jews*. New York: Pantheon Books, 1984.

Yaneev, S. *Remez Bepardes and Safot Nestarot BaTorah*. Gush Dan: Machon Meir, 1985.

Zohar. Jerusalem: Mossad HaRav Kook, 1964.

About the Author

Dr. Benzion Allswang is a social-clinical psychologist who treats children and their families in the south suburbs of Chicago. He also learns and teaches at the Kollel Kinyan Torah in Chicago. Dr. Allswang received his Ph.D. in social-psychology from Loyola University of Chicago and holds master's degrees in clinical psychology from Roosevelt University and in Religious Education from the Hebrew Theological College (Yeshivas Skokie). He has rabbinical ordinations from Rabbi Zalman Nechemya Goldberg of Jerusalem and from Rabbi Yaacob Fink (of blessed memory) former *av beit din* of the Haifa Rabbinical Court. He is married to the former Rachel Rosenblatt, daughter of Reb David Chaim Rosenblatt (of blessed memory) of the Nechbodai Chassidai Be'on and of the Gedolai Gabaai Zedakah of Jerusalem. Dr. Allswang, his wife, and four children presently reside in Chicago.